THE FACE PRESSED AGAINST A WINDOW

Tim Waterstone is a British businessman, author and philanthropist. He is the founder of Waterstones, the United Kingdom-based bookselling retail chain, the largest in Europe. In 2018 he was knighted for services to bookselling and to charity.

'[A] moving, funny take on business, family and mortality'
Jim Armitage, *Evening Standard*

'The rollicking, page-turning memoir of Britain's biggest book tycoon'
Daily Mail

'[Waterstone] writes movingly… Small, poignant images stand out… From such raw clay are great entrepreneurs moulded'
The Tablet

'*The Face Pressed Against a Window* confirms one's sense that this extraordinarily energetic and well-meaning man has been, and still is, a force for good.'
Literary Review

The Face Pressed Against a Window

The Bookseller Who Built Waterstones

TIM WATERSTONE

Atlantic Books
London

First published in hardback in Great Britain in 2019 by Atlantic Books, an imprint of Atlantic Books Ltd.

This paperback edition first published in Great Britain in 2019 by Atlantic Books.

1 3 5 7 9 10 8 6 4 2

A CIP catalogue record for this book is available from the British Library.

E-book ISBN: 978-1-78649-631-7
Paperback ISBN: 978-1-78649-632-4

Printed in Great Britain by Clays Ltd, Elcograf S.p.A.

Atlantic Books
An Imprint of Atlantic Books Ltd
Ormond House
26–27 Boswell Street

London WC1N 3JZ

www.atlantic-books.co.uk

For my children: Richard, Martin, Sylvie, Amanda, Maya, Oliver, Lucy and Daisy, with my undying love, gratitude and admiration.

CONTENTS

ix   *Acknowledgements*

1   Prologue

11   Part One
       Where the Children of My Childhood Played

133   Part Two
       I do, ladies. I do. I 'ave a go.

289   Epilogue
       Miranda Beeching
       The Carriage Clock

ACKNOWLEDGEMENTS

So many people have helped me bring this book to life that I hardly know where to start and where to stop. So let me just say this: that without the fervent encouragement of my agent, Jonathan Lloyd at Curtis Brown, I never would have finished it, so difficult did I find certain sections to write.

But support me he did, and I was at last able to put together a working draft, and then, to my delight, Atlantic Books and my old friend and colleague Will Atkinson took up the contract. Then Will and his team immediately gave me a superb insight as to how the whole narrative arc of my life, from childhood through to my old age, could be presented in a manner that I think I was before too reticent and too guarded to attempt.

I am delighted I listened. Will and his ace editor James Nightingale led the way, then the ace Alison Tulett joined the team in support, and the whole manuscript opened up.

I cannot thank too warmly those old Waterstone's friends and colleagues of mine, such as Paul Baggaley, David McRedmond, John Mitchinson, Martin Latham, Peter French and Kate Gunning, who gave astonishingly generous time to sit down at their laptops and reminisce for us about their Waterstone's days, which added so much to that part of the book.

Thank you to them. Thank you to everyone. I have been very fortunate indeed.

PROLOGUE

Required: Experienced Booksellers for a new bookshop –
Waterstone's – in Old Brompton Road. Opening in
September. The first of many. Our object is to have the
best literary bookshops in the land, staffed by the best,
happiest, literary booksellers.

This was the advertisement I ran in London's *Evening Standard* in July 1982, eight weeks before our very first Waterstone's store was due to open in South Kensington. It's an odd advertisement, looking at it now. It was certainly unorthodox, particularly the 'happiest' bit, although the sentiment behind that objective was entirely sincere. But perhaps its very oddness added a positive, intriguing quality to it. Whatever the case, through it I recruited in one fell swoop my first four Waterstone's staff members, all of them from Hatchards in Piccadilly (then owned by the publishers William Collins, but safely these days within the Waterstone's family).

Hatchards was at that time, and perhaps still is, the most prestigious literary bookshop in Britain, but it was not one whose owners spent too much time worrying about their staff's 'happiness'. Those four recruits came to me because they had not been given a salary increase for three years, which was unbelievably harsh for the time, with annual inflation running so persistently high. How lucky I was.

The telephone rang barely a minute after we had opened on our first day, and Dane Howell, one of these marvellous people, picked up the receiver.

'*Waterstone's?*' he purred into it.

Ye Gods, I thought. He has just said Waterstone's. *Waterstone's.* I've done it. It's real. I've made it. That thought was more than a little premature, given the bumps and terrors that occurred on the long and exhilarating road that lay ahead of us. But at that moment, at the very start of the journey, I felt an immense sense of achievement. From day one, every member of staff knew what I wanted Waterstone's to do and to be, and they – and all the many thousands of staff who followed them over the years – set happily about doing it with me. And together as a team – as a family – we did it.

I quote, immodestly I know, but there we go, from an article in the *Independent,* written in early October 1992, ten years later almost to the day. I do so because what the article describes was exactly, exactly, point by point, what we had all set out to do, and then did. I had never met or spoken to the journalist, and – well – it's good to read all that from another's pen. One takes enough brickbats in life...

Here it comes again, the annual kerfuffle of the Booker prize. Amid Tuesday night's celebrations – and acrimony and recriminations – one man will be watching the proceedings with wry disinterest, secure that he has won again, as indeed he has done for the past 10 years.

Neither author, agent nor publisher, the real victor will be a retailer, a businessman. In the decade since the Booker was first televised, Tim Waterstone, 53, founder of 86 bookstores, has done more than anyone to transform literary Britain.

It would be difficult to overstate Mr Waterstone's impact on the book trade, and publishers tumble over each other in tribute: he has changed the rules, moved the goalposts, revolutionised the industry. He has made book-buying a pleasurable experience, not an obstacle course. He has made high culture stylish. His shops have proved a godsend to publishers specialising in literary fiction – the Fabers, the Seckers, the Picadors. He staffed them with postgrads who had read a volume or two and were more than likely to be writers themselves. He set in motion an Eighties publishing revolution that inspired many other stores to revamp – Dillons, Hatchards, Books Etc – and with the boom in authors' advances and the emergence of the writer as talk-show star, he somehow made the whole business rather rock 'n' roll.

Before Mr Waterstone opened his first shop in Old Brompton Road in 1982, you could go into Foyles and be anaesthetised by inefficiency, stunned by confusion; it made the local library look snazzy. Or you could go into WH Smith and find little but bestsellers and gift books. In most cities outside London you couldn't find philosophy or art or science, because if it didn't sell by the dump-bin, it wasn't stocked. Such classics as there were, invariably dusty Penguins, were consigned to a dark outpost beyond Cookery.

But Mr Waterstone opened a shop you could walk around, a shop that stocked 50,000 titles, almost everything you could need. It had a sensible layout, agreeable lighting, a thoughtful kids' section. Staff didn't bother you if you read a chapter or two. It organised book readings and signings, a book search service, published a catalogue with its own recommendations and kept cuttings of the reviews. If they had bunged in an espresso bar and a chaise longue, you could practically have lived there...

'Go the other way', as the legendary Sam Walton of Walmart put it. 'Ignore the conventional wisdom. If everybody is doing it one way, there is a good chance that you can find your niche by going in exactly the opposite direction. But be prepared for a lot of folks to wave you down and tell you that you are headed the wrong way.'

And that's exactly what we did. In our model of literary bookselling of the highest class we travelled at speed in exactly the opposite direction to everybody else. For the book trade during the seventies and early eighties had talked itself into a state of dark gloom and bleak defeatism, particularly on the retail side. The independent booksellers were fast retrenching. And WH Smith, at that time overwhelmingly the market leader, was beginning to retrench from books too, placing increased emphasis on other goods – plastic toys, cheap stationery, fizzy drinks, music – and making a big deal of it to the City, looking for applause at their wisdom thereby.

Passion and independence of mind are what Sam Walton was preaching. But it is the vision that comes first – all else flows from that – and the Waterstone's vision was absolutely simple and absolutely clear. Surely all the great consumer retail businesses have been built from a picture born and carried in the founder's head, and this one certainly was. Right from the very start we had a defined picture of what the offer was to be, and who it was to be aimed at, and why it would win. And that is the point – winning. And 'winning' for the founding entrepreneur is not at all the making of a fortune. It is the making of the point, the defeating of the sceptics, the victory of the vision, the acting as a disruptive catalyst for a significant cultural and market change. It's the public projection of a personal vision, and a personal passion to succeed with it.

At Waterstone's we used not one jot of market research in determining our action plan. We just did it. And in that I would guess that we were typical of most if not all successful entrepreneurial start-ups. These arise perhaps every time from a founder's sudden, blinding epiphany – a vision of a breakthrough in an area in which he or she has market knowledge and experience. We could not afford market research. But in any case, what market research could have helped us? The fact was that the sort of bookshops we were intending to open was not out there. They were a figment of my imagination. There was nothing tangible, nothing for us there to research. As George Bernard Shaw said, 'The British people never know what they want until they are given it.' But we – not the royal 'we'; we, the staff and I – knew with total clarity what we wanted the Waterstone's bookshops to be, and we knew they would work. They would certainly appeal to me as a book buyer, so surely there must be a few million other people out there just like me. Why wouldn't there be?

The timing of our launch, thank goodness, proved to be excellent. The eighties lay ahead and, as the *Independent* piece says, what happened as the decade rolled out was something of a publishing revolution. The Booker Prize began really to gather pace and publicity saturation, driven particularly by Salman Rushdie and his *Midnight's Children*, which won the prize in 1981. There were feisty, cutting-edge new publishing imprints, dozens of them, some tiny, but all of them reaching out, and confidently, into a literary world that had previously lain fallow – and none more so in its heyday than the feminist imprint Virago. There was a chat and a bustle around it all that had not been seen in the book world for a very long time. And Waterstone's, as we grew and grew and grew, accelerating away from a standing start to open eighty-six large bookshops in our first ten years, was absolutely at the epicentre of that 1980s revolution. We benefited that revolution, and we were benefited by it, and we had no real rival to match us.

Putting this in a general context, entrepreneurs carry a self-confidence that is inviolate, whatever disasters may strike. They have their vision – tunnel vision, perhaps – and they are going to win with it. And all would embrace this simple checklist of the way to run their company's affairs: How can I inspire? How can I ensure that my dream can best be driven on its way? How can I lead more and manage less? How can I inspire creativity and imagination amongst the whole team? How can I know who our market is, and deliver to them what I know they want? How can I let our people show what they can do? How can I let our people believe that they are capable of anything, that they can reach out, and that they can grow?

'Where there's no vision, the people perish,' says Proverbs 29:18. Well, big corporates don't really do vision. The entrepreneur does little else. It is the vision that brings the win, the self-belief, the ruthlessness, the ability to ignore setbacks, the ability to lead and to inspire. Entrepreneurs are not really corporate animals at all. Other people's opinions, bureaucracy, needless, fussy communications bore them, and they have a wafer-thin attention span when time is being wasted. Bill Gates dropped out of Harvard University, for no other reason than that he was bored and impatient to get on with what he considered to be real life. Michael Dell was a dropout from the University of Texas for the same reason.

No one reads Kipling these days, and they are the poorer for it, but everyone is familiar with those great lines from 'If', which are inscribed above the door of the players' changing room at Wimbledon; that lovely juxtaposition of meeting with Triumph and Disaster, and treating those two impostors just the same.

What Kipling encapsulated in 'If' was the entrepreneurial life. Having the courage to put all your winnings back on the table and start again; meeting great triumphs and great disasters with calm resolution; risking everything; saving your breath on self-pity; dreaming great dreams.

That is what wins – tenacity, drive, and an almost insane ability to deal with financial stress. Add to that real self-knowledge, together with a certain simplicity and straightforwardness and clarity of mind. If you have it within you to add one extra dimension – a passion, linked to a sense of rightness, an instinct for what really matters, a contempt for duplicity and deception – then you will be, as Kipling puts it, a man. Wholly politically incorrectly in current language, of course, but he was someone of his time, and we all know what he means, and please don't lose contact with him just on those grounds.

If you can make one heap of all your winnings
And risk it all on one turn of pitch-and-toss,
And lose, and start again at your beginnings
And never breathe a word about your loss...

and

...If you can fill the unforgiving minute
With sixty seconds' worth of distance run,
Yours is the Earth and everything that's in it.
And – which is more – you'll be a man, my son!

Even in the early years when I was trying to prepare myself for my Waterstone's dream by gaining experience in a conventional business setting, I knew exactly what was missing. The moment I threw over that old life – the corporate life – and went off to try my hand at the new life – freedom – Waterstone's – I immediately felt comfortable in my own skin. Putting aside the fun years of my youth in India, I had never had that feeling before. I had been pretending to be X or Y – but none of it was me. I had no commitment. Or – much better put – I had no real cause to attach my commitment to. And I felt the most overwhelming need to make my own mark on the world, to fight my own fights, to win my own wars.

And thus, at last, in 1982, when I was forty-three, Waterstone's came into being and we set off on our adventure. I had no fear of failure or the consequences of that – though I should have done, in practical terms, as I had children to support. Quite simply, by doing this, I found happiness and pride. And a resolution to my life. And the Kiplingesque seeds of all of that – my successes, my failures, my ups, my downs, my triumphs and my disasters – all of these, throughout my life, both personal and professional, were set into my being by the circumstances of my childhood, in which I was the marginally emotionally battered child of a marginally battered lower-middle-class ex-colonial family.

And that is what this book is about.

PART ONE

Where the Children of My Childhood Played

CHAPTER 1

It was the winter of 1942, mid-war, and the country was tired and bombed and scruffy. I was three years old, and a few months earlier my family had moved into our house in Crowborough, in East Sussex.

Finally, after almost two years of itinerant wandering, we had settled down. My father had been enlisted in the Royal Army Service Corps in the early months of the war, and my mother had spent the years since then driving with us all around the country, following his postings.

All of that was such an extraordinary thing to do, and for some reason my mother never seemed to want to talk about it in later years. But what happened was that on the outbreak of the war she moved all of us out of our rented house in Glasgow, packed us into our small car – our luggage, Nanny, my sister Wendy, my brother David, the dog and me (a very small baby, of course) – and set off for England. Her one purpose was to follow my father. At that time he was being moved around continually from one Royal Army Service Corps camp to another. In later years, I asked my older sister why she thought our mother had done that. Wendy said that my mother was convinced that my father would never have been able to cope with army life unless he knew that she was always close by to support him.

So off we went, bridges burnt, now without a home to return to. The five of us, plus the dog, followed my father from camp to camp, up and down the country, from Scotland down to Yeovil, then up to Wales, up again to Lancashire, then down to Reading, across to Kent, back again to Yeovil, month after month after month, one bed-and-breakfast room followed by another. I knew nothing of it, if course, but it must have been an appallingly uncomfortable and prolonged experience. It led eventually to my mother suffering a breakdown, and it came to a halt only when my father was withdrawn from the Corps and posted as a technical instructor at a staff college in Kent, where he remained until the end of the war.

Shortly after my father was appointed to the staff college, he came home on leave, to see the new house. Excited at the prospect of his homecoming, I drew some pictures to give to him.

And so one day my mother called for me and there he was, in his uniform, standing in the hall. My father. Except, of course, he was a complete stranger to me.

I had expected that he would reach down to pick me up, but he made no move to do that. So I handed him my pictures, probably sullenly, as they would have been appalling, and even at that age I would have known it, as I have never been able to draw.

And then I did something that may well have served to change the character of the rest of my childhood, and perhaps thus to shape in part my life.

'Go away,' I said. 'Go away. We were happy without you! *Go away.*'

He stood there, quite still, staring at me, appalled. So was my mother. So was my sister, aged eleven. So was my brother, aged eight. So, no doubt, was the dog.

I seem to have eradicated from my memory what happened next. I think my mother may have hit me. And who could blame her? In any case, she must have understood the root of this catastrophic insult to my father. With him away for all that time, I had from babyhood frequently slept in my mother's bed. But now, each time he came home, this stranger, this big uniformed man, would no doubt be with her there, in my place.

My father remained with us then for perhaps ten days, before his leave was over. He spent much of this time in the tool shed, with the door shut behind him. He told us he was making a present for my brother David's birthday. This turned out to be a sort of wheeled toboggan. It capsized the moment David tried it out on a run down the rough lane that bordered our house, and then each and every time thereafter.

It was a disaster for my father, really. He told us he had been looking forward to making this toboggan for David for weeks, and now it had failed. It was a shame, but this was when I first saw the weakness in him, and it was a shock. My father, in his early forties, took his disappointment like a child: pouting, on the edge of tears, his bottom lip quivering, shouting at my mother, and, most infantile of all, stamping his foot when she tried to turn the situation into a joke. I saw Nanny stare at him when he did this, and then grimace as she turned away.

I think Nanny was not so much shaken by his anger, as contemptuous of his childishness. She had lived with our family since well before the war, no more than a young girl when she joined us, and was perhaps used to this kind of performance from him. But it was new to me, and it both puzzled and frightened me. Men were supposed to be strong and affectionate and gentle and protective. They were like that in stories. Fathers didn't shout and pout and sulk and quiver their bottom lips over such an inconsequential matter as this.

A few days later his leave was almost over. He was due to return to his barracks the next day. I was in my pyjamas and was just about to go upstairs to bed. I saw him sitting in his chair, reading a newspaper, waiting to be called to his supper.

Suddenly, unexpectedly, a wave of affection for him came over me. I knew I had done wrong in what I had said to him when he had first arrived. My mother had been angry with me, and I understood why. I wanted to make up for it. He was my father. I went over and stood in front of him, reaching out my arms to him. But he shrunk back into his chair and pushed me off with both hands, roughly so. 'Men don't kiss,' he said.

I pulled back, appalled. All I had wanted was for him to reach out to me, and perhaps touch my hands for a moment. I was three years old. That was all I wanted. As young as I was, the snub – the spurning, coarse, insulting rejection of it – hurt. It hurt. And his action seemed to set into being the future pattern of our relationship. For he never once attempted a physically affectionate gesture towards me. Hard to believe no doubt, but true. Not once. I saw other children laughing with their fathers, ragging with them, being picked up, swung about, hugged, pushed on swings, kicking a football, carried on shoulders. I wanted that for us, too. But not once in all the years of my childhood did he as much as touch me. Nor did he express affection for me in any other manner. Not once did he give me praise. Nor, if it comes to that, did he do so in my adulthood. Not once.

I will never understand why all this happened. One can construct reasons, and see if they can be made to fit, but none really suffice. Perhaps my arrival in the world, way too long after my siblings, had been to him an unplanned disaster, worried about money as he was throughout his married life. Maybe there had been a simple mismatch of personality. Maybe he resented the affection that my mother so openly lavished on me. Maybe it was my rejection of him in that appalling incident I had created in our hall.

Maybe this, maybe that. Maybe there is no one clear reason at all. But what I do know, and my siblings knew too, is that this was more than just emotional reticence in him, because in his other relationships within the family – with my mother, my sister, my brother – he was fully emotional. Actually, he was emotional with the three of them to the point of being positively needy. Unhappy, unfulfilled and bullied in his work, as we all in the family bore daily witness to, he was devoid of self-confidence, devoid of interests and intellectual curiosity, and allowed himself to be destroyed by perceived social snubs. In all this he clung to my mother with a desperation that in its vulnerability, in its incompetence, was painful to witness. He clung to my sister, who was at times openly irritated by it. He clung to my brother, though my father was frightened of him.

My mother knew it was her role to hold my father up in his life, and she did so, and, always, always, she held him close. She knew his weakness, she knew his emptiness, and she knew that he was her responsibility, and she never let him down. Well – except perhaps one should say this – she seldom engaged with his awful relationship with me, but sometimes, just sometimes, very quietly, her hands on mine, she would apologise to me for it. But in the final analysis there was no doubt that she knew what the essential role of her life had to be – she was the guardian and the protector and the shield of my father, her husband, from a world with which he was most ill equipped to deal.

So, whatever the reasons for it, he and I spent all those years of ours in mutual, numbed dislike. His weapon of choice – the weapon that no child can weather or combat – was sarcasm. Endless, witless, brutal sarcasm. Worst, devastatingly worst, when it was shouted at me. And it generally was.

I think now that my presence in the house gave him a punch-bag on which he could release his dissatisfactions around his own life. Even as a child of ten or eleven, frightened of him as I was, I knew that I was the stronger and the more resilient of the two of us. I knew that he was weak, and that I wasn't. His treatment of me simply confirmed his weakness. Better to let him bully his way on. I was strong. He was weak.

But there was at least one occasion when his attack on me led me to get up and escape. I was ten. He had started it at the breakfast table – a mocking, merciless rant at me – and I suddenly, impulsively, pushed my plate aside and got up from my chair and fled. I ran out to the garage, seized my bike and rode away as fast as I could, up the lane, through the high street, past the riding stables, past the barber, past the fishmonger, past every-thing until I was out into the country. I pedalled for miles and miles, through Lewes, nineteen miles away, and on and on still. Reaching the South Downs village of Alfriston, I deliberately put myself in danger by going absolutely full pelt down a precipitous and winding hill, almost with the intent to have a crash and damage myself. And then, resting by the roadside, finally beginning to calm down, I rode the twenty miles or so home to Crowborough.

It was nearly dark when I got there, and I sat down on a bench on the village green, uncertain what to do next. A few minutes later my mother drew up in her car, smiled at me, shook her head ruefully, and made no further comment other than to suggest that I follow her home. I learnt later that she had been driving around for several hours trying to find me.

And so the pattern of my childhood years wound its way on. By the time I was thirteen or fourteen, I had become much more capable of withstanding the buffeting of his attack. By the time I was eighteen, and on the point of leaving home, it had become little more than a distraction, an echo from the past, a painful experience that was there, and it had happened, but something that I could now put aside and forget about. And that is what I did. I put it aside, and resolved to forget about it. But if my resolution superficially succeeded, what had been done had been done.

For the truth is that my father had damaged me, and the damage had stuck. It's still there. Recently, one of my brother's daughters sent me a photograph of my father, which she had found amongst my brother's papers when she was tidying them up after his death. I looked at my father's face, staring into the camera, and that shock of fear – sharp, sudden fear – hit me all over again. Exactly the fear I had of him in my childhood.

All this had happened, and it was cruel, and it was relentless.

And I can recognise the legacies of it in the way I have led my life. One legacy, and it is absurdly trivial, is that I cannot to this day watch a Fred Astaire film without wanting to turn away from it, because Astaire looks so like him. But a second legacy, and this one is anything but trivial, is that I believe that without the trauma of that relationship I would never have broken out and fought the battles that I did fight to create and succeed with Waterstone's. That wasn't just for me. It was for my father too. Waterstone's was a statement of personal confidence and drive and tenacity, a statement that great things can be achieved, a statement that vision matters, that leadership matters, that culture matters, that books matter.

Waterstone's was me having the last word on him. It was proof of my worth. I needed Waterstone's. Why else would I have named it after me? Actually – it was named after my father too, if you like. I was hurling bottles at my childhood, which I could neither forgive nor forget. That was why Waterstone's won. Waterstone's, pure and simple, was aimed at my father. Well, that's what a therapist told me a few years ago. And he was right.

*

There was an interesting incident when I was in my thirties. My father called me, and suggested that we might meet that day for a family picnic. I hadn't seen him for some years, and I don't think he had telephoned me before ever – and I mean ever – except for those several times over the last years of his life, my mother dead, he remarried, that he had once more run out of money, and needed from me what we both allowed the other to refer to as 'a small loan'. Though I have to say that on some occasions they were anything but that as far as I was concerned, such were the sums he sometimes requested out of my already uncomfortably stretched family net income. But, whatever, I would then supply the money, I hope graciously, or at least apparently so. And I should mention in passing that none of these loans was ever repaid, and when my father died I found that I alone of his children had been omitted from his will...

But the call on this occasion was not a request for money. Not at all. It seemed to be, and I am sure it was, a reaching out to me. An attempt to build something between us at last.

So we had the picnic, me with my then wife Claire and our two baby daughters, he with his pleasant second wife, an Australian widow. We sat beside each other on the rug. In time, Claire took the children off to play. My father and I talked. Yes – talked. And – yes – he was trying to reach out to me. He really was. And I was quickly aware that his wife, whom I hardly knew, was doing all that she could that afternoon to aid and encourage and prompt him in that. And, looking back now, I applaud her for it.

He couldn't have known that he was so near to the day of his death. The aneurism that killed him instantaneously those very few days later could not have been foretold. But he was doing just that – he was reaching out to me. And that afternoon I tried to reach out to him. And that was the last time that I saw him alive. And so he never saw Waterstone's brought into life, for that lay five or six years ahead, and I wish he had.

It was, of course, all way, way too late. Just those very few days later my father lay on the mortuary slab. He was seventy-seven, but in death looked much older.

I sat on the chair beside the slab, and gazed at him. His eyelids had been pulled down like blinds, and they now clung close to the outline of his eyeballs, too close, accentuating them, and unattractively so. The covering lay loose on his body and I leant across him to straighten it, and tidy him.

We were alone, but for a porter down at the far end of the room, sitting on a plastic chair, reading a tabloid newspaper. He seemed to be oblivious to us, or tactfully pretending to be.

I took my father's hand, and held it for a moment. But it felt wrong, and contrived, and I didn't welcome the intimacy of it, so I let the hand go, and just stared at him. He was dead. He was gone. I was free of him.

It may seem uncomfortably offhand for me to say this, but the truth was that he had never loved me, and I had never loved him. I would have liked to have loved my father, and perhaps he would have liked to have loved me too, his son. Who knows? But in the ghastly, enforced companionship of this mortuary slab it was we two who were alone together. He was lying there alone with me, of all people. And that is how I remember that scene, and how I felt as I sat there with him.

The porter yawned, stretched, dropped his paper on to his chair, and made his way over to us.

'All well, sir?' he said. He looked down at my father and seemed to be struggling to find something to say. 'Nice-looking old gentleman,' he murmured at last. 'Very nice-looking.'

He wasn't actually, not in the least, but it was a pleasant little compliment. My father was always a carefully groomed man. He would have appreciated it.

CHAPTER 2

I remember the day so clearly. It was my third birthday, and we were moving our possessions into the house in Crowborough, which my mother had bought, as I learnt in later years, for three thousand, five hundred pounds.

It was the summer of 1942. Petrol was severely rationed, but private motoring had not yet been banned, so we could still use our car. We arrived at our new house in our Vauxhall. This was only five years old, but had run up a huge mileage, as my mother drove us all around the country, following my father's Royal Army Service Corps postings.

I caught the excitement of my brother and sister when they ran down the path to the front door of our new home, and then the scrabbling around as my mother looked for the key. I tried to keep up with Wendy and David as they ran up and down the stairs to explore the empty rooms, and then raced out into the garden.

The house was one of a group of nine built just a few years earlier by a local developer. They were all of them different, all of them ugly, but all of them with good, generous one-acre gardens. And in my eyes our garden was the best part of it. It ran all the way down to a stream, and we had inherited from the previous owner large vegetable beds and fruit trees, rose beds, a strawberry and raspberry cage, a beech hedge, a tool shed, and a straggly herbaceous border. And, best of all, a formal rectangular pond, with water lilies, tadpoles and frogs and water boatmen, those seemingly weightless little aquatic insects that our gardener a few years later formally identified for me under their scientific name of Corixidae.

We were called back into the house to have tea, which in those wartime years of tight rationing would have been no more than a glass of milk and a slice of bread and dripping, plus, if you were very lucky indeed, a couple of plain biscuits. I imagine my brother and sister had memories of normal family food, pre-war, and longed for it. But I had known no different, and was perfectly content.

Meanwhile, Nanny was busy upstairs with the suitcases, and I ran up to see how she was getting on. As the cases were emptied she was taking them up to the loft to store them away. I stood at the top of the stairs and watched her as she climbed up the fold-down ladder and squeezed through the trapdoor.

Once she was up in the loft Nanny had managed to forget to walk only on the cross-beams, and she had put one foot down on to the plasterboard ceiling. That collapsed, of course, and – well – the picture is forever frozen in my mind: Nanny's leg sticking through a hole in the ceiling. A skirt pushed up. A stocking top. A plump, bare thigh. A glimpse of knickers. Altogether an astounding sight. I was spellbound. Surely, surely, just three years old, I couldn't have found it erotic? But the guilty thing is that I think I did. Scarcely credible, I know, but I know that I did.

We five settled into the house, and all was happy and calm and pleasant. As the months went on, Nanny gave me lessons every morning – reading from a picture book, simple arithmetic, forming up of letters. My mother sang as she busied herself at the kitchen sink, her voice, as always, a thin, affected parody of Gertrude Lawrence, who I later discovered was her idea of sophisticated perfection. Wendy would bustle off every morning to a little day school at the other end of the village, girls only, owned and run by a stern lady of advanced years, who dressed and carried herself like an Edwardian Queen Mary. David walked up the hill to a local day school too, grey blazer, grey shorts, his satchel in his hand, his dark and light blue striped cap pulled down over his ears.

The difference in my mother now that we were settled in our own home must have been stark. Much credit to Nanny, really, rather than her, but the house was organised, we children were busy, and my mother was singing. The five of us made a comfortable group together. We were properly housed now, the ceaseless travelling was over, life was ordered, and we were peaceful and content. All was well. My father was away in the army, and I was secure within what was to me our happy nuclear family group.

I knew of nothing else, of course, but life, which for me was the war, seemed to be the greatest of fun. Crowborough lay on the flight path of enemy planes to London, and I could lie on my back in the garden and watch sporadic fighting up in the sky. Fighter planes ducking around each other, chasing each other, puffs of smoke. And, occasionally, the burst of an explosion, and then perhaps a solitary parachute – a beautiful thing, silent, floating, calm and gentle, in extraordinary contrast to the preceding violence.

There was a moment when violence crossed my path rather too close for comfort, although I didn't at all realise that at the time. I was with my sister in the fields opposite our house in the summer of, I think, 1943, when I would have been just four. Wendy was holding my hand and walking me along a path. As she reached out to open a gate we could first hear and then see a fighter plane heading straight for us, and flying very low indeed. It was German.

My sister grabbed me and pushed me – hurled me – into the brambles by the gate. They were firing at us, but in a moment the plane had flashed past overhead, over the hill and away. I extricated myself from the brambles, screaming and weeping and shouting at Wendy that I would tell on her to Mum. It was a little tough on the poor girl. She knew that German fighter planes on their way home had a habit of firing off their last spare rounds at anything that struck their fancy; Crowborough, being on their route, had experienced this before.

Some months later a German plane crashed to the ground just on the outskirts of the village. We hadn't seen it come down as it had been in the night, but the word soon spread, and Nanny and I rushed off to where the postman, Nanny's young admirer, told her it was.

A small crowd was already gathering by the time we got there, and although three or four policemen were holding everyone back they allowed us close enough to look into the smashed and mangled cockpit. Nanny pushed me through people's legs so that I was at the front. I had hoped to see a dead German pilot, as

I am sure we all did, but the body had already been taken away.

The pilot's parachute, however, was still there in the cockpit, caught up and torn and entangled, but intact. One of the policemen pulled it out, and started to cut it into sections to share amongst the onlookers. Parachute silk was highly prized in those days of clothes rationing. The sections he cut for us all were generous, as an entire parachute represents a considerable square footage of silk.

I went up to claim our piece, and we took it home to my mother. She divided the silk into three, and shared it between Wendy, Nanny and herself, with the intention that each should make themselves something with it – a petticoat, perhaps, or a blouse or scarf.

And all this time my poor brother was sheltering under the piano. The piano, a baby grand, was never used as an instrument, as it was never tuned and anyway no one could play it, but it fitted, just about, in our front room. It had been bought from a junk shop in Tunbridge Wells. To own a piano was part of the minutiae of a family's social ascent, and my mother kept it polished to the highest of sheens.

David, later in his life an SAS tough, and then some, was the frailest of little boys. He was undersized and perpetually ill – scarlet fever, rheumatic fever, indestructible nettle rash, a brush with polio. He only gathered full robustness, both physically and mentally, when he was perhaps eleven or twelve. In these final couple of years of the war he was nine or ten, and the clamour and aggression of the aerial combat above us terrified him. Whereas I, so much younger, would sit in the garden happily – more than happily – gazing up into the sky to watch the planes fight, and later in the war to watch the flying bombs, the doodlebugs, as they chugged over us to London, poor David was frightened by it all to the point of trauma. So, when it all got too much to bear, he took his blanket and his pillow, made his camp under the piano and refused to emerge.

He was there for weeks. My mother couldn't get him out, and even Nanny, whom he loved, couldn't get him out. It must have been my sister Wendy who did. Theirs was a very strong sibling bond, and it stayed with them all their lives. They were very, very close. I think it must have been her.

One incentive that may have been offered to him was that we would all go by bus to Tunbridge Wells, to visit the travelling fair. We always enjoyed a bus ride. This not least because Nanny had read somewhere in her magazines that Germans were infiltrating their spies into the country by dressing them as nuns, and that they could be identified by their hairy legs, most easily glimpsed on places like buses, as they climbed the steep and winding staircases up to the top deck. That always gave us something to do, and anyway none of us had been to a fair before.

My memory, however, is that I thoroughly disliked the whole event. I went down the helter-skelter on a mat and landed on the base of my spine. I then went on the bumper cars, with Nanny as my passenger, and steered drunkenly around while Nanny screamed. Someone rammed our rear, I was thrown forward, and I cut my chin on an exposed metal rim of the dashboard. I have never been able to stand bumper cars or indeed anything else about fairs ever since.

Afterwards we went to have lunch at the nearby British Restaurant. British Restaurants were a national facility of some thousands of communal kitchens, set up at the beginning of the war by the Ministry of Food to make inexpensive meals available for all. They were truly a national treasure, and I loved going there, and so I am sure did everyone else. I have a memory of the wonderful wartime cheeriness of it all. Nanny thought having lunch at the British Restaurant was a real tonic, as she put it. And so it was.

The entrance passage to the restaurant was curved between high mounds of sandbags, this to provide protection against bomb blast. Once we were through we were in a large dining hall, which I imagine in peacetime was a church hall, or an assembly room, or something of that kind. The room was noisy and happy and steamy, with rows of women standing behind tables, their hair tied up in knotted turbans. They were chatting away, laughing together, dishing up simple and pleasant hot food. No second helpings were allowed, but there were generous first, and always an additional illicit spoonful on the plate for a child. And – delicious – to follow was a bowl of steamed pudding, poured over with golden syrup. Wonderful.

I recall looking across the table at my mother that day, as I finished the pudding and pushed my plate aside. Her face is so pretty, I thought. My mum is so pretty. And so she was, at least in my eyes. But when I see photographs now of her at that time I find it difficult to justify her prettiness to anyone looking at them too.

She was in her late thirties at this point. She was of medium height and medium build, brown hair in a simple cut, blue-eyed, full-cheeked, perhaps a little jowly – actually, I suppose she looked much like everyone else in the British Restaurant that day, particularly the dinner ladies, as my mother's hair was tied up in a turban just as theirs was.

But there was prettiness in her, and I think now it must have come through her smile, which was delightful. At least it was delightful to me. The smile of her mouth itself, the wrinkling up of her eyes, the sheer happy, lovely good humour of it.

It was the warmest of smiles really, and it brought out what was always for me her most positive feature, within a personality that contained a whole mass of balancing faults. It was this. My mother was very good at familial love. To me, as a young child, that was everything. She was never angry, and she was never critical. She was tactile, and she was warm, and she sang, and she hugged. She planted sudden impulsive kisses on the back of one's neck. You were told that you were delicious. She was quick and impulsive with endearments.

Trivial and momentarily indulgent as all this most certainly was, I loved it. No doubt partly, or perhaps primarily, because of my father's aggressive, endless disdain for me, I loved it. And I loved her.

Some would say – and my brother certainly did say, for he claimed to have actively despised her – that my mother's life had been at best mediocre. Vapid even, her decently intelligent mind – and it was indeed that – left negligently undeveloped in a silly and trivial world of deep philistinism. Her laziness. The anxiety she had over the precariousness of her and my father's class status. Her prejudices – her casual anti-Semitism, and her mindless racism. Her minute calibration of where other people stood on the 'commonness' scale. Yes – some, and perhaps most of that is true. But she gave consistent love, and she gave consistent loyalty, and those are two pretty essential attributes both in a mother and in a wife.

No more profound loyalty to her husband could have been expressed than by her driving us around the country to be in present support of him in the early years of the war, before we settled in Crowborough. But eventually my mother seems to have totally broken up under the formlessness of that life. Rather than my father, it was she who succumbed to what sounds to me to have been the full-blown mental breakdown that I mentioned earlier. And then she, in a neat reversal of roles, was rescued by Nanny, and by Nanny's mother. And in that way, of course, Nanny and her mother rescued the rest of us too.

Nanny's mother, the widow of a treasured servant in the country house near Oxford of an aristocratic family, had moved to spend her last years in a tiny terraced house in Oxford's Jericho, which the family had bought for her. It was to this house that Nanny took us all, while my mother declined into her breakdown. I am told that Nanny's mother was a lovely fat old lady, and that she bounced me on her knee, and made me laugh, and gave me kippers for my tea.

We stayed there for at least six months, perhaps rather longer, and my sister told me in later years that it had been a particularly happy period for all of us, appallingly cramped up together though we must have been. And then, as time passed, my mother was able to gather her strength again. She steadied up. She abandoned any idea of further travelling, and rented a basement flat in Tunbridge Wells for a month or two, once more to be within my father's reach, now at his staff college in Kent, and there we went. And then she bought the house in Crowborough.

Nanny remained with us for another four or five years, until a little after the end of the war. In all the years she was with us she was absolutely at the epicentre of our family. My mother totally depended on her. My father, when he returned to the family in 1945 on his army demobilisation, was jealous of her, and showed it. We three children adored her, cherished her, for her perpetual good humour, and her kindness, and her efficiency, and her sense of fun, and, perhaps, given everything, her sheer dependability.

And of all of us it was probably my brother who cherished her most. Nanny had nursed him through all his periods of illness as a young child with a devotion and purpose in which my mother, he believed, had failed him. In his version of events, my mother had as good as abandoned him. I don't know if this is true or not. Knowing my mother as I did, I doubt it. But whether true or false, that construction of her dominated David's thinking of my mother for the rest of his life. Strictly true or not, it was strictly true to him. He would never let it go.

After she left, Nanny was to remain nearby for a period, in her new position as housekeeper to an elderly retired colonial couple in a large house at the other and more substantial end of Crowborough. David once told me that there were some considerable back wages owed to Nanny. I don't know if that was the case, however it was clear that she thought my mother and father were in financial straits, and she was probably right in that. They usually were. Our house was very small, and, as I well remember, and hated, my parents used to bicker noisily about money in the kitchen late into the evening and I suppose Nanny had overheard them.

My mother and father never kept in touch with Nanny after she had gone, and they never saw her again. And nor did Wendy or David, which in my brother's case I found rather surprising. But I did, though many, many years later. She had seen my name in a newspaper and wrote me a little letter, wishing me well. The letter was sent from her late mother's Jericho address, so I drove down to Oxford to see her, and subsequently a few times more. She was by then a very old lady indeed, fragile, totally sweet-natured, and possessed of a dogged and literal devotion to a version of Jesus so simplistic that it might have been straight out of a child's picture book.

A few months later, after my last visit, I had a call from the Social Services in Oxford to say that Nanny had died. It seemed that she had left my name with them. I went to her burial. I was the only person there.

CHAPTER 3

Crowborough is situated in the Weald, on the edge of the heathland of Ashdown Forest, thirty-five miles or so south of London. It stands on a hill, fully 800 feet above sea level, and it was marketed in the early years of the twentieth century as a health spa. Thus several substantial residential hotels became established in the village between the wars, acting predominantly as places of comfortable retirement for mostly ex-colonial people. In the days when our family lived there, Crowborough had a flavour wholly in keeping with that. Such were the members that the golf club could have been a planters' club in the foothills of India's Nilgiri Hills, and the little tennis club even more so, where you helped yourself to Rose's Lime Juice on the veranda after a sporting mixed doubles on the rough and ready grass courts.

There are some pretty villages around that part of the Sussex and Kent borders, but Crowborough was never one of them. It had developed in an eclectic sort of muddle from the early nineteenth century onwards. The ugly little artisan houses in the valley to the east had straggled untidily up the hill to meet at its crest one or two quite decent Edwardian villas, and a plug-ugly

Anglican church built up there in the late eighteenth century by the local benefactor, Sir Henry Fermor. The church stands beside the village green, off which in our time unassuming and sleepy roads meandered around lightly built residential areas of sturdy houses for the middle classes. These were of no architectural interest or cohesion whatsoever, but pleasant enough, and the sprawling gardens, where the children of my childhood played, were characterised by wheelbarrows and bonfires and rhododendrons and neat beds of standard roses.

The Crowborough of our day was a clean, ordered, quiet, unpretentious sort of place, and it had what its residents needed. The village wandered in its anonymous way over quite a substantial area, but the population was only then two or three thousand at the most, so as one walked along the high street faces were familiar, and names were known, and people smiled and nodded at each other in greeting. Crowborough had become a place for quiet retirement and quiet family life, and within these constraints it did very well.

Our house lay halfway down a rough and unfinished road – Mill Drive – which was there to access the nine houses that faced on to it. There never was a mill, and nor was this really a drive, more of a cul-de-sac, but the development was a pleasant enough place to be, and it was perhaps one rung up on the ladder from what would have been expected of us as a family.

There were no books in the house apart from a single grouping of three in a small bookcase in the front room, the sitting room – a *Pears Encyclopaedia*, an illustrated book of *Our Heroes of the Great War* (which I was deeply attached to) and a handsome abridged version of Dickens's *The Old Curiosity Shop*, with compellingly theatrical colour illustrations by Frank Reynolds. One of these illustrations was of Daniel Quilp, the malicious, hunchbacked moneylender. When I was three or four, and had first discovered the book on the shelves, I used to open it up just to have a quick little peek at this Quilp picture, then shudder in delicious fright, and slam the book shut again. After all these years it has finally found its last resting place with me – I have no memory by what route, but I am delighted to have it.

The rest of the bookcase contained my mother's knick-knacks: little china figures, a pair of glass ducks, a tiny brass bell, a porcelain cup and saucer. The dining room was furnished all in dark teak, the badge of identity for ex-colonials home from the Far East. Squeezed in there was the teak table and the six teak chairs and the teak sideboard on which my father placed his bottles of drink: gin and sweet sherry to mix for my mother's evening cocktail 'Rusty Nail', whisky for him, and a solitary bottle of Curacao. This was two-thirds finished at one early Christmas, and then remained there, dusty and untouched, until the house was sold in 1958.

All in all the house, with its crude and dark kitchen, overlaid with oily black dust settling on it from the coal bunkers lying immediately adjacent, was perhaps a little scruffy, and certainly somewhat tight for space. But it was what it was, and Burnside, as it was called, was not a bad place to be. For me, its main virtue was its garden, with its stream at the bottom of it, and the tunnel through which the stream flowed under the road. I used this to crawl to and from my friend Rose Robert's garden, playing a wounded and heroically gallant English officer escaping from a villainous Nazi prison camp. She played either a brave nurse or a farmer's wife. Once I was spotted in another garden on the other side of the tunnel and was shouted at, and I rapidly crawled back the way I had come, fantasies of heroism abandoned.

Rose had been adopted, but had not been told that she was, and my mother had learnt of it through village gossip. Rose was then somehow treated by my mother as if she was less worthy than all the rest of my village friends. I am sure she must have sensed something amiss in my mother's approach to her, and wondered why. My mother did much the same with a 'rough' young girl I brought home for tea from the 'wrong' end of the village. She also looked down on the greengrocer's son – 'the village idiot'. I didn't admire my mother for the way she labelled people, and so pejoratively.

There was a family of foxes by the stream, their earth in the undergrowth quite close to the wired-in hen run that was watched over by the preening cockerel. My mother had allocated to me the task of shutting up the hen house every night. She clearly had no idea how frightened I was of the dark, and for some reason I didn't want to admit that to her. But the truth was that at that time I was absolutely terrified of it, to the extent that I used to go to bed on dark winter nights with my cricket bat tucked under the blankets, in case we had robbers.

So this shutting up the hen house business proved quite an ordeal for me. My dread grew hour by hour on winter afternoons as the dark began to draw in. It was no good going down there early because the hens would not have settled inside for the night. It had to be done when it was dark, and it was a long way down to the bottom of an acre garden. The only way I found I could get up the nerve to tackle it was to wait until it really was dark, and not before. And then, cricket bat in hand for protection, sprint, sprint, sprint, heart pounding, and rush into the cage, slide home the bolt, padlock the cage, and sprint, sprint, sprint, all the way back.

The garden through which I sprinted back to the house was not exactly a model of thoughtful design, but it was big, and I loved it – the fruit trees, and the autumn bonfires, and the pond, with its frogspawn and water boatmen, and the tall beech hedge, and the wild and thinly planted and unkempt herbaceous border – lupins mainly, I think, and white phlox, and tall, straggling Michaelmas daisies. At the end of the border there were two rose beds, also somewhat thinly planted out and weedy. These our gardener (two hours on Friday afternoons, weather permitting) used occasionally to hoe, complaining about his back. He never seemed to busy himself much in the garden, but he was useful to me. He had two countryman's skills, both of them I imagine illegal, and when I was ten or eleven he taught me both.

The first was trout tickling, which quite definitely involved poaching and illegal trespass, as the stream on which he taught me ran off a secluded and privately stocked lake. Trout tickling entailed letting oneself down into the stream and walking along slowly, watching for a shadowy shape under the overhanging riverbanks. The secret was gentleness, stillness and patience. In time you might just detect a dark shadow and a tiny movement under the bank. Slowly, slowly, calmly, calmly, you then put your hand into the water and gently, gently push it along. And then – yes – keep icily calm – calm – then, so, so calmly, gently – yes – you can feel it – it's a trout. Now, gently, gently, just with the tips of your fingers, soft as lace, gently, gently rub the trout's belly. It will remain so calm, so calm, so happy with that. Now, still rubbing, gently, softly, so softly, work your way towards the head. Then – not too suddenly; keep calm! – squeeze your grip to the head, grip it, grip it, and, holding hard, lift the fish upwards out of the water, and lay it down, thrashing now, on the grass, well away from the bank, so that it doesn't drop back into the water. There. Done it. Exhilarating stuff. Wonderful. And all this was done just with your hand, and your gentle, caressing fingers.

Yes – well, that's the theory, but in truth I was hopeless at it. I was too blundering in the water and could never get near a trout before it shimmered away. But finally I almost caught one. I changed my technique. This time I lay on the ground, at right angles to the stream, and leant over the bank. Gently I slid my hand into the water and – gently– I could feel the tail, and then my fingertips were stroking the belly, and up, up, slowly, slowly towards the head, and the grip tightening and – whoosh – it had gone. Lost, damn it. I had tightened my grip too fast.

The second skill that our gardener tried to teach me – and I am not at all proud of this – was snaring rabbits. This I was better at. We went out into the fields on a wet afternoon, and he taught me how to identify in the long grass the tracks the rabbits were following to move to and from their burrows. What we then had to do was to peg down our wire lassoes and loop them into just the right shape and size, so that when the rabbit runs through the lasso it instantly tightens around its neck, thus breaking it. An instantaneous death probably, but, well...

This became a major pursuit of mine, and a lucrative one. Each morning I would creep out of bed just after dawn, slink out of the house, then sprint down the garden, jump the stream, climb through the undergrowth, and there I was, in the field opposite, shielded from view from our house and its bedroom windows. Apart from the fear of being caught by the farmer it was not just my parents I was concerned about, but my sister too. She would have been outraged at my cruelty, and quite certainly would have reported it to my mother. My brother would probably have kept quiet, as a gesture of indifference to my mother's views on the matter.

I would then make my way along the hedgerow for a few hundred yards to where I had set the lasso snares the previous day, and see what I had caught. Some days a single catch, other days three or four. Those rabbits were worth a shilling each to me (about two pounds in today's money) when I took them straight to the village fishmonger. He sold not just fish but game too – hares, my rabbits, pheasants – hanging from hooks outside the shop.

I guiltily hid the loot money each day in my bedroom, but I no doubt grew careless with it. My mother became suspicious, and asked how I was suddenly rich enough to buy so many sweets, which were still officially rationed, but by that time almost always illicitly available from under the counter. I claimed that I had made money from finding lost golf balls in the gorse of the golf course, and selling them back to the club professional, which actually was true. But my mother remained suspicious. And then all was revealed. One day she caught me absolutely red-handed. I was at that very moment handing my dead rabbits across to the fishmonger and pocketing his payment. She was absolutely, blindly furious. She cuffed my ears, took my money, and sent me straight home, and up to my bedroom. She was equally furious with the fishmonger, and threatened to report him to the police.

Across the lane from us on Mill Drive lived a retired couple from the Hong Kong police, whose drinking was legendary, and language worse. During the school holidays I sometimes used to help in their garden, weeding, mowing, cutting back brambles, and I was grateful for the money. I did the same for an old lady who lived right at the end of the lane, Miss Dorothy, as she invited me to call her. Or rather I tried to do the same gardening tasks for her as I did with the Hong Kong couple, but it seemed all she really wanted from me was to sit with her in her kitchen and talk.

I was struck by Miss Dorothy, actually, and remain so. It was the first time I had consciously come into contact with someone who was, quite literally, dying of loneliness. And I mean just that. I learnt some years later that it was exactly what had happened to her. She was found one morning, dead and cold on her kitchen floor, where it was clear she had lain for some days. She appeared to have had no relatives. In Crowborough, at least, I believe she had no real friends. I think I may well have been one of the only people she ever had conversation with in her last years, and I was just a child. For whatever reason, I have never forgotten Miss Dorothy, and I hope I never will.

CHAPTER 4

In the middle of the little high street, on a section called The Broadway, was a bookshop called The Book Club. It opened for business shortly after the war in, I think, 1947, and later became a major part of my life, especially during the school holidays. Considering that the population of the village and its surrounding area was so modest in those days, it was a shop of a generous size, with a quite excellent and wide range of stock.

The owner was the dauntingly severe Miss Santoro, assisted by a kindly man in his fifties, who was burdened with the most chronic asthma that I have ever seen, his chest sunken in, his shoulders bowed. I said that Miss Santoro was severe, and I often heard her being coldly unhelpful with various customers' less than informed enquiries. But once she got used to my incessant presence in her shop, browsing away for hours along the shelves but never buying anything, she treated me with great kindness, and led me to books she thought I would like. She provided me with a bench that she pretended was reserved only for me, and smiled whenever I entered the shop. She was angry with me once, when she saw me lick a finger before turning a page. I still think of that – and her – if I ever catch myself doing that now.

I don't think I ever bought a book from her, though in my single but short period of exhilarating affluence – the illicit rabbiting money bulging in my pockets – I should have done. Miss Santoro was greatly forbearing in allowing me simply to arrive at her shop and explore away as I did. I am sure I never thanked her properly at the time. I do so now.

And I do so particularly, as I have no doubt at all that it was Miss Santoro who kindled within me the bookseller vision that three decades later emerged into life as Waterstone's. Much of Waterstone's inherent values, perhaps most of Waterstone's inherent values, were being tested out there by Miss Santoro before my very eyes. The quality of her stock range, which, as I have said, was broad and decidedly literary in style. Her marketing outreach into the community. The comfort and warmth of her shop. Her extraordinary personal knowledge about books and their quality and their titles and their authors, and her enthusiasm for promoting her favourites. Her assistant, the asthmatic gentleman, whose knowledge and enthusiasm was fully the equal of hers. And – yes – me too really, the boy, the browser, sitting quietly in his allotted place and left undisturbed to read just as much as he wanted, and as often as he wanted, even though he never bought anything at all. If Miss Santoro had lived long enough to see it, my suspicion is that she would have watched me driving Waterstone's into existence without a single ripple of surprise.

The Book Club benefited from Crowborough's quite surprisingly rich literary connections, and Miss Santoro marketed that aspect of it mercilessly, with her window displays promoting 'local authors' and all that sort of thing. Graham Greene's mother, for example, had owned a house in Crowborough for many years, and he spent much time there. Her house was on the fringes of the village, out near the golf course. Indeed very close to the Canadian army camp, which was based there during the war. Bizarrely, I still remember the name of their regiment – the Lincoln and Welland. But then I was a great fan of theirs, standing cheering and clapping with all the other village children when they marched by, all of us shouting our pleas for them to toss chewing gum to us.

The Canadians certainly added a touch of energy to the place, packing the pubs, chasing the girls, teasing the matrons. Nanny was pursued by one of them for a time, and with rather charming ardour. He used to arrive at our house in freshly pressed uniform, smelling of carbolic soap, standing in the hall with his cap in his hands, calling my mother 'Ma'am'. He lost out, though, to the heightened passion of our postman, who had Nanny in a considerable flutter for a while.

On one occasion my mother was paid a saucy compliment by one of these Canadian soldiers as we were walking along the high street. She laughed, while whispering in my ear that she thought he was terribly vulgar. I can only have been four years old, so I am surprised I knew what the word meant, but it was one she used often, so I suppose I must have worked it out.

But before the Canadians left Crowborough to join Operation Overlord, the Allied invasion of Normandy in June 1944, there were a couple of disasters. First the unpleasant rape case of an eleven-year-old girl who was intellectually disabled. And then there was an absolutely dead-plumb hit by a V1 bomb, a doodlebug, which came down on top of the Canadians' mess tent, killing its occupants. A stone memorial in tribute to them, placed where their camp had been, stands there to this day alongside the fourth hole of the golf course.

The Graham Greene connection with Crowborough was through more than just his mother, for also his mistress Dorothy Glover lived and died in a house just a couple of miles away, and Greene was often with her there. Greene's great friend the notorious double spy Kim Philby and his family also had a house in the village, and I knew Philby's daughter Josephine, who was much the same age as me. Philby was, of course, eventually exposed, and only just in time fled to Moscow, but before that happened Greene and Philby used to drink and gossip together in our local pub. I have often wondered since whether Greene knew of Philby's real life. It would have been perhaps in his character if he had, and was intrigued and excited by it.

And there were other famous literary links to the place. Edwin and Willa Muir had lived and worked in Crowborough for most of the 1920s, and their cottage was where they completed their iconic translation of Franz Kafka's *The Castle*. A. A. Milne's house was a mile or so out on Ashdown Forest, and Arthur Conan Doyle lived for many years in a substantial house on the village outskirts. A. A. Milne died when I was twelve, and Conan Doyle years before, but dead or alive they and all the others were still 'local authors' as far as Miss Santoro's windows were concerned. And someone who was very much alive and active in Crowborough, and frequently to be found pottering around in The Book Club, was Minnie Louise Haskins. A retired LSE lecturer, an amateur poet, and a wholly obscure elderly lady, she was taken by absolute and total surprise when King George VI, wrestling with his speech impediment, closed his iconic Christmas Day broadcast in 1939, the war just begun, with these opening lines from her poem 'God Knows'.

> I said to the man who stood at the Gate of the Year:
> 'Give me a light that I may tread safely into the unknown.'
> And he replied:
> 'Go out into the darkness, and put your hand into the hand of God.
> That shall be to you better than light, and safer than a known way.'

The national press loved the story, and even though Miss Haskins and her poem may have been wholly obscure up to that point, they both became immediately very well known indeed. An astonished Crowborough was very, very proud of her. And all the more so when the King died, in 1952, and those words of hers were engraved on the gates of his memorial chapel, at Windsor Castle.

Minnie Haskins lived to see that, but passed away four or five years later. She was missed when she went, for she had become, in her celebrity, the village's star opener of fêtes and jumble sales and school sports days. The vicar was never content to let her rest. He had recently got himself into serious trouble over an indiscreet relationship with a young girl from the village, which his wife, his bishop and his congregation all got to know about, and in his attempts to rescue his reputation, his marriage and no doubt his career, he had changed from being dreamingly inert around the place to being furiously proactive. Minnie Haskins was a trophy member of his congregation for him to employ in that.

Between the vicarage and our house lay a small group of shops. The village barber was one of them, and in the school holidays my mother dispatched me there every second week for a short back and sides and a smear of Bay Rum hair tonic. And there I really did hear the famous words of 'something for the weekend, sir?', murmured softly into the ear of the man in the adjacent chair, as a final splash of eau de cologne was massaged into his scalp. I knew him. He was the vicar's verger. It was a decade and more later before I realised what the barber had been suggesting...

Beside the barber was the music shop, which I first discovered when I was around eight or nine. I was vaguely looking for a record I might try out on the radiogram that my parents had recently bought, very proudly, for the front room.

The radiogram was jammed up against the piano, which I had by this time learnt to play. Learnt to a most modest standard, I have to emphasise, but good enough for my mother to want to show me off to her lady friends who visited to tea. She would make me join them to play some fiddly little Mozart show-off piece that I was learning at the time. In my opening bars the audience would be in devout, aesthetic silence. Before long, conversation would break out again, first in whispers, then in full voice. At the final chord there would be a sudden shocked silence, and then clapping and exclamations of joy. If my brother caught sight of me afterwards he would aim a kick at me and call me a foul little swank, and how right he was.

The little Mozart piece had raised my curiosity, so I wandered into the music shop to see what I could find. I was enthralled, sifting through the stock of records, to realise what a superbly rich culture I had stumbled into and yet knew absolutely nothing about. Mozart, Schubert, Bach, Elgar, Richard Strauss – I had no concept as to how to begin. The shop owner, another severe asthmatic I noticed, perhaps The Book Club man's brother, asked me what I was looking for. He could see I had no idea. He asked me how much money I had, and laughed when I replied. He told me the best thing for me to do was to get hold of a scratched record or two, and learn from those what I liked best. So he would give me one to start with, and then if I liked that I should come back and he would give me another to try.

LPs had just come on to the market, and he gave me one from his scratched rejects at the back of the shop. I took it home and my mother was out, so there was no one in the house. I put the LP on the turntable and lowered the arm. The music burst out, and I thought it was absolutely beautiful. I had no idea that orchestral music could sound so ravishing. I turned the volume up as high as it would go, then opened the French windows into the garden and sat on the doorstep and listened and listened. The needle stuck when the scratch was reached and I got up to move it, then looked at the label to see again what I was playing. It was the Rachmaninov second piano concerto and the soloist was Cyril Smith with the Liverpool Philharmonic conducted by Malcolm Sargent.

The music shop owner knew just what he was doing. Accessible, emotional, sweepingly romantic, it was absolutely the right choice of music, at least for me, the small boy he had found in front of him that morning.

Close by the music shop was the greengrocer, whose handicapped son was known by my parents and their friends as 'the village idiot'. They meant it casually, I suppose, unthinkingly, much in the manner of the time, but I hated to hear them use that term. I am glad I met him, actually. He introduced me early to an awareness of innocence. I wish I could recall his name.

I remember passing him in the street one day, and I smiled at him, the first time I had done that really, and he smiled back at me. At that point two spinster sisters, perhaps in their sixties, well known in the village, rode past us. They were always seen on horseback, and dressed in formal, rigidly presented black jackets and ankle-length black skirts, with their hair secured into buns. They rode sidesaddle on their beautiful and identical black, gleaming horses. One of them had their tame parrot sitting on her shoulder, as they always did when they rode out. An extra-ordinary sight. They knew me, I think, but then as ever failed to acknowledge me. That mattered not at all, but what disappointed me is that they took no notice either of the greengrocer's son, who stood beside me waving and waving at the sisters as they passed us.

I remember joining company with him at that moment and we walked further along the street, side by side, his hand clasped gently on my forearm, to me a distressingly moving gesture of friendship and trust. A few minutes later a gaggle of olive-skinned young men arrived, unsupervised, relaxed, happy, laughing. They waved a greeting at the pair of us as they passed by. They were our Italian prisoners of war, off for the afternoon to work for some local farmer or other, as they did most days. They were safe and sound, away from the fighting, and they had absolutely no intention of escaping anywhere, not that anyone bothered much about locking them in to prevent it. They thought

Crowborough a marvellous place to be. Some of them had found girls whom they promised to marry once the war was over, and then settle down to spend the rest of their days in the place. I hope they did. Perhaps they would have made friends then with a German prisoner of war who was also in the village, in his case under some sort of guard, though as he had had his legs blown off, together with various other bits of him, that would seem to have been hardly necessary.

The German most certainly did marry a Crowborough girl when the war was over. I remember them well. They lived in a simple farm cottage down on the other side of the railway station, and the love she so patently bore for him was absolutely luminous.

CHAPTER 5

The war was over, it was the early spring of 1946, and I have this darkest of memories of seeing my parents off to India, from a wet, cold, terminally gloomy Tilbury, downriver from London. My father, who had worked for the same Glasgow firm of tea garden agents and warehousemen since the age of, I think, fifteen, had unexpectedly been sent out to India for one final term of service in Calcutta before the promise of becoming a departmental manager in his firm's little London office, and my mother had decided to accompany him.

Wendy and David must have been there beside me, and surely Nanny too, but I have no memory of that. All I recall is standing on the dockside, watching the ship draw away through the river fog, taking my mother away from me for what I had been told was to be 'just' two and a half years, but sounded to me to be as good as for ever. I am not sure I have ever again experienced a moment of such despair.

But these were colonial times, and that experience of mine would have been duplicated over and over by other colonial children; they, like me, about to be dumped in one of those quite dreadful cheap prep schools that were in those days littered across the land especially to house the likes of us as boarders.

I was six, and in every sense far too young. My brother had already been at the school – Warden House, on the outskirts of Crowborough – for a year or two, so at least I arrived there straight from Tilbury that same afternoon with some company. We went immediately into the dining hall for tea, whereupon my brother left me to it, joining up with his comrades.

The meal was no doubt disgusting – probably something the cook optimistically called 'Fritters', which was her normal offering – and shortly thereafter the headmaster's wife, who was a complicated woman, but capable of kindness, took me up to my dormitory to put me to bed. She knew I am sure that I was exhausted, homesick and defeated – and apart from anything else I was the youngest in the school. She sent for my brother. He arrived, and stood in the doorway, and was then told to kiss me goodnight.

'Do I have to?' he asked miserably.

'You most certainly do, Waterstone One,' she said.

So poor David duly came to my bed and did as he was told, and I don't know which of us loathed the moment more.

I stayed at Warden House for a further two and a half years, and I was then sent to board at another prep school forty or so miles away. I am not entirely sure why my parents moved me from one to the other, but they may have gathered from some source or other that there was an aspect of Warden House that was absolutely disgraceful, even by the standards of those days. I told them nothing of it, and when I asked David shortly before his death whether he had done so, he confirmed he hadn't either. But some other child from a family more communicative than ours must have revealed at least some of it.

The disgrace was not over the food, which was beyond appalling. Nor the brutal lack of heating, which was beyond appalling too; in a Victorian building of icy, frigid draughts we had in the hall but one single radiator to warm us against the unprecedentedly savage winter of 1946–7. We boys took turns in small groups to stand pressed against it, five minutes each group, those with colds drying their sodden cotton handkerchiefs on the top, for we were allowed only one clean handkerchief a week. Nor was the disgrace over the standard of teaching, which was again beyond appalling, consisting mainly of chanted tables, chanted Latin declension, and chanted history dates. All those aspects of the school were probably quite typical of a great number of rotten prep schools of the time. No – the disgrace was that the place was actually a near brothel of sexual abuse.

That sounds too dramatic, and too modish and obvious these days to claim. And, in its scale, too unlikely. But just a few years ago I learnt a most salutary lesson. I had been interviewed by a journalist from a major academic journal, *The Times Educational Supplement*. She was there to ask me about my childhood education, and in my description of it I was painfully jocular and trivial and false. *All that stuff never did me any harm!* And that sort of nonsense. A couple of weeks later the *TES* interview was published, written closely in line with what I had told her, and in that style.

A week or so after that a letter was forwarded on to me by the journal. It was from the wife of a California-based academic. She told me that her husband had been at Warden House as well, a little after me. She told me that she profoundly resented the trivial manner in which I had treated the sexual abuse at the school in the interview. And in particular she objected to my tone of voice, my joking about it rather, as if it had been an amusing little eccentricity of an amusingly eccentric little school.

And here was the dreadful thing. She told me that her husband, ten years or so before, in his forties, had killed himself. Killed himself because, she said, he had been destroyed by the sexual abasement he had been through at Warden House at the hands the headmaster. Despite years of therapy, he had never recovered.

In the following weeks I had, I think, four further letters forwarded to me from other former pupils of the school, and all in just that sort of vein, if none so ultimately tragic as the first. I felt reduced by them, and crass.

So because of that, and as a tribute to the dead academic and his bereft wife, this is the truth as far as I know it, and it is going to be unvarnished.

The day boys were probably safe, but I doubt there was a boarder at Warden House who was not submitted to the headmaster's attentions at some time or another. We knew that the abuse was about to happen when he walked about the classrooms with a prominent erection sticking out in his trousers, which was quite obviously on active, deliberate display. On those occasions a boy would be summoned up to his study, on some vague charge of untidiness or insolence or indolence, or something of that sort. Having locked the study door, the headmaster (a clergyman, incidentally) would tell the boy to take off all his clothes and then get down on hands and knees on a wicker deckchair with its back let down. When the boy was on the chair and naked and kneeling, the headmaster then pressed the boy's head down, along with the small of his back, so that his bottom was pointing up at him. He would then stand behind the boy, gazing at his bottom, caning it intermittently, hard at first, then quite lightly, as if playfully, while he opened his trousers and masturbated himself, grunting his pleasure. When he had finished he would button himself up, tell the boy to get up and dress, and say to him something jocular and pleasant and friendly. He would then unlock the door, chuckling, and, quite unabashed, send him on his way.

It was the jocularity of the dismissal, and especially the chuckling, which was perhaps the most repulsive part of this performance of his, certainly for me. I remember that chuckling particularly. It was the implied suggestion that it was all, all of it – the nakedness – his unbuttoning of his trousers – the caning – his masturbation – just a playful, harmless game.

Apart from a general habit of him insisting on personally taking our temperatures when sick by means of inserting a thermometer up our bottoms, that was the total and complete pattern of it, as far as I know. There may have been more devastating occurrences for others, but I don't know of it. That is my own account, and it is the sheer brazen self-confidence of the man that strikes me in its telling.

And there is another factor lying in this, which may be the most sinister of all. For the headmaster's wife was always about the place, bustling around, doing this and that. She would have been there in the building when the headmaster was walking freely around displaying his erection, just as we boys were. Was she complicit in all of this? Did she know what was going on?

In truth, I don't think that this was a great source of damage to me. But I emphasise *not to me*, for it clearly was to others. Somehow I accepted it as a part of life – I didn't at all understand what sexual appetite was about, and anyway what upset me far, far more than this was the unrelated fact of having my mother away from me in India for such a devastatingly interminable time. When a few years ago I asked my brother David about this aspect of life at Warden House, he said he had weathered it too, and thought it was all 'just silly', as he put it, and placed it rapidly behind him.

Others couldn't and absolutely didn't, however, as I saw in those letters. They were so critical of me, and I accept that the criticism was deserved. For whatever reason I hadn't grasped the potential for real evil in what had transpired; the real evil of that chuckle; the real evil of introducing transgressive sexual abuse into the psyches of prepubescent minds, with the danger that it then becomes fixed there for life, and fixed as the norm. I should probably have done so, because as I write this I remember one day I came across two of the older boys hiding in the tall bracken on the far side of our sports field, one naked, the other unbuttoned, quite clearly playing out those scenes for themselves.

And there is one more thing to say. Google 'Warden House School Crowborough'. Scroll down and follow the link to Stop Church Child Abuse, and, on page 22 of their report you will find this:

Rev Noel Christian Moore was originally arrested in 1950 and convicted on eight counts of indecent assault against minors in 1951. He was imprisoned until 1955 but then returned to working as a priest and chaplain. In the 1960s he and a lay teacher abused upwards of four boys in Warden House, a private school in Crowborough. Some of the abuse was committed by both men working together in the Chaplain's Lodge at the school. This involved alcohol and boys were abused by each man in separate rooms and then swapped. The Rev Moore died in 1973.

So – the years went on, but nothing much seems to have changed, judging by the above, for this man clearly joined the staff some years after I had left the school.

The school eventually closed down, I think in the early seventies, and the buildings were sold off as a care home. But – and here is another coda to this depressing tale – it should have been closed down actually in my time there, and could have been, by us boys ourselves.

The story had evidently leaked to the extent that Department of Education inspectors descended on the school, and interviewed each of us boarders, individually and separately. And we all lied, each and every one of us. It seems inexplicable, I know, but that is what we did. In that curious form of rigid, unbending loyalty, in good times and bad, that institutionalised small boys perhaps in particular are so ready to adopt, we stayed silent. The school needed protecting. There were other schools in the neighbourhood, our enemies on the playing field, and we must not let our side down. Anyone who spoke out to these terrifying Department of Education inspectors would be a traitor, and a sneak. These people weren't parents. Parents were different. These men were officials, and outsiders. We would never sneak to them.

So no one did sneak to them. The inspectors went away empty-handed. They had contributed to their failure by the aggressive manner in which they questioned us children. By the standards of today their interrogation technique was crude and insensitive beyond measure. But away they went. And the headmaster carried on, no doubt just as before.

CHAPTER 6

With my parents now in India there arose the question as to what was to be done with me in the school holidays – and of course what was to be done with my brother and sister too. They, though, were really old enough by this point to organise themselves, which they did, arranging to stay with school friends and favourite cousins.

But someone had to arrange matters for me, and that was largely undertaken by my mother's brother, Lester, a country solicitor in Suffolk. Staying with Lester himself was my favoured option, for he gave me a flavour of what fatherly banter and relaxed affection felt like in a normal tactile family, and I had never experienced that. Looking back, I wonder if he was daunted by what, as a consequence, grew into my perhaps overly tactile affection for him. I hope not, and I think that actually he came to realise that there was a problem in me, and that it needed to be eased. In any case, he treated me in exactly the same way as the four children of his own, who were around my age. We were gathered up by him, all of us as one, which for me was perfection.

I did also enjoy staying with another member of that branch of my mother's family, my great-grandmother. She lived in a pleasant villa in Bournemouth with two of her daughters, Alice and Daisy, both then in their sixties, and both unmarried. It was an unusual household, and, perhaps surprisingly for a small boy, it appealed to me.

Burra (from the Hindi – large, important) Granny lived until she was ninety-four. Dressed always in a coal-black mourning silk dress and a coal-black choker, with stiff white hair, she was regal, upright, powdered and totally humourless. There was a son, Charles, born only a year after Lilian, Lil, my mother's mother, but the two unmarried (and surely virginal) daughters, my grandmother's sisters, spent their lives locked in as their mother's companions. I imagine Alice and Daisy received very little from her for their pains, apart from the prospect of a comfortable financial provision for their retirement years on their mother's death.

However, that never worked out for them. Burra Granny seemed determined to hold her primacy over them by living for ever, which she pretty well did. And then, when she did die, poor Alice and Daisy found that there was disappointingly little money left in the pot. Maybe my mother had been right in suggesting that Burra Granny had been prone to a private little daily bet on the horses. Given her marital background she may well have done just that, but it was as it was, and Alice and Daisy had waited until they were both around seventy to discover that their inheritance was disappointingly modest. They then lingered on together for almost another twenty years, in dwindling health and in dwindling circumstances. And then they died, just a few weeks apart, Daisy just before Alice, who despite her habit of speaking sometimes sharply to Daisy, perhaps found that her life held no further purpose with her younger sister gone.

The other legatee was the small, mild, delightful Bunn, Burra Granny's gardener, chauffeur, manservant, cook and odd-job man. Mild he might have been, but he had had a war service of quite startling gallantry, and startling is not to put too strong a word on it, for he was a highly decorated rear gunner in Bomber Command, a role which carried just about the lowest life expectancy of any in our entire armed forces. But apart from his period of war service he had spent all those long years of his working life entirely in Burra Granny's employ, probably imagining that he would be amply rewarded for it on her death, perhaps with a generous annuity. He was to find, however, when the will was read, that he was to receive exactly and only fifty pounds. And no annuity.

Nevertheless Bunn lingered on all those years thereafter, tidying up behind Alice and Daisy. Possibly he was diverted by the fact that Daisy, never very strong in her mind, and perhaps drifting by this time into dementia, began to demonstrate an overt and unseemly erotic compulsion towards him. This took the form of her each evening walking decorously naked from her bedroom to her bathroom and back, leaving the knickers she had worn that day on the carpet by her bed, for Bunn to retrieve, admire and launder.

As a small child, I liked Bunn very much indeed, perhaps loved him, and particularly because he used to take me down to the beach to play cricket on the sand. I still have a box camera photograph of me setting off to do just that, six years old, possibly seven, bat in hand, wearing, bizarrely, my school uniform of grey shirt and tie, and jersey and shorts and long grey socks. Odd clothes for holiday cricket on the beach, but it was just after I had been deposited into boarding school at Warden House, so the uniform was quite new, and perhaps I was proud of it.

Poor Bunn, poor Alice, poor Daisy. I was fond of all three of them, and they all three seemed to be fond of me, and they took pains to show it to me, which was a kindness.

Bunn was just always, reliably, beautifully, Bunn. Alice, mild, bespectacled, softly spoken Alice, if sharp sometimes with her sister, had at least found a daily escape from the house by teaching English at the girls' school down the road. And I imagine she taught it rather well, for she was a voracious reader, and clearly an intelligent woman. And Daisy was hilarious really, at least in my very young eyes. She was always startlingly unkempt beside her neat and tidy older sister. She sat awkwardly, her knees never reliably together, her hair askew, glasses askew, shawl askew. Even her smile and laughter seemed somehow askew as she played the most infantile card and board games with me, this with clearly quite genuine personal excitement. It was Daisy who always wanted to play these games, not me. I am sure I was the only one who was ever prepared to play them with her.

And although I can't claim to have been exactly fond of my great-grandmother, I was rather proud of her really. That's too slight – I was very proud of her. She was quite magnificently, unbendingly, Burra Granny. The daughter of an Islington parlour maid fresh up in London from a peasant Cornwall farm, she had married at nineteen to a young Jewish man of German extraction, who was just setting up as a pawnbroker in Lambeth, in south London. The business prospered, perhaps emphatically so. And when Charles Kessell (changed from Cässell) died, just short of his sixtieth birthday, Burra Granny sold the pawnshop, pocketed the cash, and with her two unmarried daughters set off from grimy Lambeth to genteel Bournemouth and the demure villa. There she was to live for a further thirty-four years, and they more than another fifty.

Nothing of her peasant background remained in Burra Granny. Well, nothing but a pronounced cockney accent, which never left her, and which she never made the slightest attempt to hide. Daisy and Alice seemed to have upgraded their accents to match their Bournemouth social status, Alice particularly so. Burra Granny never did. Her clothes, her house, her furniture, her bearing, her dignity – yes, absolutely. But never her accent.

My mother coloured when I mentioned this to her once in later years. She tried to explain it away by saying that the better social classes of Burra Granny's days tended to have a cockney lilt in their accents, as a matter of fashionable society affectation.

My brother, who happened to be in the room at the time, guffawed at the attempt. For once, I rather agreed with him.

On other occasions, arrangements would be made for me to stay with my father's parents, in their neat and dusted and polished little house in Patcham, on the outskirts of Brighton. There, my insurance agent grandfather had prematurely and voluntarily adopted a retirement spent entirely in bed. He was a man of ferocious ill will, his most memorable characteristic being the banging of his walking stick on the floor if he could hear the faintest sounds of life going on below. But at least up in his bedroom he was out of sight, and when in the house I spent all my time with Granny and her daughter Peggy, known as Poor

Peggy within the family on account of there having been in her history some quite ghastly disappointment at the altar, or so the legend told.

Granny was dry, and not in the least affectionate, but she was kindly in her way, and she talked away with me, and I liked her. And Poor Peggy I liked a lot. If she really had once been abandoned at the altar, she had certainly put that behind her in the years that followed. It came to light only on her death, when the lawyers were tidying up her modest little estate. They discovered that she had a tiny flat, not more than a mile or so from Granny's house, where for years she had been in regular and illicit rapture with a married-to-someone-else gentleman friend. My mother was vastly amused at the revelation. My father appalled.

And all of this rather opened up a line of what had always been a mystery around Peggy and her finances. On a bewilderingly frequent basis she would announce that she had won a payout on one of her Premium Bonds, and that she was going to use the money for a nice cruise or a nice little trip abroad. She only had a very small holding of Premium Bonds, so it was indeed a remarkable run of good fortune that she enjoyed. Or was it so? Looking back, it seems much more likely that they were gifts from her gentleman friend. If that was the case, I find it delightful. And I hope that Peggy and her lover adored each other, heart and soul, and were able to travel as man and wife and in blissful rapture and accord on those nice cruises and nice little trips abroad. These 'won' with Poor Peggy's Premium Bonds. I am quite sure they did.

As I have said, I liked Peggy a lot. She was a tall and ungainly woman, and extremely plain in conventional terms, but I thought that she had in her way a delightful face, animated and vivacious, and she made me laugh, as she was a fluent conversationalist.

In summer months I really welcomed staying with Granny and Peggy, as it allowed me to spend day after day at the nearby Hove ground of the Sussex County Cricket Club. There, in my belted raincoat, I used to sit on the benches, marking the scores in my score book, ball by ball, over by over, spare sharpened pencils and ruler and rubber in my satchel. In my satchel, too, I was armed with the packed lunch Peggy would make for me of sandwiches, Spam usually, or jam, spread with margarine, and a slice of plum cake and an apple. She seemed to be only too happy to pack me off for the day to somewhere I enjoyed. She and Granny could then get on with the dusting.

But it was indeed such happiness for me, for the county team players were my heroes. In those days almost all of them were born and bred in the Sussex villages, and lived in them still. The villagers knew them, and were proud of them, and they felt part of us and we felt part of them. The whole setting of that Hove ground was perfect. I can picture it now – Denis Compton, notoriously as always probably only just out of bed, striding down the pavilion steps one Saturday morning to go out and bat against us for Middlesex, Brylcreemed hair slicked back, twirling his bat, yet another beguiling century on its way. That time when the ball was hit to the boundary, and I ran off to collect it, so that I could throw it back to the Sussex fielder. And not merely any fielder – it was James Langridge, no less, who played for England. I threw it to him. He caught it. He smiled at me. 'Thanks, son.' I had thrown the ball to James Langridge, who played for England. And James Langridge, who played for England, had caught the ball that I had thrown to him. And James Langridge, who played for England, had spoken to me. To me. James Langridge had said 'Thanks, son' to me, to me, to me. And he had smiled, at me, at me, Timothy Waterstone. How could life ever be so perfect again?

Then, the day's play over, I was back on the bus to Patcham and supper in the front room with Granny. And Peggy too, if she had not just popped out for an hour or so 'to see Mrs Harris', or whatever excuse she used to get to her gentleman friend. The wireless on so that Granny could listen to a play. The walking stick banging on the ceiling if my grandfather caught the faintest sound of it.

The telephone was kept in this room, in the corner, behind the standard lamp with the big flowery shade. It stood on a little table, and was covered over by a tea cosy. I imagined this was to deaden its ring from my grandfather's hearing. Partly that, perhaps, but mostly I think because Granny thought telephones were vulgar, common things, and best kept disguised.

Writing all this I realise now how fond of Granny and Peggy I was. Both of them. What an exact relic those two were of a class and a culture of their time. Not such bad lives at all. There was a familial loyalty in that little household that was touching and empowering and true.

A dry old stick, I have tended to think of Granny. I could see immediately that she was emotionally contained in the very extreme, but in her wholly undemonstrative way she was kind to me, and I was grateful for that. What she couldn't do was warmth.

Which leads me to wonder about my father's childhood. He left his grammar school at such a very young age to work as an office boy in the Glasgow firm he was employed by for all his life, which subsequently sent him off to India to be a tea planter at the tender age of nineteen. He'd had quite a radically foreshortened childhood therefore, one that I would imagine was not characterised by much warmth or affection shown to him by either of his parents, such were their personalities. That might go a little way to explain the pattern of his life that followed, and above all that clutching, desperate, needy emotional attachment to my mother, as well as to my sister and brother.

But what it doesn't explain was his relationship with his youngest child. Me.

CHAPTER 7

When my parents at last returned from India I was dispatched to a new school, Hawkhurst Court, over on the other side of Sussex, at Wisborough Green. It had been recently established in a rambling, dilapidated Edwardian country house, set amongst pleasant fields and deep woods. The boys I found there were of just the same sort as I was accustomed to – colonial children mainly, and all of us homesick.

That first night there we were as one: miserable, cold and drearily fed at our inaugural supper. I imagine that every one of us was missing their mother, though none of us could or would admit publicly to that. But in the way of children we got to know each other very quickly, and squabbled a bit, and fought a bit, and teased a bit. We were institutionalised children and this was a way of life with which we had become familiar.

The army had occupied Hawkhurst Court during the war, and even three or four years after their departure there were still relics of their presence all over the place: Nissen huts in rows, which were used now as our classrooms; white-painted cobble-stones bordering the rough drive up to the house; coils of rusting barbed wire lying abandoned in the woods. But it was a nice old place, that house, and I could appreciate that after my quite awful earlier school.

The teaching was incomparably better than at Warden House, and the dormitories warm, and the headmaster a pleasant if distant man. There were certain aspirations towards social grandeur about the place, too. For example, our shoes were cleaned overnight by the gardener's boy. We left them out under our names on a long rack and they would be there, freshly polished, in the morning. All this rather went with the headmaster's history as an officer in the Royal Navy.

But what the headmaster cannot have realised was that the gardener's boy was also a bookie's runner. Each morning newspapers were laid out on the hall table, and we would grab them to pore over the racing form, race meeting by meeting, and make our selections.

The minimum stake the gardener's boy would accept was a shilling (two pounds today). We would write on a piece of paper our name and the name of the horse and the race, wrap that around the shilling coin, and push it up into the toe of our shoe. If our horse won, our winnings would be there in our shoe a day or so later. What ecstasy it was to scoop it out. I have never forgotten the name of the horse that won for me on my very first attempt. *Summer Rain*. I loved you, *Summer Rain*, as I put my hand into my shoe and felt around for my cash.

We had a Boy Scout troop at Hawkhurst Court, and a jolly games master, and we had our racing bets to place in the toe of our shoes. It wasn't so bad. And the school got me through my state eleven plus exam, which meant that I would be going on to one of the East Sussex grammar schools, my mother having explained to me that money was too tight for more years of private school fees. I didn't mind at all. However, it never happened. I don't know what turned events, but my mother rang me at school to say that I would not be going on to a grammar school after all, but would be staying as a boarder at Hawkhurst Court until I was thirteen, and then take the common entrance exam for Tonbridge.

Had someone offered to pay my fees at Tonbridge? It could certainly not have been either pair of my grandparents, such were their circumstances. So who could it have been? Maybe my godfather, a man-about-town who appeared to have an affection for my mother, or so she believed. He had no children of his own, and he was certainly a man who would always reach for his wallet and press a note into my hand every time he saw me. This passed to me with a little smile, and a pat on the shoulder, and a wink, as if he and I were co-conspirators in some secret plot. Perhaps we were. But if there was a plot, what was it?

My godfather had already done me one great kindness. As an eighth birthday present to me, in 1947, knowing of course that my parents were still out in India, he rescued me from Warden House one Saturday morning and drove me up to Lord's to watch the first day of England's test match against South Africa.

I was cricket infatuated at that age, and knew the name of every single player in the England team, and most of the South African too. I had been excited beyond excitement ever since he told me what he had arranged, and I woke that morning impossibly early, desperate not to miss his arrival. But as soon as I was awake I noticed that some small, red, raised spots were showing on my stomach. I knew what it was immediately – it was chicken pox, for some other boarders had already gone down with it. The great thing was that the spots were only showing on my stomach, and possibly also on my back, but none on my face. I dressed immediately, so that the spots were all concealed, and sat there waiting on my bed.

Eventually the headmaster's wife came in to say that the car had arrived, but she noticed nothing of the spots, and so I was safe and away in the Wolseley, with its rich godfatherly smell of deep leather upholstery and leather polish and eau de cologne and cigar smoke. At least that was the smell of my godfather. He and his immaculate car always smelt just the same as each other. Every time I met them, and they always seemed to be together, it was male, and strong, and comfortingly reassuring.

It was just a perfect day for me, despite the fact that I sensed that the spots were beginning to spread, and rapidly, and were even now up on my face, though my godfather never appeared to notice. I scratched a bit, and probably felt ill, but if I did I ignored that, for now he and I were sitting high in the packed stands, and – this wonderful, wonderful, incredible moment – the South Africans were coming down the steps of the pavilion and on to the field in their cream flannels and long-sleeved shirts and polo-knit sweaters and dark green caps, and there a minute or so behind them followed the two legendary England opening batsmen, Len Hutton of Yorkshire and Cyril Washbrook of Lancashire, Gods to me, both of them. Gods. And there they were before my eyes, and here was I.

And when these two in time lost their wickets – but not before beguiling me and all the tens of thousands of us there – following them to bat for us were two more Gods, even greater Gods, Bill

Edrich and Denis Compton. They were playing on their home ground, cheeky and cocky Londoners the pair of them, both of them not out at the day's close, each of them with impudent, delicious centuries to their name, the entire crowd standing for them as they returned to the pavilion. Would there ever be, could there ever be, men as great as this again?

What a day. What a godfather. And when the Wolseley finally drew up that night in front of the appalling Warden House, and he handed me over to the beamingly avuncular clergyman figure of the headmaster, my chicken pox was so advanced that even my godfather must have noticed it as he slipped me my ten-shilling note, and patted my shoulder, and went on his way.

But anyway – back to my mother's phone call – something had transpired, and I was to stay at Hawkhurst Court. And those remaining two years passed quickly enough. I was unable to do any trout tickling or rabbit snaring there, but one of the boys, John C, like me an ex-tea planter's son, had old skills to teach me as a birds' egg hunter, and he and I used to set off to the school woods after afternoon class to clamber up the trees in search of nests.

John C and I were both keen Boy Scouts, and leaders of rival patrols, mine the Fox patrol. The Scouts meant the occasional summer weekend would be spent camping. The bachelor scoutmaster, in real life our geography teacher, was happiest strutting around in his khaki hat and shorts. He liked uniform, he liked barking orders, he liked discipline, he liked us putting up our tents within his strictly marked-out lines and he liked a Scout song sung around the campfire of an evening ('Underneath the Spreading Chestnut Tree' – King George VI's favourite too, which the King used to like to sing, complete with the appropriate knuckled knocks to chest and skull, sitting cross-legged on the ground in full Scout uniform).

A feature of the Boy Scout life is, of course, 'Bob a Job' week, a 'Bob' being a shilling in our then currency, and exactly what I used to earn from the fishmonger for each of my snared rabbits. We individually spent our afternoons that week going around the local houses in our Scout uniforms, showing our 'Bob a Job' certificates and asking for a task to complete so that we could earn said Bob.

I got off to a bad start, but at the second house I called on, a pretty, well-kempt sort of place, I was met with immediate and smiley kindness by the lady of the house, and after she had thought for a moment I was given the job of mowing the back lawn. It already looked beautifully mown to me, and needed my attention not a bit, but for twenty minutes or so I pushed the hand mower up and down, keeping as best I could in straight lines. I kept going at this, until, a decent interval perhaps having felt to be elapsed, she came out of the house again, stood in apparent rapture at what I had achieved, told me I had done brilliantly, hastily took the mower from me, replaced it in the shed, filled in my form, gave me my Bob, my shilling, and called me in for tea in the kitchen. During those twenty minutes when I had been fighting with the mower she had laid out an offering on the tea table that was absolutely and fantastically superb, at least in the eyes of a child who had been locked away in board- ing schools for far too many years. Scones with raspberry jam and clotted cream, chocolate cake, gingerbread, home-made lemonade. And it was all there just for me.

She sat at the end of the table with her cup of tea, and gestured to me to eat and eat. And so I did. And when her husband appeared he came over and put his hand on my shoulder and laughed, and complained that I had not been offered enough. Then entered their daughter, a young woman in perhaps her mid-twenties, who I learnt later was a West End actress. She laughed too and clapped her hands together when she saw me there in my Scout uniform sitting at the table, a scone poised en route to my mouth as I looked up to her, a blob of raspberry jam sitting on my chin.

I finished eating and sat there smiling, looking at the three of them, too shy to talk, but basking in the totally unexpected good humour and warmth of it all. I was enjoying just sitting there, my hands tucked under my thighs, looking from face to face as the others talked happily between them about some family arrangement or another, and then the wife turned to me. She had seen on my Scout form that I was from Hawkhurst Court, and asked about that, all three nodding and smiling at me as I began to talk now, anxious to encourage me, and with that my confidence rose by the minute. They asked me further questions, taking it in turn, laughing with me when I said anything funny, pulling sad faces when I told them that my parents had been obliged to send me to boarding school when I was only six as they were going off to India, laughing again when I said my brother had been made to kiss me goodnight on my first evening at school. I had never before had such a conversational success. I would happily have sat there talking to this wonderful audience for hours, but then the daughter glanced up at the kitchen clock, and told me I had better run off back now or they'd all get into trouble.

Then they all three went with me to the front door.

'I'm Helen, my husband's Mark, and Laura is Laura,' said the wife. 'And what's your name?' And I told her, and she said it was one of her favourite names, and they waved me goodbye as I ran down the path, uncomfortably aware that it would be noticed that I was late back to school.

Theirs was the most extraordinarily warm and kind family. I had never met one quite like it before, and not many since. I abused it, though, I am afraid. Innocently, childishly, but I abused it. I went back to their house at teatime the following day. And the day after that too. And the day after that. All of it uninvited. And on that final day I took John C along with me as well.

Somehow I thought they would be only too pleased to see me, or rather us, when I brought John C with me. Perhaps they were. Perhaps, as they told me that last day, they really did have to be away then for a month or two, so the house would be closed up for that period. But anyway I never saw them again, as the summer holidays soon arrived, and I was off home to Crowborough. And even I was perceptive enough to realise then that it was conceivable that I had outstayed my welcome in their quite wonderfully generous family household.

It was in the following Easter term that my mother gave me my first evidence that my brother's scorn of her contained within it some element of fairness. Her behaviour in this was trivially stupid, and in the circumstances I think now just about unforgivable.

It was her birthday. Two or three days before I had posted to her a present – a book. I had been into Petworth and chosen it with pride, enclosing with it a flowery birthday card, hideous probably, but to the taste of a sentimental and affectionate eleven-year-old boy.

We were eating supper in the school dining hall. The head-master came across to me and said that my mother was on the telephone. I went out to the entrance hall and up the stairs to his study, where I saw the receiver lying on his desk. I picked it up, and there sure enough was my mother, and my heart leapt at her voice.

'Happy birthday, Mum,' I cried, so happy that she had got my present, and was now calling to thank me for it. '*Happy birthday!*'

'Well, *thank* you,' she said, but there was something wrong with her voice, something unexpected, a tone in it that was a sur-prise, an acidly sweet, sarcastic quality that was commonplace from my father, but unique for me in her. 'Such a shame, though. Quite honestly I was rather hurt. I've given it to someone else. You gave me the same book last year.'

And that was the sum purpose and content of the call. It had hurt me, gone through me like the thrust of a knife, and sixty and more years later it still does, in the telling of it. It was the shock, above all. I never saw it coming. Suddenly, immediately, my mother felt to me to be a totally different woman to the one I had so treasured in my heart for all my years. Giving their mothers presents and birthday cards and the birthday wrapping paper and all the rest of it is an exquisite pleasure for young children. It had been exactly that for me.

I replaced the receiver and in a moment of total, brutal, now adult clarity I thought this: I am away from home, and I am not very old, and I shouldn't have been cast away in this far-away boarding school in any case. What on earth am I doing here? By this time she is months returned from India. Unless it is to keep me away from my father, there is no reason now for me to be sent away. She is at home, she does no work, she has next to nothing to do, she is in strong health, and there are no calls on her time but for her wretched monthly golf club committee meetings.

Why am I away at all? Bronchial, small, perpetually home-sick – why have I been sent away at all?

CHAPTER 8

A few months earlier we three siblings had stood waiting on the platform of Crowborough station, huddled in coats and scarves. It had been so long, so long, and at last my mother was home from India. Or nearly home, or would be when the wretched train came out of the tunnel, and round the bend, and hissing, hissing, drew up in front of us. And once home, she would always be home, and the years of India ended.

And then, suddenly, it was there, the engine thrusting its way out of the tunnel, enveloped in steam, then slowing as it rounded the bend. And as it crept past us we could see my mother releasing the leather retaining strap for the window to drop, waving at us, smiling, waving. Then the hugs from my mother, big, big hugs for everybody, and feverishly rapid attempts at talk from everyone, and – well – they were home.

And now we climbed into the taxi, which was in those days Crowborough's one and only taxi, and an unpleasant one, always littered with cigarette ends and sweet papers, and driven by a particularly surly owner. Then we were in front of our house, and the heavy old trunks were being hauled down from the taxi's rear platform, their sides covered in the labels from their travels to India and back over the years. My father dragged them down the path to the house, and through the front door into the little hall, where stood our disembowelled and deceased grand-mother clock.

My mother had said in her last letter from India that there was a special treat for us packed at the bottom of her trunk. My brother had a particular line in scornful irony about my mother, and here it was employed to the full. He particularly disliked her taste for dainty knick-knacks. There had been over the weeks a riot of guesses as to what we might expect in these treats. A brass bullock each? A china suttee widow? A miniature glass Buddha? But now, there on the hall floor, the trunk was opened and my mother reached down into the bottom of it. She drew out nine thick stems of sugar cane – three for each of us. I was delighted. Wendy pretended to be. David handed his to me, saying that he had developed a sugar intolerance.

Now that my parents were back home I had a Saturday job at the riding stables that were in the middle of the village, mucking out and cleaning and polishing the tack. Roughish ponies and elderly ex-hunters could be hired from there for hacking out on to Ashdown Forest, or around the country lanes down into the valley. My friend Alan B joined me there, and together we forked out the dung and straw. Alan was a member of a seriously devout Roman Catholic family who lived down the road, four children, and an endlessly hospitable father and mother. The father was reduced to one arm, having lost his other in some horrific tussle with a shark in Singapore harbour at the time of the Japanese invasion. He played tennis, though, at the little village tennis club, as did all of them, as a family, and I often played with them.

Near to Alan's family's house in Crowborough there used to be a chicken farm, which had a notorious history, as in the 1920s it was the scene of a most lurid murder. It was quite a cause célèbre in its time, dubbed by the national press as The Crowborough Chicken Run Murder. It was made the more notorious by the fact that no less that Sir Arthur Conan Doyle himself, Crowborough's most proudly beloved resident, had declared that in his opinion there had been a miscarriage of justice, and that the hanged Sunday school teacher had been innocent.

The case was most prominently featured in the 1949 Edgar Lustgarten national bestseller *Verdicts in Dispute,* so Miss Santoro, who never missed a promotional trick, piled copies of it up high in The Book Club window. One day she asked me if I would cycle out to a house down in the valley to deliver a copy of the Lustgarten book to a housebound old lady who had asked for one, and bring the money back to her. I did that, and before long the idea had occurred to Miss Santoro that I could do more deliveries, and that she would pay me sixpence (say one pound today) for each one I did. Not wildly generous, perhaps, but then she had had me sitting in her shop day after day and not buying anything for two or three years by this point, so I can hardly blame her for that.

So of course I agreed, and Miss Santoro's local free delivery service, open only in my school holidays, grew very pleasantly for her and indeed for me. In time it became difficult to keep up with the number of orders, particularly as the distances we were covering were sometimes to villages quite a few miles out, so Alan did some of the runs as well, he being as pocket money impoverished as I was.

At the peak, Alan and I were each doing perhaps three or four deliveries a day, or say twenty a week at sixpence a time. Our pocket money was now reaching a level where we could afford to sit in the baker's little café some mornings and have an iced bun or two, and a glass of Coca-Cola with a scoop of vanilla ice cream in it – a Cola Float, I think it was called. All came to an end, however, rather sooner than we would have liked, as Miss Santoro's customers so appreciated her new home delivery service that they pressed her to make it available all the time, rather than just in our school holidays.

So – she bought a little van, The Book Club name was painted on its sides, and the asthmatic gentleman drove it around making the deliveries, for all fifty-two weeks of the year. From that Miss Santoro developed her marketing yet further, exchanging the little van in time for a larger one, which she fitted out with bookshelves, and acted thereby as a mobile bookshop to take to villages further afield on a regular schedule. As I said earlier in the book, she had a go, did Miss Santoro. And how brilliantly she taught me what proactive, imaginative, knowledgeable bookselling is all about, even on her relatively modest village scale.

All this meant that this source of school holiday income was now closed for Alan and me. We had our Saturday mornings mucking out the riding stables, and there was lost golf ball searching that could be done, but that market was becoming crowded, with new searchers out there in the best spots, and the golf club professional becoming less generous in what he would pay to buy the balls back for his shop. There was charcoal burning out on Ashdown Forest, but most of the professional charcoal burners out there would not let minors be involved, and quite rightly so, as the process of carbonising wood in those circular charcoal piles of theirs was heavy work physically and the fumes were hazardous. So, there was nothing else for it, we caddied at the golf club, which we regarded as a weak alternative, but there it was.

There was no fixed fee as a caddy, one simply had to depend on the player whose golf bag one was carrying to tip well at the end of the round, and some did, and some didn't. It largely depended on how they had played. Most started off being friendly and smiling, but once they had sliced and hooked a few balls into the gorse they usually behaved appallingly, and tipped accordingly. In any case, I didn't enjoy being a caddy. I was never one much given to meekly subservient roles, even at that age, and caddying is the very worst of meekly subservient roles. However, I needed the money. We always needed the money.

There was in the village at that time a Dr Barnardo's Home for orphaned and abandoned boys of school age. Perhaps sixty or seventy boys were there in the place, aged I think up to fifteen, at which time they were transferred elsewhere, mostly for technical training. The village in general, and the vicar particularly, resented their presence and labelled them 'rough'. But they always seemed to me to be nice enough kids – of course they were, for heaven's sake – and they had a cheerful, anarchic air about them on the few times they emerged from the place.

One such occasion was a cricket match between the Barnardo's boys and the Crowborough junior under-thirteens team, which I used to play for sometimes in my school holidays from Hawkhurst Court. The match was played in the pleasant grounds of a local country house, whose owner not only welcomed the Barnardo's boys with a warmth and sincerity the rest of Crowborough should have been ashamed of, particularly the vicar, but also laid on a splendid tea, to be eaten between the two innings.

Alan was playing in our team, together with the son of the headmaster of a nearby prep school that thought rather well of itself. He arrived in immaculately laundered cricket whites, with a striped silk cravat tucked in around his throat. The Barnardo's boys first stared at him, and then mimicked him, and mercilessly. They probably mimicked all of us, or at least any of us who showed the slightest sign of social pretension. Thank goodness I hadn't worn my white cricket trousers, but just a crumpled old grey pair with a torn right pocket and a shrunken Aertex shirt. Apart from the prep school headmaster's son I think all of us were similarly dressed, as of course were the Barnardo's boys, but it all made up to a rather awkward start to the match.

They batted first, and practically every ball we bowled at them they dispatched into or over the long grass on the boundaries, struck each time with an identical hearty cross-bat scything blow, indifferent to the ball's length or pitch. By the teatime interval, which automatically ended their innings, they had run up an enormous score. They then settled in to eat, with fervour, and although we tried to capture a share of what was there, they guarded and shielded the plates from us with crafty forearms and elbows. That done, we went out to bat ourselves, our lovely private school straight-bat forward defensive strokes to the fore. They took turns to bowl at us, just as fast and as viciously as they could, particularly enjoying the moment when the headmaster's son with the cravat was struck straight on the point of his elbow.

We lost, of course, heavily, and made our way home on our bicycles. The Barnardo's team disappeared back to their cruelly enclosed institution in their coach, pulling hideous faces at us from the back windows as they went, and quite rightly so.

Also in our under-thirteen team that day was Philip D, a boy who had not played with us before, but I remember him well. When I was five or so I used to be asked to his house to tea. He was a mild, very well-mannered only child whose mother had been widowed early in the war; as a consequence, her only apparent purpose in life was to heap adoration on her son, born just a month or so after his father's death.

Four or five years after the cricket match, when he was seventeen, he and an older accomplice were caught in the small hours of the morning in the act of burgling someone's house in the same quiet road as Sir Arthur Conan Doyle's substantial villa. He was sent to borstal. All of which made the more pathetically sad his gentle mother's response to this quite awful disappointment, let alone humiliation. She held her head high, went to Sunday church and shopped every day on the village high street quite as if nothing had happened. I am not sure my own mother was not one of those who gossiped so unpleasantly at her expense. I hope not, but I fear that she did. And the most pathetic moment of all was when the fishmonger, my friend from my rabbiting days, kindly asked after her son, expressing the hope that he was coping all right. She replied that indeed he was, and that she was so proud of him because he had been given the borstal governor's prize, for being the best-behaved inmate...

*

Alan B was such a good friend of mine. By the time I had gone my way and he had gone his it was to be another fifty years or so before I saw him again. It was in the autumn of 2005. I was working in my office one morning, and there was a call from one of his sisters, whom I had not met or spoken to since our childhood days together. She told me that Alan was dying in a Windsor hospice, and he had been asking to see me. I got into my car and drove straight there. He was still alive, but now in a comatose state. I sat at his bedside for an hour or so, then had a brief conversation with his wife, whom of course I had never met, and left.

Alan B died that night. I have no idea why he wanted to see me, but I was very glad to know that he did. Perhaps he just wanted to relive with me before he passed away some trivial but to him important memories of our childhood days. They would have been just as important to me too. He was a charming boy. He might even have wanted to recall once more our Saturday mornings mucking out at the Crowborough riding stables.

CHAPTER 9

It was 1950, and my father was now travelling each day to his office in London. My mother spent her time looking through illustrated caravan catalogues, as they had met someone who was a devotee of the things, and they now wanted one for themselves.

By the time David and I came back from our schools, three months later, the deed had been accomplished. My father had felled a section of the hedge at the end of the garden by the lane, and brought the caravan in through there, and there it now stood, stark and ugly, on what had been before a rather pleasant corner of long grass and spring bulbs. David made no effort whatsoever to conceal his scorn for the thing. I felt the same, but was too polite to show it. Wendy, now off to London, and medical school, and, although she didn't yet know it, love, just ignored it altogether. My parents were clearly taken aback, but only momentarily so, as it was their new toy and they were already planning a holiday in France in it the following summer.

Well – as things turned out it was not the next summer that they braved France with the caravan, as they were still practising with it around England. But a couple of years later they did, and I went with them. By that time it was only me left in the house, just turned thirteen, as David had decided to all but abandon Crowborough. He now spent all his school holidays in Suffolk with our uncle's family, whether my mother liked it or not. And Wendy had found the love that awaited her at St Thomas' Hospital medical school, and was on the point of getting engaged, and by this entering a marriage of sixty years and more, a lifetime.

So, on my mother's invitation, I went with them to France alone, with a little tent to sleep in for myself. I had hesitated as to whether to go, and I was right to, as it was not at all a success. Even before we were halfway to Dover I knew it would have been much better if I'd stayed at home. My father was already attacking me all the time, sarcastically, mercilessly, made worse by the fact that I tended towards car sickness in those days, not helped, as my mother pointed out to him, by my father chain-smoking all day and every day with the car windows shut. On one occasion my mother made him stop the car to allow me to get out and vomit, and he shouted his impatience at me when I got back in.

He kept on scraping the caravan's sides in the narrow French village streets, then sulking. He shouted at my mother in panic whenever a road direction sign loomed up in front of us. And this was capped by the final indignity of the car – still the old Vauxhall – failing to have the power to tow the caravan up to the top of a mountain pass. The road grew steeper and steeper, the car struggled and struggled, and none of us said a word. Finally we came to a standstill.

My father hauled on the handbrake. Still no one spoke. Then my mother suggested that my father should take advantage of a little section of widened road we were parallel with, turn the car and caravan in that, and go back down the mountain. He attempted to do so, shouting at both of us to keep completely silent, me particularly. He fought with the steering wheel, puce in the face, turned too sharply, and the car and caravan jackknifed and jammed. He tried again, backed a bit, tried again, backed a bit more, and then my mother screamed, and I mean screamed. By the force of providence he had just stopped, but one of the back wheels of the caravan was partially over the edge. And over that edge one looked straight down hundreds of feet to a little ribbon of a river.

Heaven knows what would have happened had not a car now appeared from around the bend, heading down the mountain. It braked sharply to a stop, the front of the Vauxhall blocking the road. My mother, weeping, weeping, near hysterical, appealed to them for help, and a couple of young men got out, went to my father, and speaking seemingly quite deliberately quietly and calmly, helped him out of the driving seat and told him to stand clear. At least he would no longer be in the car if it and the caravan slipped further and fell. They then, still so calm, and in what seemed tiny, tiny stages, pushed and pulled and gently manoeuvred both the car and the caravan, so that in time the back wheel of the caravan was well clear of the edge, and the angle was straight, and the car's nose was pointing fractionally downhill. One of them then climbed into the front seat, released the handbrake, and allowed the car to roll a few feet further forward. They then put my father back behind the wheel, my mother and me in to join him, wished us *bon courage*, and with a smile and a wave disappeared from our lives.

It took us a further couple of days to reach our seaside campsite – by a different route, of course. Once there my father cheered up enormously. Particularly so when he and my mother discovered that the other campers were not only English, but of a marginally lower social class. They then became the squire and his wife, sweet with everyone, graciously condescending, their accents upped just a notch to accentuate their comparative standing. Their adjectives too. Suddenly, my mother found everything 'divine'.

The incident on the mountain pass, suitably edited, became a charming little tale. And it was all such a success that they invited everyone in the camp to come to our caravan for an evening drinks party. Delicious little fishy things on biscuits, cocktails – we might have been back at the Crowborough golf club. My mother wore a pretty frock, and affected a cigarette holder. My father wore his military blazer, his RASC tie, and – this always to my sweating embarrassment whenever it appeared – his monocle screwed into his eye socket. The monocle was of plain glass, though hotly denied to be, and thus entirely false, and indicative of his quite devastating lack of pride and self-esteem.

And that was the last of our family holidays. And – well – thank heavens. There is a photo somewhere of the three of us standing beside the wretched caravan and the poor old Vauxhall, I think possibly on the Calais dockside as we were returning home. My parents are arm in arm and look marital and happy and as one. I look wan and miserable. I hope I didn't spoil their holiday for them. In any case, we never holidayed together again, and nor was it ever suggested that we should.

But there had been some good summer holidays in the past. For a period of three years after my parents returned from India in 1948, until I was eleven, and while Wendy and David were still just about young enough I suppose to want to do it, we used to set off each August for our summer holiday in Thurlestone, a pleasant small seaside resort in South Devon.

Thurlestone had two decent-sized and good hotels and one small and bad one, and we stayed in that. Well, most years we sort of half stayed in that, for there never seemed available when we got there the number of bedrooms that my parents claimed to have booked, so some of our party would be shunted off to a bedroom or bedrooms in a neighbouring farmhouse annexe. I was thought to be too young for that, so my brother and I were allowed to remain in the hotel itself, in a shared room.

Each year was pretty much the same. It would take us two days to drive down from Crowborough in the old Vauxhall, with our trailer rolling on behind with the luggage. My mother's current cocker spaniel would travel in the back with the three of us children, snarling and snapping at us if we momentarily impeded its comfort. There was a night's stop en route, always in the same pub in Honiton, and always in beds from which we all five would emerge in the morning covered in bites. I think it was in the final year that my mother's spaniel bit the chambermaid when she came into their bedroom bearing their tray of morning tea.

Excitement would grow the nearer we got to Thurlestone. Now the Devon lanes were so tight and narrow that each meeting with a car coming at us from the opposite direction would entail the same puce-faced, panic-stricken, cursing attempts by my father at manoeuvring and reversing the car and trailer.

The more he panicked the more they would jackknife and lock against each other, just as the car and the caravan did on the mountain pass a year or so later.

But – finally – we were nearly there, and we came over the hill, and there – at last! – was the sea, and there was the arched rock formation in the bay, and there was the first of the good hotels, and then the little tennis club with the golf course beyond, and then the second good hotel, and now the sharp, wrenching turn to the left, and then there was our little hotel, the bad one. Then the ringing of the bell in the hall, and the long wait for anyone to come, and then the argument as to how many bedrooms we had booked and what could be done to house the 'unreserved' balance of us.

Then the settling into the bedrooms, and the first walk down to the beach, the spaniel leading. And then back up the hill again to the hotel dining room for our evening meal, amid much anxious checking of watches and shouting to any of us who had strayed, because we had to be exactly on time or we would be refused service. Prawn cocktail or melon. Lemon sole or lamb chop. Ice cream or tinned fruit salad or cheese and biscuits. Always the same. Not too bad, either. Actually, in my eyes, used to both the dead monotony of my mother's cuisine and a trail of several thousands of boarding-school meals, it seemed the absolute epitome of exciting and fine dining.

Soon it was morning, and we would meet at the breakfast table, straggling in one by one, my father chain-smoking over my watery scrambled egg and toast, stubbing his cigarettes out on his plate. Then my parents and the cocker spaniel would set off to play golf together, and my sister was off to the tennis club and the teenage boys she might find there, and my brother would disappear for his fishing, refusing to let me join him.

And so I would run off along the cliff path to the sea, and climb down the rocks into the coves that were accessible at low tide. I collected cowry shells, I poked around in the rock pools, I caught shrimps in my net, I made sandcastles, I dug out moats in the sand. Other families would clamber down too, and then there would be other children to play with, and compete with when it came to the shrimping. The weather was of course Devon weather – sunny days, rainy days, days of both. It didn't really matter to me. I loved it all. I enjoyed every single day of every single holiday we had at Thurlestone, and I wished we had had more of them.

Tennis, cowry-shell collecting, picnics, hotel meals, golf for my parents and the dog, some good humour, some ill humour, and we were all back in the Vauxhall and off on the two-day journey back to Crowborough, our third and last Thurlestone holiday finished. And just in time, as Wendy in particular was now too old for them, but David as well really. On that final Thurlestone holiday he had not been good company for any of us. Including, I am sure, himself.

CHAPTER 10

This is the moment I think for me to explore David's character in just a little detail, and a good place to start that is when, in 1967, my mother suffered a stroke. She was only sixty, and it was wholly unexpected. She was found by a neighbour, collapsed by her open front door. Her doctor called me, finding my London office telephone number in her kitchen. My father had fallen into a state of such intense distress that the doctor had steered him to his bed and given him a knock-out sedative.

I called my sister, who was by then living and working in Canada, and then drove to my brother's house in west London to tell him. I called the East Grinstead hospital, where my mother had been taken, to hear that she was at that moment still alive, but fading. I invited David to drive down with me to be with her. He said he wouldn't go. That shocked me, I suppose, but it didn't surprise me. He had allowed a disdain for my mother's way of life to have become for him an obsession. He grew to be in the end totally unforgiving and totally relentless in his disregard for her. It was uncomfortable to hear him express it, and I eventually told him that I refused to do so.

I went on my own to catch the last of our mother's life. I found her laid on her back, face buckled, ugly, coarse, rasping snores coming from her as her lungs fought their last struggle for life. I sat down beside her and listened and watched. I had only just been in time. Within ten minutes of my arrival there came one last rasp from her, the loudest and coarsest, and for a moment I thought she was trying to sit up, and I jumped up from my chair to help her. But it wasn't that. It was her death throes.

And all this time David had remained at home. It was not so long afterwards that I learnt from his wife what had happened. When I had left him, David had walked around his house punching out windows and mirrors, and in doing so brutally, brutally lacerating both of his hands.

Grief indeed, one might say. And that may be right. In David's own way he might well have grieved my mother's death as much or more than I did. I think that he did. And I had loved her, and he had hated her. Perhaps the key to it lies in that.

All his life there was so much simmering rage in David, so much howling against the world, so much absence of peace. All that anger – but against what? Who was the enemy? He had been a gifted boy academically. He was handsome, slim-bodied until later life, articulate. He was loved by both his parents, and particularly loved by his sister. Nanny had cherished him when he was so ill as a young child, as he never stopped reminding us. All the basic building blocks were surely in place for him to have had a sense of security and a calm hold on life. So what had damaged him? Where did the belligerence stem from? That hatred of my mother? That difficulty in making friends? That lack of inner calm?

As to that, I look back and believe that one of the only times I felt that David had found true peace in the years I knew him best was over a period when, as an undergraduate, he was planning to get engaged to a Spanish girl, Christina, to whom he was most deeply attached. Her parents required of him that he first converted to Catholicism, so he took instruction from one of the priests the Jesuits had at that time in and around the university. This particular priest was a man of the greatest charm, who was well known, some would say notorious, for his ability to nurse clever and curious young Cambridge minds through to Rome.

For some reason David's engagement to Christina never happened, and he was broken by that for a time. He always said afterwards that he had only been cynically playing around with conversion to Catholicism for the purpose of securing her. That is what his children have always believed to have been the case, and I imagine his wife too. Certainly, that is how it started. But I know something that no one else knows, because I am the only person in his family who experienced it. What happened was that while under instruction he was first cynical, as I describe above, and then intrigued, and then captivated by Catholicism. He talked to me about it, frequently and intensely. He was scornful of my personal ignorance on the subject, and my feeble line of debate. He was both excited by Catholicism and calmed by it. He had found a home. And when Christina was no longer in his life the Catholicism stayed there for a bit. Initially undisturbed, it seemed it was well rooted within him. But then, for whatever reason, it eased away, and in time it had gone.

For myself, I wish the Jesuit at Cambridge had managed to hold on to him. If he had, I believe that given the stresses that seemed to be intrinsic within David's personality, his life would have been the happier, and calmer, and quieter for it. And more valuable, actually, both professionally and privately. But he didn't, and David's calm gave way again to anger. And the ongoing anger turned to drink. And drink destroyed his first wife, the mother of his children, and then drink destroyed their marriage too. And drink fed the anger that served in the end to kill him.

Putting aside for a moment any consideration of his relationships with either and each of his two wives – for who has the first idea of what really happens in other people's marriages? – the clearest, cleanest, strongest relationship of his life was quite probably with Wendy. Not quite probably – quite certainly. He drew very greatly indeed on her, and that I am sure of, and in return perhaps she drew just a little from him. Whatever the balance of that, what is certain is that they were extremely close friends. All through their lives. That was the dynamic that drove the family's affairs, matched against my father's desperate clinging on to my mother, and his clinging too with David and Wendy. As for me, I was way outside the intimacy of the David and Wendy relationship, but at the same time I was close to them both individually.

David was a difficult man, and a difficult brother, and by no means, absolutely by no means, always loyal. But although I was four years younger, all through his life I felt protective of him, his strengths so obvious, his faults so obvious, his vulnerability so acute. As we progressed together through the same family environment and the same schools and then the same college at Cambridge, I was painfully aware that he was never, never a popular boy, nor, I have been told by a close colleague of his, ever a popular man. But I wanted him to be. All my life, I wanted him to be that.

In contrast, with Wendy it was all so simple – I loved her, she, I know, loved me, and in my childhood she worked as best she could on my father to ease his persistent aggression towards me. She was the only member of the family who did.

I am going to try now to finally portray Wendy as, in my eyes, she was. First, her appearance. She was of middle height and middle build. She had a calm and pleasant face, and a most attractive smile. Her best feature, though, was her hair, which in her childhood and through her twenties and thirties was the most wonderful, rich red. Absolutely beautiful and absolutely striking. That was why my father was always having her portrait painted, though on his pocket, and by his taste, it was done by such awful amateur and near amateur artists that they never caught the beauty of the hair. And nor actually did they ever quite catch anything much, including her face, which had a touch of real beauty about it at times too, though fleetingly, and in snatches. And then her character – a little humourless, a little over-literal, a little unimaginative, but strong, intelligent, professional, steadfast, loyal, hard-working, responsible, and, beneath a protective veneer of pronounced reserve, capable of considerable emotional spontaneity and depth. Which she showed to me personally, and always, and movingly so. I don't think she ever once let me down, not once in my life.

And when she died, well into her eighties, plagued for almost a decade by her wretched Parkinson's disease, I hadn't realised before quite how acutely I would mourn her, and for how long.

Her Vancouver family organised a simple and lovely remembrance gathering. It was secular, as she would have wished, but in my eulogy I strayed a little away from that, and did so only on a sudden, concluding impulse. For I did want rest eternal to be granted unto her, and for light perpetual to shine upon her, and for her to rest in peace. I knew that it would. So I said so. I hope nobody minded that I did.

And at around the same time, a little earlier, David died too, abruptly dropping to the street, aged seventy-nine. His last words were impatient, directed at his gentle and forbearing second wife, in the car, David late for a hospital appointment. I spoke at his funeral, held on a lovely autumn day in an exquisite little village church on the outskirts of Bath, where he had lived for many years. And when I was brooding over what I might say, the old adage came to me that you never know anyone else in your life as well as you know a sibling. No one. Good stuff, bad stuff – everything is revealed in family childhoods, one sibling to another. Everything. And the converse of that applies as well, of course. You are never known yourself ever again in your life as precisely and as accurately and as objectively as then.

Everything that David was and became was there in his childhood, and I saw it and knew it: his drive, his courage, his tenacity, his sharp intelligence, his anger, his contempt, his bitterness, his loneliness, his vulnerability, his difficulty in making friends, his inability to ever, ever hold to him happiness and contentment – all those things he carried within him. But there is one thing more – that striking degree of personal fortitude that he also carried within him. He was one of the more physically resilient people I have come across. His sword of honour in the

RAF. His service in the SAS, when he was unusually hauled out of the RAF national service ranks after they had been quietly observing him in one of their brutal boot camps. He was never very big but he was as tough and resilient and aggressive as they could have wished for. His accidents, broken limbs here and broken limbs there, but most painful of all to observe was the damage done to him in a ghastly motorbike accident when he was already an old man, one side of him smashed and broken, and David calmly stoical and silent and courageous. What a contrast of character that was to that of his and my father.

So that's what I talked about at his funeral. I tried to present him in the round, as he really was, or at least as he really was to me. And after the service a man came up to me who introduced himself as having been the First Secretary in the Tokyo embassy at the time when David, straight from Cambridge, had come out to serve there in his first posting as a diplomat. He told me that he would have spoken in much the same way. It was just he and I together, so we talked about David's more complex characteristics, much on the lines as I have done above, and as I had approached in hopefully acceptable terms in my eulogy for him. And then he said that – yes – he agreed – perhaps David's most characteristic positive features were indeed his physical bravery, and his resilience, and his tenacity.

'But I hope in the end he found happiness,' he said, nodding to me and turning away. 'I hope he did. He was such an interesting fellow.'

Yes – he was. That's exactly right. David was a very interesting fellow indeed. And he was my brother, and I loved him.

CHAPTER 11

My initial memory of Tonbridge School was chapel on my first morning. We new boys were grouped in the front rows dedicated to our house, and I imagine we were all of us taken aback by the sheer blasting noise – there is no more delicate way of describing it: noise, noise as I had never before heard it – as three-quarters of a thousand male adolescents rose for the first hymn, and each and every one of them then bellowed it out.

> *Lord, behold us with thy blessing*
> *Once again assembled here*

I really liked that. I liked the idea of the Almighty being required to behold Tonbridge School once again assembled here, with me amongst the throng. And typing this now makes me realise that I still to this day not only know pretty well by heart the words of a good proportion of the matins collects, but also, and perhaps even better than that, know and love the tunes and words of dozens of the great Methodist and Anglican hymns. And that is because, and only because, of my life at Tonbridge, which would have been of course replicated by the hundreds and hundreds of thousands of girls and boys who passed through at one time or another the private and grammar schools of Britain.

I suspect that has been a considerable aesthetic resource for all of us. It's not piety I am referring to. It's simply an aesthetic pleasure to savour for life, just that, and a real one. As Father Ronald Knox said, 'It is impossible to describe to people brought up on Catholic lines of devotion what an enormous part hymns play in the spiritual life of the not-very-religious Englishman.'

Chapel was daily, and twice on Sundays. After several services I had got the hang of it all. Masters sat in the single row behind the boys, and scowled and mouthed threats at those misbehaving. The headmaster sat in a sort of Gothic booth of his own, mouthed threats at no one, and gazed silently, prayerfully, wistfully at the roof, looking saintly. The chaplain was a High Church man, given to dramatic ecstasies of personal devotion, for which he liked an audience. Preachers were brought in from the ranks of colonial bishops and the like, and preached to the total and obvious indifference of masters and boys alike. The head boy and his praetorian guard of school prefects, David amongst them, entered the chapel last, and paraded together to their special seating. We arrived in no order, but we left in sequence, the head boy and his prefects parading out first, and then we peeled off row by row, house by house.

It was very pleasant and very ordered and much enjoyed by everyone. There was no great sense of religion involved at all, except for the chaplain's much admired and imitated pantomime of prostrate writhing on the altar steps. But the key to it was the singing. Almost always it was the whole school that sang, not much being allocated to the choir alone, which was small and unimpressive. The point was that we all should sing, and we did so with the greatest enjoyment, just as loud as we could, the masters too, the headmaster, all of us.

The masters were a mixed bunch. On the one hand we had perhaps half a dozen enthusiastic young Oxbridge rugby or cricket blues, who taught either geography or French to the lower forms. Ranking above them were cadres of men of middle age, housemasters some of them, most of them not and clearly never to be so, unless it was to be to one of the then two day boy houses, which were considered to be appointments beneath contempt. These teachers spent much of their time in the town's public bars. At the other end of the scale were wizened old men with snuff down their jacket lapels, who taught the sixth form Latin and Greek, and lived their lives out in nostalgia for days of old. And not least in their memory of the gallant ranks of their pupils past, who, in the Great War, from their Tonbridge classrooms marched straight out to their golden deaths in France.

Cleverness was not much admired by either the masters or the pupils, and was most wisely kept concealed. Being good at games absolutely was admired, and a boy's standing in the school largely depended on it. Some very stupid boys indeed became heroes and school captains. Some very clever boys got absolutely nowhere. The former loved the school, and no doubt were never in their adult years as happy or as secure in their self-esteem. The latter were universally miserable. David was amongst them. At school he was feared, respected, clever, lonely and remote.

In a le Carré version of life, David was perhaps the quintessential candidate for recruitment into espionage, via one of the dons, as in the traditional Cambridge way. Which was, I think, exactly what happened when in time he got there. Indeed, I know it was exactly what happened, unless David was lying to me, bragging to me, some years later, the two of us alone together one late night, and both in our cups. The English tutor at our Cambridge college was Tom Henn, a renowned Yeats scholar, an elderly Anglo-Irishman of a military background. Undergraduates were generally convinced that he was connected with our intelligence agencies, to which they guessed he fed chosen candidates for recruitment. David said that Tom Henn had approached him. That struck me as likely to be true. And certainly David's initial career was in the Foreign Office, posted to Japan and then, after a spell in Whitehall, to Switzerland.

But all that was in the future. As for me, I found my first year at Tonbridge pleasant enough. I was reasonably content, largely because I seemed to fit into the place quite well, being a middle-of-the-road games player and middle-of-the-road, too, in the classroom. I was accepted, I wasn't bullied, I pottered around, I made people laugh a bit – it was all a fairly pleasant experience for me, and I think I emerged at the end of that year having neither suffered much harm nor done anything particularly right.

My housemaster's report at the end of my first year was perhaps near the mark: *Not, I think, a boy of advanced ability in any direction, and mildly subversive, but he does perfectly well.*

I had a lot of trouble with my parents when they read that. 'Mildly subversive' sounded to them alarmingly Labour Party and left wing. But I showed it to Richard Bradley, who taught me history and English and was an amusing and most pleasant young man. He was delighted with it. He loved the phrasing – 'not a boy of advanced ability' and 'mildly subversive' and 'does perfectly well' – and copied it all down on a piece of paper and put it into his wallet, saying that he was going to plagiarise it in one of his own reports at the first possible opportunity.

It was Richard Bradley who gave me perhaps my first experience of really tangible success, and that was in my first summer term. I was fourteen late that May, and he was that year the judge of the school's annual literary prize, the one prize spread across all classes and age groups in the school, from thirteen to eighteen. A short story of mine won it, and I received the award at the June Speech Day celebrations, at which Field Marshal Lord Ironside presided. The prize was an inscribed cloth-bound volume of the Somerset Maugham collected short stories.

'You're a bit young for this, aren't you?' the Field Marshal muttered, frowning disapprovingly as he handed it to me. I then spent hours poring through the stories to try to find the bit or bits that he thought I was too young for, but found nothing. My good friend Roger Ordish thought that I must have been given an expurgated edition. We had experience of this, as our edition in the house library of Nicholas Monsarrat's *The Cruel Sea,* a huge bestseller of that time, was an expurgated version for school and family use, specially (and perhaps prayerfully) edited by the Bishop of London. A member of Judde House, our house, had checked the text of our edition against the normal edition, and then written the bits back in that had so shocked the bishop.

Bullying was under control in our house, but it was in general deeply engrained in the school's culture of the time. But the staff-room model, certainly amongst the older masters, was for the school to continue much as it already was. The voices of change, from Richard Bradley and the odd supportive colleague of his, were scorned and ignored. The accepted view was that if the younger boys found life difficult, then they must toughen up. It was not the school's job to mollycoddle. The regime of compulsory cold showers, and lines of exposed lavatory bowls, and compulsory boxing, and senior boys beating younger boys, and fagging, and – yes – perhaps a little bullying in some of the houses – why not? All that was what turned boys into men. Men for the Empire.

Thus the school song:

And teacher and taught touch hands and part,
But the school, the school remaineth.
Greetings Tonbridge, Tonbridge!
Farewell, mother of men!

and

So shall Tonbridge flourish, so shall manhood be,
Serving God and Country, ruling land and sea.

The late-Victorian concept of the English gentleman, one might say – typically described perhaps as manly, straightforward, stubborn, unimaginative and gentle. Tonbridge aspired towards that, but it had spun out of control. The 'gentle' element of it had got lost in a coarse aggression. The notorious bullying of the younger boys and the weaker boys in some of the houses was unacceptable, and the school was heading towards moral collapse because of it.

Even so, I do believe that in its own desperately flawed and misdirected way, Tonbridge was a well-meaning place. The school was puzzled really, clumsily so, as to what its role should be in a post-war world in which Harold Macmillan's winds of change were blowing. It didn't understand what the winds of social change were about. It held on to pre-war colonial values and codes of conduct that were traditional and well rooted, but wrong. It had drifted into being, accidentally really, a caricature of a school of outdated character, lost and struggling in a changing world.

If there was anything in the *mildly subversive* comment in my housemaster's first-year report on me it would have been that I never felt part of the culture, and he sensed it. My protest was hardly heroic, or indeed bravely proactive, but I was lightly cynical, and lightly ironic, and lightly amusing about it, and making other boys laugh is an effective way of navigating a school community. Rather like Richard Bradley in the staff common room, I am sure.

CHAPTER 12

I t would have been so much easier if we had been encouraged to meet and make friends with girls. The girls' high school was no more than a few hundred yards away, and it would have changed the whole complexion of our school life if we could have shared activities – drama, perhaps, art, music, and some of the sports too, tennis, athletics. Roger Ordish and I were so keen on the idea of this shared participation with the girls' school that we asked our housemaster if the pair of us could add Domestic Science to our list of O level subjects. He couldn't decide whether we were in jest or not. He refused.

One barrier was eased, however, but not until my final year. Astonishingly, it was agreed that our sixth form and their sixth form should hold a joint dance. The proposal came from our side, I believe, and if so I detect Richard Bradley's influence in there somewhere. The dance was to be held in our main school hall, and the anticipation around it became absolutely feverish as the day of it dawned. Hours were spent shaving and re-shaving our sparse stubble, brushing our teeth, squeezing out blackheads, blowing into our cupped hands to check our breath. The ground-staff men had been put in charge of the decorations, and they had drooped ferns over the banisters and ivy from the wall lights in some ghastly parody of South Kensington chic. Tables were stood around the place with bowls of nuts and crisps and trays of soft drinks, and we were organised to be there in our best school suits and clean white shirts fifteen minutes before the invitation time of seven o'clock.

We stood there together in the middle of the hall, waiting. One of us attempted a joke, and raised a shrill burst of laughter, betraying our nervous tension. And then they arrived, three or four dozen seventeen- and eighteen-year-old schoolgirls in their party frocks, entering through the double doors, giggling most of them, all clearly as nervous as we were. I am not sure really if it was to our relief or dismay that they were followed in by three or four of their teachers, who then took chairs over to the exit doors, and sat down in front of them, arms crossed, meaningfully.

They were the girls' chaperones, we realised. No one was going to be able to leave their sight. But at least their adult presence served to help break the ice, as I am not sure how otherwise the two groups would ever have split and intermingled. For the first few minutes we hesitated, the girls giggling, we boys blushing and fingering our collars. And then someone put a record on the gramophone turntable, and there was a cautious advance from one of our ranks towards the girls, and then another, and eventually the girls all had partners and were dancing, and most of the boys did, but there were more of us, so some were left as wallflowers, that not necessarily to their immediate disappointment.

The girls all seemed to know about ballroom dancing. None of us knew a foxtrot from a tango. We had had a couple of lessons in preparation for the evening from a wife of one of the masters, but as there were no girls available for those we were obliged to dance with chairs, which was somewhat less complicated than the real thing, as chairs do as they are told, and they don't have toes. But – well – it all worked out, really. The girls began to find our dancing incompetence delightfully funny, rather than painfully embarrassing, so we laid that on a bit, and there was laughter at last, and noise. And in time the chaperone ladies even allowed us a last dance with some of the wall lights switched off, so there was just a touch of cheek-to-cheek shuffling around in the shadows to Al Bowlly and 'Goodnight, Sweetheart' before it all ended. We returned to our houses flushed and happy, wildly excited, great lovers all of us, great claimers of romantic conquests already won and delightful assignations bound yet to follow.

Our housemaster was an ineffectual man, but kindly. We were all of us most deeply enamoured of his daughter, a girl of most fulsome maternal build, who to our surprise had arrived as a member of the girls' high school team that attended the joint sixth-form dance. She was my partner for the moony Al Bowlly number that closed the evening. The following day I had an appointment with her father in his study. She came around the corner just as I was knocking to go in. There had been just the barest hint of cheek to cheek between us that few hours before, and she blushed the brightest pink at the sight of me now, and I am sure I did too, my boulevardier bravado of the night before wholly evaporated in the light of day.

CHAPTER 13

So there we were. There was the classroom, there was cricket, there were friendships, and the terms rolled by. And the school holidays became much the easier for me as I grew older, and I was less and less in the family home, and thus less exposed to my father. I kept just as absent from him as I possibly could, which was pretty well all the time, and this must have relieved him as much as it did me. I played tennis, and golf, and rode my bike great distances around the Sussex and Kent countryside. I was usually staying with a friend or somewhere out in the country, and always with the books that I had borrowed from the school library – invariably fiction, and mostly nineteenth century and early twentieth: Dickens, George Eliot, Aldous Huxley, Dostoevsky, Graham Greene.

There was no great teenage angst in me really. Now that I was almost clear of my father, my whole life felt cleaner and stronger and mine. It was beginning to come home to me what a burden all that had been. As a young boy I had been so severely frightened of him. But it was sinking into the past now. I was coping with life. I always had coped with life. I was all right.

At nearly sixteen I remained small while everyone else in my year grew tall. Then when I did start to grow it was late, it was sudden, and it was most emphatically.

I had arrived at the school three years before as the smallest boy since the First World War, as evidenced by the school shop fitting me out with a uniform that they had had in stock since 1918, and had been waiting ever since to sell. Now, overnight it seemed, I had grown to five foot six. The next thing I knew I was five foot ten. None of my clothes fitted, as no one could keep pace with them. My trouser-leg turn-ups perched inches above my ankles. My shirt collars throttled me. My jackets imprisoned me. And having grown so fast, too fast, my neck was perpetually stiff, and I consequently held my head at an extremely uncomfortable and totally absurd angle.

In my discomfort from all this I was perpetually grumpy, but I had my consolations. Best consolation of all was the understanding I had one term with the sister of one of the younger boys in our house. She and I met a few times, and we held each other's hands, and we glimpsed paradise. We arranged to listen simultaneously at our respective schools to the Radio Luxembourg weekly hit list on one late Sunday night, me with my tiny radio buried under the bedclothes to smother the sound, she in her dormitory I don't know how. She told me that I was to listen to Peggy Lee's 'Mr Wonderful', as a message to me, and I told her she was to listen to Frankie Lymon & The Teenagers' 'Why Do Fools Fall in Love' as my message to her, which, looking back, was perhaps rather less generous.

Richard Bradley saluted me every time he passed me in the sixth-form classroom block, giving as he went an uncomfortably accurate impersonation of how I was holding my neck. He had taught me both history and English all the way through, but having been offered a house mastership at another school, he left the winter that preceded my A levels, much to my dismay.

There was, it seems, a difficulty in immediately filling the vacancy, and when I returned to school that next term I found that one or two of us had been allocated to be taught English in our final weeks by the wife of the school's assistant chaplain. We were to be taught by her at her home and one to one. Buried as she was under the babies that the assistant chaplain apparently seeded in her every nine months, but a quite recent Cambridge graduate, a Girton scholar, and an extremely good natural teacher, this proved to be an excellent development. Mrs Alton taught me immediately something that Richard Bradley had of course attempted to do, although he had never quite reached me to the same effect. She gave me to read D. H. Lawrence's short story 'The Odour of Chrysanthemums' , and when I came back on the Monday to report to her what I felt about it, I launched into my customary Richard B format of purpose/narrative drive/imagery/language/style, etc., only to be stopped short.

'Sweetheart,' she said, waving her hands, 'not that. All good – but not that. I want to know something else. What does it *mean*, sweetheart? What is Lawrence *revealing* for you? What does his story *mean*?'

We then discussed the story in that light, and the simple clarity of her insights was such that I suddenly grasped the essential heart of not just literature, but art and aesthetics in general. All this had never struck me before with quite such immediacy, despite all Richard Bradley's efforts. She posed me questions such as: Is literature, is poetry, is art itself only an aesthetic experience, or does it carry within it a moral component? Can poetry work its magic without one interposing on it one's own mind and emotions? Does fiction add a dimension that the purely documentary and historical cannot aspire to? What did Hemingway mean when he said, "I make the truth as I invent it truer than it would be?" What is the purpose of art – to *convey* the truth of something, or to *be* the truth of something?

Mrs Alton was asking me, for the first time really, to put my mind around these sorts of issues, and the thinking of them through, even at a rudimentary level, helped me a good deal. And when the end of the year came, and we all set off into our post-school lives, I knew that Mrs Alton had raised my whole level of intellectual grasp over our two or three months together, and had put me in a better position to tackle life living within my own skin, for I was beginning to understand more of what that actually meant for me.

Yet that seventeen- and eighteen-year-old period of one's life is an odd one in some ways. Suddenly some of the bits and pieces of the adult world are thrust at you whether or not you are responsible enough to take hold of them. I had, for example, no idea at that point as to what my career should be. My mother wanted me to be a doctor, to follow Wendy, and I thought to please her I might as well at least explore following that path. So I went for an interview at St Bartholomew's Hospital – Barts – to become a medical student.

I was shown in to be interviewed by some consultant or other. He had just got to that part of my CV that showed I was a lance sergeant in the school corps, and nodded approvingly at that. I can't imagine why. Perhaps he was an ex-army man himself.

Anyway, we chatted away for a bit about this and that, none of which seemed to have much to do with the medical profession, and then he asked me what I was currently reading. I had the book in my bag, as I had been engrossed in it on the way up to London. It was *The Outsider*, by the then modishly popular existentialist Colin Wilson, and I took it out and showed it to him. He laughed, reached into his drawer, and held his own copy aloft. We then talked about that book and nothing else for the next twenty minutes, at which point he looked at his watch, cried out in alarm, and got to his feet. As he reached for his raincoat he said that I seemed a good sort of chap, bright sort of chap, nice sort of chap to talk to, the sort of chap who would fit in with the other chaps, and offered me there and then a place in the medical school for the following September.

I cannot imagine anyone anywhere who would have made a worse doctor than me. Thank heavens the reality of that prospect then struck home, and when the Barts letter arrived a couple of days later confirming my place I hid it from my mother while I worked out what to do. But there was no way of avoiding it. I had no intention whatsoever of becoming a doctor. This had all served to concentrate my mind. I knew now that what I really wanted to do was to go up to Cambridge and read English. I faced up to it, and I told her. She was disappointed, but mollified by the thought that if I managed to get in she would have two sons at Cambridge together, as David was already there. And that would be something to drawl faux modestly about at her wretched golf club committee meetings.

So I self-crammed, desperately so, sat the Cambridge entrance exam a few weeks later, and, after an interview at my prospective college, I was offered a place. Meanwhile, there were five months to kill, and I needed to make some money to sustain myself over the summer, before the county scholarship, which I had been awarded on the back of my Cambridge place, kicked in at the beginning of the academic year to cover my weekly living expenses.

Then providence struck. The telephone rang, and on the line was Logie Bruce Lockhart, who had at one time taught me at Tonbridge, and was now headmaster of Gresham's School, Holt. I had talked with him a few days before at a reception in London, and he had jotted my number down. The news was that one of his English teachers had suddenly collapsed and died with a heart attack. The school term was to start on the very next day, and he invited me to come up and join the staff for just that term, while he made arrangements for a permanent replacement. I immediately accepted. I told him that I would come up to Norfolk that afternoon. And that's what I did. Bed and board provided. Salary £135 for the term.

I had never been to Norfolk before, and as I looked out of the train window at the green, flat, quiet country, I felt, I knew, that I was going to have a magical summer. I was on a little branch-line train from Norwich to Holt, where I had been told I was to be met. A momentary flicker of fear went through me at the thought of that – new people, strangers, and where was I going to live? And how would I cope with the teaching? But I had forced that moment of fear on to myself actually, just to test myself more than anything else. I was fine. I had the whole summer to enjoy this. It was an adventure. And here we were drawing in now at Holt station, and there was a small, dark-haired woman in perhaps her mid-forties waiting on the platform. That must be her. I glanced again at the scribbled note in my pocket – Margie K, that was the name. The wife of one of the housemasters.

I dragged my suitcase down from the rack, and climbed out on to the platform. I looked hopefully across at the woman and she smiled and walked over to me and shook my hand, then led me out to her car, which was an absolutely filthy old Land Rover. She put my suitcase in the back, and I found it comforting that she chattered away incessantly, asking questions but then not pausing for the answers, with a cackling laugh at my expense when I started on some stiltedly polite nonsense about how grateful I was that she had met me, and how good of her it was to take the time.

I asked if she knew where I was being put up for the term, and she said it was with her and Jack, 'you nincompoop'. The cackle of her laugh grew familiar as the weeks progressed, and the nincompoop bit did too, as she called me that a lot of the time. Particularly if she thought I was being intense, which she told me I really must grow out of. She also didn't like my clothes, and said so, and a week or so later got me out of what I regarded as my rather smart new military twill trousers, and into something cotton or corduroy and casual and way less proclaiming of the class-strangled posturing of my Crowborough background.

When we reached the house Jack was there too, holding a tennis racquet and dressed in ancient and stained cream tennis shirt and shorts, talking to a boy of late teenage years. He waved across at me but continued his conversation, and watching them both for a moment I thought the boy actually looked at least as old as me, and probably older, and I wondered how on earth

I was going to cope with the likes of him in class.

I found that Jack was head of another department, and therefore nothing to do with the arrangements around English, but he explained to me that I was to see the headmaster after breakfast the next day, and that he understood that the plan was that I should teach all the twelve- and thirteen-year-olds in the Junior School, and also some of the thirteen- and fourteen-year-olds in the Senior School, which turned out to be correct. He also confirmed that I was to live in his house for the term.

I was relieved. Now I knew where I was going to live. I liked the look of them both. Margie was, as I have said, small and dark and around forty-five. Her hair was of a coarse texture, and rather roughly cut. She wore little or no make-up. She was by absolutely no means beautiful, but that wouldn't have worried her in the least. As I was to discover, she had that sort of physical self-confidence that has contempt for beauty, in full knowledge that she could have for herself just any man she chose to take, and immediately. As for Jack, one's first impression of him was of considerable personal beauty. He was tall, slim, forty-five also I would guess, fairish-haired, blue-eyed, wrinkled smile, Hollywood looks really, rather of the Gary Cooper sort.

I could not have realised what an impact they were going to have on me as the weeks of my stay with them rolled out. What happened was this. I hesitate to say that over the weeks I fell in love with them both, but the truth is that I sort of did. Or rather I fell in love with the idea of them both. And with their marriage, which as I was to discover was in part a train crash, in part delightful, and the complexity of it, the passion of it, was to me a revelation of what adult life can bring.

Meanwhile, I had to get through the stage fright of my first night in the Ks' house, and then breakfast with the boys in the dining hall in the morning, and then my meeting with the head-master, immediately after that. I knew him quite well from our Tonbridge days, and liked his self-confident informality. It was much in character when his first action was to hand me, unasked, a five-pound note from his wallet as a personal loan until my first tranche of salary was paid. This was a relief, as one of my concerns during the night was how I would survive until that had happened.

He then took me across to the main part of the school to show me my classroom, and then into the staff common room to be introduced around, and particularly to the head of English. This teacher was so like Tonbridge's Richard Bradley in both manner and appearance that I felt somewhat less terrified as to what I was to do next. He talked me quickly through where my five or six forms were in their syllabus, apologised for the muddle that the sudden death of the teacher I was standing in for had caused, and promised to spend proper time with me that afternoon to work out matters in more detail. Meanwhile, I was to weave my way through this first day the best I could, and he hoped I was all right with that.

I didn't have much choice but to be all right with that, and it was now ten o'clock, and I was shown back into my classroom where my first class was already waiting. They all stood. I gazed at them in dismay, wondering what on earth to say, and what to do, and suddenly extremely and hideously aware as to how close we were in age. My introduction had been so chaotic that I had absolutely no shape or plan in my mind whatsoever. But anyway

I asked them to sit, checked again which form they were, and looked into my scribbled notes from the so-called briefing in the common room a few minutes earlier. They were thirteen- and fourteen-year-olds, just completing their first year in the Senior School, and to my great relief I found that they were currently studying the Thomas Hardy canon, and had just all read *Jude the Obscure*. Fortunately I knew the novel well, and I gave them subsequently the Hardy short stories to read too, once I had persuaded the librarian to order in copies for us of one of the collections, *Life's Little Ironies*, which I knew from a weekend reading project from my sixth-form days at Tonbridge.

My first lesson over, I was beginning to think that this was going to be fun. Next in were the twelve-year-olds from the Junior School, and I saw from my notes that a collected edition of World War poetry was to be their main study of that term, with Steinbeck's *Of Mice and Men* as their fiction lead. Easy – first Thomas Hardy and now this. Perfect. The librarian arrived with their copies of both, so I handed these out, and launched straight in to a plagiarised version of Richard Bradley's riff on the comparative voices of the four or five major poets of the war.

Belatedly, seeing the glazed faces looking up at me, I realised that it might be rather better for them to read and enjoy the poetry first, and discuss the poets' relative voices later. So I did that – a poem or two of Owen's, a bit of Sassoon, a bit of Henry Reed, and we were away. I asked which poem they had liked best. Hands shot up all around the room. We took a vote, and Henry Reed and 'Naming of Parts' won. We were just starting to discuss why, when the bell rang, and they all started chattering and laughing their way out of the classroom, their books stuffed into their satchels.

And so my very short career as a teacher proceeded through that summer. I enjoyed doing it so much that I thought at the time I might make a career of it. With the twelve-year-olds we performed a semi-staged version of *A Christmas Carol*, the adaptation written by me. LBL buttonholed me to say that there had been complaints over the noise made by our rehearsals of it during classes, mostly laughter, and told me to quieten it down. Also with them I invented a poetry recital competition, initially with the Shakespeare sonnets, which didn't really work, and then with a double act of A. E. Housman and Betjeman, which really did. I can't reliably remember what the prize I awarded was, but I think it may have been a ride in Margie's filthy old Land Rover, which she occasionally allowed me to drive: 'Listen, nincompoop, don't you *dare* dent it.'

The fourteen-year-olds I led through a range of my favourite literature from the first half of the century, sticking to their modern texts and poetry syllabus as rigidly as I could, but it was all too rushed, and I would have achieved more by attempting much less. I gave them the Rudyard Kipling short story 'The Gardener' to read over one weekend and comment on, that iconic and enigmatic piece that I had only discovered myself a few days before.

I sat the younger boys down one morning to brief them on the US invasion of Lebanon, news of which had just broken. I wanted them to develop a proper interest in current affairs, which was a reasonable thing to do. The way I went about this, however, turned into a disaster. One boy in the front row of desks burst into tears. His father was serving there, and in my desire to make them understand the seriousness of the situation I had much overdone my presentation of the danger and dramas of it all, thus terrifying him as to his father's safety.

I was horrified by that incident but – yes – I really enjoyed the teaching. And as I settled down at the school, and the staff grew used to me, I got involved in other facets of school life, outside of the classroom itself. There was, for example, a drama society in the Senior School, which met after supper in the rooms of the English head, the Richard Bradley lookalike and sound-alike. Each Thursday we read a play through, each taking a part, shared around so that if we got a small role one week we had a better one next.

R. C. Sherriff's *Journey's End* was the first of these, which I had previously acted in, and, thus knowing the play, I hoped to get one of the wonderful parts of Stanhope or Raleigh, and to give either of them my full am-dram emotional blast for the delect-ation of the others, but I had to do with Private Mason, the cook. Another evening it was Rattigan's *The Browning Version*. Then Arthur Miller's *Death of a Salesman*, J. B. Priestley's *An Inspector Calls*. Noel Coward's *The Vortex*. Female parts were by necessity shared around with the male, but sometimes, not always, if the role was important it would be played by the English head's wife. She always attended, always served a heap of sandwiches, and always produced a bottle or three of white wine, which would have been absolutely fine by LBL, but probably not by the school governors.

We never, at least when I was there, attempted Shakespeare, partly perhaps because of the length of his plays, and probably more because the English head and his wife wanted these Thursday evenings to be after-dinner occasions, and fun. Shakespeare in the classroom, though, and certainly in the annual and most ambitiously staged school play, in my summer there led by an extraordinary young actor, son of a famous actor father. But they wanted Coward, Sherriff, Priestley, Miller, Rattigan, and so on, for their lovely, homely, winey evenings with the school drama society, and how right they were.

I salute them. Who wouldn't? What a lesson in education, real education, they gave us all. He and his wife were more like Oxbridge dons in their style, comfortable tutors in a comfortable college. Many decades later that was exactly as I found him. By chance I was on a visiting committee of the university being dined one night at a Cambridge college, and he was a Fellow there, and, as a very, very old man indeed, more like Richard Bradley than ever.

And then there was cricket. I played at Tonbridge for various elevens over my years there, but never the first. I found it not very difficult to get into the staff team at Gresham's to play against the school side, mostly because I had no doubt talked up my ability and record more than a little in the lead-up to it. Cricket at Tonbridge was a matter of high importance, with huge prestige involved, make or break as to whether you rose to the highest ranks of office and esteem. An extraordinary number of future England players came from the school – indeed, over the post-war years I believe the most from any single school in the land. I could see immediately that the standard at Gresham's was much lower, but also much more fun. Many of the boys there came from local farming families and the like, and all sport seemed to be played with a degree more good heart and humour than at Tonbridge, and they played their cricket rather like a jolly Norfolk village match.

I opened the batting for the staff, and after an interminable innings – stylish, I thought, cultured, but I admit interminable – I was bowled, for I think seven runs. The next man in, who passed me on my way back to the pavilion, taught physics, though I had never dared speak to him in the staff room, as he looked too furiously florid and apoplectic. All I remember of his innings is turning back to see some immediate and violent flails at the ball, most missing by some distance, and then he was bowled too, and back in the pavilion with me while I was still unbuckling my pads. And so it went on. Our captain, a young Oxbridge blue, did some highly successful play down the order, all with dismissive modesty and calm. But in short time we were all out. Then the tea interval; then out we went to field. One hour later, if that, and the boys had won, and we were all, including the boys, off to the pub.

I was so enjoying Gresham's. What a good place it was. I was enraptured by my English classes and the Thursday-evening drama society – actually everything I came across, not least in its sense that personal unorthodoxy was admirable and accept-able. Being different, being happy in one's own skin, was here a goal, an achievement. Much of this, I have to say, stemmed from Logie Bruce Lockhart himself. Although a most considerable games player, with an international career recently behind him in the Scotland rugby team, he never made a false idol out of games. His leadership was much more centred on a love of lan-guages, a respect for scholarship, a respect for the arts, a respect for behavioural standards of civility, kindness and courage, and above all else the importance of self-development through the disciplines of the meditative life. I liked a school led by a head-master who taught that these values mattered. And matter they did at Gresham's. Just on the arts side alone the alumni list was and is quite extraordinary for quite a small country school. Some glittering names are there. Ben Nicholson. W.H. Auden, John Pudney and Stephen Spender. Benjamin Britten and Lennox Berkeley. Philip Dowson. Peter Brook, and now Olivia Colman.

And, remarkably, arriving there straight from Tonbridge, I could find no evidence whatsoever of bullying. Gresham's had no aspiration towards following the traditions of the great schools by parodying them. There was too much self-confidence in its own virtues to want to do so. This was not a school geared towards providing leaders of the Empire. It was a school for Norfolk. Gresham's was wholly integrated into its local society. Content to be itself. And doing that very, very well indeed.

CHAPTER 14

Which brings me back to Margie and Jack K. I was out of my depth with them initially, and rather painfully so, looking back at it. Except in childhood, with relations, I hadn't lived with another married couple before, let alone of this sort, and they made me nervous. Or rather, Margie made me nervous, quick to criticise my clothes, or my ignorance around something or other, all rather as if I was a slightly disappointing member of her family. Even as if I was her son, for I had learnt that she was childless. Jack just smiled at all this, and left me to cope.

She sent me out to the garden to cut asparagus one night during my first week with them, from the vast, unkempt old bed of it she had shown me earlier: 'Here, good sharp knife – got it? – you *cut* them, nincompoop, *not* pull them out – you *cut* them at the soil line – Christ! – got it?' And then again, '*more* of them, you *nincompoop*', three times more she wanted, '*Christ!*' she wanted *six* times more, until at last we three sat down at the kitchen table, with a heaped, heaped plate of this lovely stuff that I had never eaten before, I suspect now not even seen before, and a big jug of hot melted butter and Margie's vast white plates. I saw that she hadn't laid knives and forks and so I got up to get them for us.

'Put those bloody things down,' she said as I walked back, she and Jack already eating the asparagus with their fingers, napkins tucked into their shirt collars, butter dripping on their chins. I did so, returned, and ate like them, greedily, just like them, the big white napkin tucked into my collar, just like them, dipping hunks of bread into the pool of butter on my plate, just like them.

I have never eaten asparagus in that quantity at a single sitting ever again, or even approaching that quantity. Or drunk Chablis out of half-kilo mugs, as French peasants would do, and seldom in that quantity either. Or laughed as much at Margie's incessant stories, the punchline always signalled in advance by her bending forward and cackling in that extraordinary way of hers, then straightening up to deliver it.

'Oh, darling,' she said once, wiping her eyes, 'you're such a bore, dear. You must learn to talk, darling. Talk, talk, talk. You're a nice boy, but you're a bore, sweetheart. Talk, for Christ's sake. Talk. Just copy me.'

All this was not exactly how I had thought life would be. I loved it, of course, but it took a few evenings before I could really manage to hold my end up, for all were exactly like the first, great mounds of extremely good and extremely simple food, way too much Chablis, and Margie in fullest flood. But it was delightful. Though on one or two occasions it turned, badly, in the other direction. Something Jack happened to say, or something she noticed in his appearance – whatever the trigger, Margie's mood would suddenly switch, and, instantly, instantly, she was shouting at him, insulting him, all this in front of me, with Jack glancing over at me, then he shouting at her. I stayed with them the first time while they were doing this, quite certainly too long and wrong to do so, but I was taken aback and didn't know what to do. That time they suddenly stopped, as immediately as they had started, and after a moment or two of silence Margie cackled her laugh, and Jack smiled, and Margie said to me, 'Look, piss off now, darling, would you? Go to bed, for Christ's sake. I want a hug with Jack. You're a sweetie, of course, but – look – piss off would you, darling?' And I did. Hastily.

A few weeks later I was walking alone one Sunday afternoon at Blakeney, right out in the dunes there where seals could always be seen at low tide. I had been there the previous weekend, when Jack and Margie had led a picnic with the junior boys, and had wanted to explore it again, so remote and lovely had it struck me. I had gone out now to the furthest promontory, but realising that the tide was turning started to walk back to the little village, to catch a bus back to the school. The quickest way was to leave the path and climb for a bit over and down through the dunes themselves.

As I did this, I suddenly glimpsed, half hidden, a head, a shock of black hair. Thinking this looked like Margie's, I went over and looked down into the dip in the dunes where I had seen the head. It was indeed Margie, and she was with a man that I didn't recognise. She immediately grabbed a towel and shooed me away. I hesitated, then made off as quickly as I could. I didn't really grasp at first what I had disturbed – I was highly unversed in those things at that age – but as I walked on and thought about it, the truth of it hit me.

Later that evening I was in the kitchen when she came in. I started to mumble an apology, but she shook her head to stop me. Then she tried to say something, but then just shook her head again, and stopped too, and shrugged. And then, in time, her back to me as she did something or other at the sink: 'It doesn't make any difference to me, dear. Nor Jack. Jack and I, we just...' Her voice tailed off. Then Jack came in, smiling as he always was, and Margie went across and hugged him, laughing, then kissed him loudly, smacking, theatrical kisses on each of his cheeks.

'I could eat you sometimes, Jack,' she said, and pulled her head back to gaze at him. Then, still hugging him, she turned to me. I was smiling, as it all looked to me so affectionate and marital and happy, but it was difficult to understand what on earth was happening. She kissed Jack once more, then withdrew and returned to the cooking. Then there was a rapid, brief, deliberately quick-fire exchange between them, unexpectedly in French, way too rapid for me to follow, though I tried, and I think it was something about love, and they both laughed, and that was the end of a very curious incident indeed.

One of the older masters talked to me about Jack and Margie one day. He was fond of a round of golf on his spare afternoons, and if he had no one else to play with he took me, two or three times I think it was, for a game at the legendary course at Hunstanton, a dozen miles or so away on the county's north-west coast. On perhaps the last of these days, by which time we had got to know each other a little better, he asked me if I was getting on all right with Jack and Margie. I told him that I really liked them both, and was very happy there with them, and how much I was enjoying my time in general.

He puffed on his pipe for a bit, then said something along the lines that he had known them for years, ever since all three of them were young teachers together at I think it was Malvern, and then Jack had gone to teach at Eton, and Margie in I think he said a state school nearby. And, finally, they had all three found themselves together at Gresham's. He then spoke very carefully and in coded terms, so much so that I couldn't really quite grasp what he was saying. But I think what he was implying, no more than that, was that Jack was impotent, or had become impotent, perhaps through injury, perhaps through some psychological impairment, I don't know, and that had made their marriage stressful for them both. That did somehow fit with what I had witnessed in their relationship. So I guess what may really have happened to Jack and Margie was that she had by necessity been released into a world of sexual freedom, and from it a guilt must have arisen in her. And that guilt added to the shrill pain in her, as I now think it was. Pain. Guilt. That voice, that cackle of a laugh, that aggressive drive.

I thought Margie was a superb woman, actually. She was totally delightful with the boys, who found her funny and involved and kind and wonderfully unorthodox. Jack was popular too, for his gentle manner, and his unceasing smile, and – well – the stillness in him. There was a centre to Jack, a heart, a dead, still calm. I thought he was pretty superb as well, as it happens.

When I look back at them I feel that they were, for just those very few months, an integral element for me in the process of leaving childhood and growing up. I was looking at and living with a totally different marriage to the one my parents had, as different as it could possibly be. And it was, in its own way, perhaps – no, certainly – a better one.

I really learnt from that. And I really learnt from them. And I hope and wish they had managed to stay together. A Gresham's ex-pupil I came across many years later thought that in the end they hadn't. I hope he was wrong.

The term wound its way on, and the skies were blue, and the birds sang, and the summer was golden, and I taught the thirteen-year-olds some Tennyson and Browning, and life could not have been happier. This stop Norfolk, next stop Cambridge. That's all I could see in front of me at that moment, and that was enough, and it was wonderful.

And it was in that mood that I met Shanie Dyson, the eighteen-year-old daughter of a recently widowed wife of one of Gresham's masters. Shanie was soft and beautiful and gentle and when I saw her I could hardly speak. When term end came, I first lingered in Holt for a week or so to be near her, then went back to Crowborough. That was hopeless. All I could do was pine. So I called Margie to ask if I could come back and stay again for another couple of weeks, and she said I could, but I would have to bring some Chablis with me. My mother was away on holiday with my father, so I borrowed her car, a little open-topped Morris, signed for a case of Chablis on my mother's account at the village wine merchant in the hope that in the circumstances she wouldn't mind, placed it on the back seat, and set off for Norfolk, not half an hour after I had spoken to Margie.

Four hours later I was in Holt, I had unloaded the Chablis, and I was in Margie's kitchen once more. I was home again, home again, for that is how it felt to me.

The Dyson family came to supper that very evening: Mary, the widowed mother; Tom, her older son, perhaps fourteen; James, aged eleven, and Shanie. Margie was in fullest voice throughout the meal. Jack was smiling. Mary Dyson was in the company of her old, old friends and was at ease. And her Tom and her James were polite, and very young and very solemn and very intense. Tom particularly so. And James was – well – you know what happened to him. I have no idea what Shanie was. All I could do was look at her.

And looking at her was pretty much all I did for the next couple of weeks. And on my last evening there in Norfolk we sat alone together in Mary Dyson's sitting room, playing Charles Trenet and 'La Mer' time and time again on her radiogram.

So that's where the long arc of my childhood closed. In Holt, beautiful Holt, to where I have only once returned in all the years. With Shanie, beautiful Shanie, whom the winds blew away from me, and whom I only saw once again as well.

As I write this, I rather hate leaving it. But I have to. It was just another childhood really – all of it. But it was mine, and I had lived it through, and now it was time for me to live the real world, the adult world, for good or ill. And over the decades I came to know plenty of good and plenty of ill. Of course I did. As do we all.

PART TWO

I do, ladies. I do. I'ave a go.

CHAPTER 15

L ooking back, I can see that we were a Cambridge generation at a crossroads. It was 1958, the war was thirteen
years in the past, and yet the country was still in a state of
passive exhaustion, and perhaps the university was too. Inward-
looking, quiet and conventional, it was as if the place had reverted
to its pre-war days, completely unprepared for the dissent, unrest
and excitement that was to spring into life throughout European
universities just six or seven years later.

We students were conservatively dressed in gowns, jackets
and ties, corduroy trousers, duffel coats and stout shoes. The great
majority of male undergraduates had come up to Cambridge
having just completed their compulsory two years of National
Service. They were thus accustomed to the military world, to
discipline, and they were in every way more mature than the
minority of us who had not done National Service and had
arrived mostly straight from school.

I was in one of the first groups to receive automatic deferment
from National Service to go to university, because the National
Service cut-off date was set to be 31 December 1960, and our
three-year university course would have still been running at
that point. Anyway, the truth of it was that the military really

didn't want any of us around, and never had, and welcomed the chance now to be rid of the whole burden on them, and to get on with conventional and professional military life.

Social protest at Cambridge was then unknown, apart from that shyly articulated by the various evangelical Christian groups, and even what was coming from them was more than socially conservative in tone. Recreational drug taking was unheard of in my time, though only those few years later, by the time of the mid to late sixties, it was rampant. And there were most certainly way too few women undergraduates, with no co-ed and only three women-only colleges on the campus, of which one was absolutely tiny.

It was a very, very male environment indeed. And a consequence of that was probably that we engaged in too much male role playing. Most of us were extremely heavy beer drinkers, though even this was conducted in a conservative manner – pint tankards in ancient or faux-ancient, timbered pubs, leather-elbowed tweed jackets propped on the bar, college or military ties part of the uniform, pipes in our mouths.

Truly, beer drinking was of prodigious volume. Four, five, even six pints would be considered the standard evening's consumption. And more than that if one was on what was then known as – and for all I know is still known as – the King Street Run. For this, the form was to have a pint in every one of that street's pubs, which I seem to remember was ten. And all of that was of course followed by vomiting, either in the streets en route to our colleges or in those colleges when we got there. At my college – the small, beautiful, central, welcoming, but perhaps rather less than academically distinguished St Catharine's – the accepted form on completion of the King Street Run was to hold on until one had passed through the porter's lodge, and then vomit in the lavatories in the pretty little court just the other side of it. A slightly depressing memory of the joys of youth perhaps, but there we go.

Amongst those at St Catharine's in my intake was Ian McKellen, like me set to read English, and I was paired with him for our weekly supervision (the Cambridge word for tutorials). We had stood in a group, looking up at the notices to see who was paired with whom, and when he saw his partner was to be me, he came up in his roll-neck jersey, smiling, to say hello in a pronounced Lancashire accent. I found him to be friendly, and gentle, and modest, and Ian and I made pleasant minor acquaintance together. It was not so many weeks later that I realised what prodigious talent he had. Harold Hobson of *The Sunday Times*, at that time indisputably the most eminent theatre critic in the land, had travelled up to Cambridge to see a Marlowe Society production of, I think, *Richard III*, and wrote astonishingly expansively about Ian, picking him out for individual and extreme plaudit from a cast that would have included all or some of Corin Redgrave, Margaret Drabble (straight off to the Royal Shakespeare Company after Cambridge), Clive Swift, Eleanor Bron, Derek Jacobi and Joe Melia.

How prescient Harold Hobson was, and how superb the acting was generally in the Cambridge of my day. I had arrived there half planning to act myself, but was frightened off by the sheer quasi-professional brilliance of the others. What I did instead was to play around on the very outer circumference of the Footlights, and the very outer circumference it may have been but I loved it. Of the actors mentioned above both Eleanor Bron and Joe Melia moved seamlessly between Marlowe Society Shakespeare and Footlights satirical review with equal facility, particularly Joe Melia, the son of a Leicester Square busker, and the funniest human being I have ever, ever been in the company of. Also amongst those in the Footlights of my day were David Frost, John Fortune, John Bird, Jonathan Miller (a Cambridge graduate, by then working as a doctor at Addenbrooke's Hospital), and also of course Peter Cook, who for some reason declared one day that he liked my rooms at St Catharine's more than his own on the other side of King's Parade from us at Pembroke, and for two or three weeks or so pretty well moved in with me. He used me as a feed, a stooge, for his private rehearsing, either in his learning and perfecting of a formal script or just as often in his wild drifts into experimental (but, as I saw, often quietly rehearsed) improvisation.

The English School was in good heart, and fun to be a part of. When, for example, Downing College's renowned F. R. Leavis lectured, the hall would always be totally packed out, not least because he was by this point of his career perhaps at his fullest, most contrary, most quarrelsome, dogmatic, opinionated, contentious, belligerent, obnoxious peak of fame. When he allowed questions from us, every hand in the hall immediately thrust high – our only purpose simply to try to wind him up yet further. That wasn't difficult. In my first year he was consumed to the point of positively unhealthy obsession with a loathing – and a highly personalised loathing – for the novelist C. P. Snow, whose reputation and standing at that time was considerable. Thomas Hardy's work in fiction he savagely, brutally downgraded, and Charles

Dickens's too. His enemies abounded, and who can wonder at that. Edith Sitwell famously described him as 'a tiresome, whining, pettifogging little pipsqueak'. All of this made his lectures quite extraordinarily good entertainment for an undergraduate audience. No wonder we packed them out.

Entertaining too, in a very different way, and equally heavily attended, were the lectures of C. S. Lewis, who had four or five years earlier accepted from his lofty Oxford perch the newly founded chair of Medieval and Renaissance Literature at Magdalene, and he was at that time probably at the highest point of his very public persona, in his case as a revered novelist, scholar and Christian apologist. Amongst other lecturers who also attracted an absolutely packed-out audience was the Marxist Ralph Miliband, up from the London School of Economics. I think he was a guest speaker only for that one day, and hundreds of students were turned fruitlessly away. I date my subsequent unshaken fealty to the Labour Party from hearing him speak on that bitterly cold Cambridge winter morning. A morning as cold, I swear to this, as only Cambridge winter mornings could be: a bitterly fierce north-easterly wind blowing straight in on us from over the Fens.

All round, I made happy acquaintanceships and one or two significant and lifelong friendships in those Cambridge years. An embarrassment was the quite awful third-class degree with which I slunk away at the end of it (this subsequently a matter of constant glee, joy and gloating from my very unkind children). But I am in the best of the best good company as far as the English Tripos (the three-year degree course) is concerned. For one delicious example – Richard Eyre – are you there?

That degree would suggest that my time was wasted, but it absolutely wasn't. I loved, and in my own way used, every single day of my time at Cambridge. I led a pleasant and persistent social life in the company of clever and interesting and amusing people. I talked and talked and talked. And I read absolutely prodigiously, in the company of people who also read absolutely prodigiously, and who also talked and talked and talked. How can that be wasted time?

And, vitally to any account of the rationale of my life, I spent a great deal of time browsing in Heffers, Cambridge's anchor bookseller. For it was in Heffers one term-time afternoon that my moment of epiphany came to me – the epiphany as to what in time I would do with my working life. Because that afternoon I stood there in Heffers, staring around, enraptured, and when a friend passed by me I told him that one day I was going to do this, like Heffers but better than Heffers, the best in the land, and all over the land. He reminded me of that very recently, delightedly, when we met as we are now, old men, at a high table Cambridge dinner. That was a stunning moment of sudden, unexpected, joyful clarity. I was very lucky to have had it, and the moment it came I knew that it was true. It served to give my life a career and personal goal, however unattainable it seemed to be for many years, and in the end of course I did it. Waterstone's.

My friend Francis Warner, at that time a mid-twenties post-graduate, with whom in due course I was placed for supervision, paid me a very pretty compliment a couple of years ago when he described what he saw in me in those days, and why the saga around Waterstone's had never surprised him. And I confess, given my third-class degree, which I hoped he had forgotten about, I was rather relieved after all this time to hear it...

Francis was the most beguiling teacher, who went on to have a distinguished academic career at St Peter's, Oxford, and then back again to St Catharine's, Cambridge, as an Honorary Fellow. He was originally assigned to me so that I should make some better progress with the Early English portion of the Tripos, in which I was struggling. His rooms overlooked the river, on the other bank from Magdalene, and were beautiful, but largely bare, apart from two beyond elderly and fading sofas, and a keyboard instrument that I think was a harpsichord. I recall arriving for supervision one week and walking in to find him playing a baroque piece, perhaps a Handel suite.

'Can you read music?' he asked, playing on, faced away from me. I said I could – well, yes, a bit.

'Then come here and sit down beside me and turn the pages for me.' This I then did for the next few minutes, clumsily no doubt, nervously, and he clicked his tongue sometimes in faux annoyance, and laughed.

We continued on, he now playing one of his beloved Bach partitas I seem to remember, and then – he still playing, me still turning – he asked, 'Have you read *Mrs Dalloway*?' and I confessed that I hadn't. Then, cursing me momentarily when I lost my place in the score, consequently fumbling with a page-turn, he told me that he couldn't face Early English with me that afternoon (not unreasonably, I thought), so why didn't I go and buy myself a copy of the novel at Heffers, which was just around the corner, and come back again. So I abandoned the page turning, in some relief, bought at Heffers an Oxford University Press paperback edition of *Mrs Dalloway*, and took it back to Francis. He was still at the keyboard, but stopped, took the book, flipped rapidly through the early pages, then found the little passage he was searching for.

...But he could not tell her he loved her. He held her hand. Happiness is this, he thought...

He ran a pencil line down beside it, told me how that passage and indeed the whole novel haunted him, and invited me to not only read the novel through two or three times straight away, but also to dwell with intense focus on that single passage, and turn it into a poem, which I should bring to him at our next supervision. So this was the passage, and if I could find the poem I wrote around it (which I am almost sure is somewhere in my boxes, and I am still looking for it) then I would quote it here now, however failed it might be. But the little passage itself has always remained with me, as of course has the whole novel, which, with Ford Madox Ford's *The Good Soldier* and Giuseppe Tomasi di Lampedusa's *The Leopard,* is one of the three works of twentieth-century fiction that I perhaps am most captured by.

I think Francis must have realised that my interest in Early English was not perhaps an obsession, for that was not the only occasion when we spent, illicitly of course, all our time together on wholly other matters. I recall him once, the moment I walked in, laying before me this quote of John Maynard Keynes, on which we spent the next hour in lively discussion and debate, and how enjoyable for me that was:

The Artist walks where the breath of the spirit blows him. He cannot be told his direction; he does not know it himself. But he leads the rest of us into fresh pastures and teaches us to love and to enjoy what we often begin by rejecting, enlarging our sensibility and purifying our instincts.

How very Cambridge, and superb, all that stuff with Francis was. How very Cambridge so many of the funniest and sharpest memories of my life are. How very Cambridge it is that I dwell on them a lot. They were happy days. But there was a piece in the *Mail on Sunday* some time back, headlined 'Old School Ties That Bind Two Book Men', that rather puts into perspective for me my career at school and Cambridge. I was a swot in both places, and possibly too intense about it...

Tim Waterstone and writer Frederick Forsyth have more in common than their passion for books – they are old school mates. Waterstone, a thrice-married father of eight, and *Day of the Jackal* author Forsyth, both attended 500-year-old Tonbridge in Kent in the Fifties. The Insider managed to track down old boys who remember the dashing Forsyth, but whose memories of Waterstone are somewhat less vivid. He was, by all accounts, something of a swot.

'Quiet, thoughtful and reserved is how I remember him,' says David Kemp, Waterstone's former housemaster. 'He was a leader and was generally acknowledged to be able and dynamic. Freddie was an interesting chap.' Kemp went on, 'He wasn't the orthodox pillar of the community. He was very much his own man. It's difficult to compete with some-one like Freddie.'

CHAPTER 16

I am not sure my decision to go straight out to India immediately after leaving Cambridge was based on much more
than an awareness that I was still very young and still
very immature – sort of twenty-two going on twenty, perhaps.
Fortunately, through a friend of my godfather – back in my life
once again – I had received an invitation to join a broking firm
in Calcutta, now Kolkata (produce brokers – tea and cardamom
mainly, and the general financing of the harvesting thereof).
With no other clear plan afoot, I thought that I might as well take
it up and get away as fast as I could. Going to India for a couple of
years or so would be an adventure. I really wanted to travel, and
I really wanted to see that particular country, and to draw an
income while doing so seemed a perfect solution. And so I went.

I caught an Anchor Line boat out of Liverpool one rainy and
miserable winter afternoon, the boat old and creaking and still
shabby from its service as a troop ship in the war. For three days
we wallowed and plunged and swayed our way down through
the Irish Sea and then the Bay of Biscay. All that time I lay,
heaving with sea sickness, in my tiny cabin in the boat's bowels.
I hugged a bowl to me, my shirt sodden with sweat, unable to

touch either the ham sandwich which at some point a lower deck steward had placed on the shelf beside me or the mug of tea, by now hopelessly cold and slopped.

I carried in my trouser pockets two crumpled photographs. The first was one of me with a group of my friends at my Cambridge college, resplendent in the tweed jackets and corduroys and duffel coats of the period. The other was a lovely snapshot of my Crowborough friend, Tricia, with her open smile and her pretty, vivacious face. Both gave me some level of comfort, as they brought to mind not so much a glimpse of home, but of familiarity, of remembered contact, of belonging. My sea sickness was so appalling that I absolutely had a need of that.

But on the fourth morning I awoke to find that the storms had passed overnight, and the boat was now calmly, steadily chugging along. From the tiny porthole up above me I could see a glimpse of the bluest of blue Mediterranean winter skies. And – at last – I no longer felt the heaving hell of nausea.

So, gingerly, I undressed for the first time since I had come on board, wrapped myself in a towel, and set off down the passageway to find the communal showers. There, with an over-precipitate twist of the tap, I nearly caught the full deluge of the scalding sea water that plunged down from the pipes above my head – a near and glancing miss. I then turned the cold water tap too and stood there in naked ecstasy after the days of sweat and vomit. I held my mouth wide open to fill it with the salty water, rubbing myself clean with one of the vast bars of carbolic soap that hung from above, pierced through and secured on long, thin cords. Then, back to the cabin; clean, fresh clothes, and a bite at the stale ham sandwich, before venturing up to the top deck, where I had last stood watching the iconic buildings of Liverpool disappearing into the grey, sodden mist.

The boat was small, mixed cargo and passenger, and there were no more than seventy or eighty of us on board. The main group, perhaps twenty-five or so strong, comprised Methodist missionaries. Amongst them were some married couples returning to India together for another long term of service. Others were young men and women setting out for the first time, some of them not much older than myself. Their whole party was clearly determined to have a positive, happy time of it on the voyage. They had commandeered a little saloon for their twice-a-day homily and prayers and Bible readings and hymns. This saloon was optimistically called the library, but stocked only piles of elderly magazines, grubby Agatha Christie paperbacks, doctor-and-nurse romances and tales of heroic colonial adventure.

The missionary party sat together for all meals at one big table in the dining saloon. They were always the first to breakfast, and the first in to lunch and dinner too, smiling, laughing, their pots of tea and their jugs of lemonade laid out on the table before them. When they were not at a prayer meeting or at a meal, they played games on the deck: the inevitable deck quoits, of course, deck tennis too, but also a form of play golf. The point of this game was to use a long-handled broom to push a large flat disc, a puck, from point to point, or rather hole to hole – eighteen of them, positioned around the entire area of the deck. The winner of each match was the one who completed 'the golf course' in the fewest pushes. It was infantile, and somewhat embarrassing too, as one kept getting in the way of other passengers trying to take their quiet strolls around the decks.

By the time we had reached Malta the missionaries decided that I was lonely (which I wasn't), and keeping too much to myself. They insisted that I played these games with them, as if I was one of their party. It was an invitation passed with great kindness, and I thought they were delightful people, so I played with them for a day or two, but I couldn't get away from them, even for a moment, so concerned as to my apparent loneliness were they. It got to the point that I thought I might well have to feign another attack of sea sickness in order to escape them. I wanted to get down to some decent reading. I had packed in my two trunks books that I had been much looking forward to settling down with, including a great many Graham Greene and Evelyn Waugh novels and the six parts of Trollope's Barchester sequence.

The other passengers were a mixed bunch. There were planters and their wives returning to India for yet another spell, their children left in England to cope no doubt with the horrors of the Warden House equivalents of the period, just as I had been in my time. There were some businessmen and their wives, who spent the voyage together playing bridge, and there were two young men in their late twenties, who were going out as special advisers to the Indian Forestry Service. These two spent the entire three weeks of the voyage in the bar. There they were in the company of an Irish priest, who appeared to drink nothing but pint mugs of Black Velvet (Guinness and champagne). He kept that up all the way from Liverpool, including I was told through the three days of the storms before we reached the calm seas and blue skies of the Mediterranean. Drinks on board were duty free and very inexpensive, of course, but I wondered how on earth he was eventually to pay for them.

The priest was an appealing man to talk to, an excellent, richly fluent raconteur. Though already of middle age, he had never before been out of Ireland, not even to England, apart from his ferry trip to Liverpool to catch our boat. He had been dispatched now for a seven-year spell at a mission in Vijayawada, right down in the south-east of India. Without any great show of enthusiasm, he pointed Vijayawada out to me on a map. He told me that the prospect of those seven years stretching ahead of him felt like the prospect of eternity. Thus the incessant pints of Black Velvet, I suppose. In fact, it was probably exactly that, for Vijayawada is in the state of Andhra Pradesh, which in those days had strictly held laws around alcohol prohibition.

There were half a dozen or so other Roman Catholics on board, including the chief engineer. The priest celebrated Mass for them somewhere on board each early Sunday morning of the voyage, I imagine in the so-called library where the Methodists held their prayer meetings. Then it was back to the bar. He never left the boat when in port, at Port Said, then Aden, as the rest of us did, his curiosity apparently satisfied by carrying his pint tankard out from the bar to the deck, and leaning on the rail to look down at the bustle there beneath him on the dockside.

Memorable were the truly beautiful late evenings sailing through the Red Sea, the temperature at that hour at last cooling, phosphorescence dancing and sparkling on the calm, moonlit water in our wake. Each night the stewards secured a vast canvas screen across the upper deck so that we could watch a film in the open air. The missionaries were always there, and the young Forestry Commission men too. But the priest remained on his bar stool, alone with the smiling Chinese barman, who possessed, apart from the names of drinks, barely one single word of English.

Three weeks in, and early in the afternoon I watched the coast of Pakistan draw near and there, suddenly before us, were the teeming docks of Karachi. Soon we were berthed, and cargo was lifted by crane in and out of our holds all that afternoon and deep into the night. On our loudspeakers Peggy Lee was singing Jerome Kern's 'The Folks Who Live On The Hill', a soothing presence over the shouted chatter and bellowed instruction and counter-instruction coming from the coolies on the dockside, as they pushed and pulled and knifed apart the unloaded cargo bails.

... Some day we'll build a home on a hilltop high, you and I,
Shiny and new, a cottage that two can fill...

At that moment, leaning against the rusting rails of our Anchor Line boat, I told myself that I would never forget the moment. And to this day I can hear Peggy Lee's lovely voice and picture that Karachi scene: the heat and noise and colour and energy and the heaving masses of humanity.

Then we set sail again to Bombay, and two days later the voyage was over. First one of the missionary ladies hugged me, and then another, and then another. Then one of the planters (an indigo planter, I think) shook my hand in a gruff, manly sort of way, and said that perhaps he would bump into me in Calcutta one day, when he was up from Bihar on business. The Irish priest nodded and smiled at me, and set off mournfully down the gangplank en route to his eternity in Andhra Pradesh.

I followed behind him. My two tin trunks were waiting for me on the dockside, guarded by a small boy who held out his hand for a tip.

Shortly afterwards a clerk, a babu, cherishing his officiousness in his flapping white dhoti, came trotting up to me holding a large card with my name on it. He shooed the little boy away, shook my hand and welcomed me to India. His office was the appointed local correspondent of the Calcutta brokerage I was due to join. He had with him my train ticket for the sleeper train I was to catch that night, and an envelope containing some petty cash for me to buy refreshment on the journey. He came with me to the station and saw me off. He was still standing on the platform, waving and smiling, as the train pulled away.

*

My young Indian colleagues and I had an absurdly enjoyable time in Calcutta. I made lasting friendships that I have cherished all the rest of my days. On my very first evening, the head of the firm, William Goldsmith, took me to a drinks party which he said would give me a chance to meet one or two of the firm's other assistants. He introduced me to one, Kamal Bhagat, who looked immaculate, buttoned up to the neck in a cream Nehru jacket. William G moved away to talk to someone else, and Kamal looked me up and down. 'God,' he said, with shattering disdain, 'more white trash.' Then, thank heavens, he laughed. So did I. It's almost sixty years later now, and we are still the closest of friends.

None of us in the assistants' office were exactly hard stretched in our work, apart from the acute bustle around the preparation and follow-through of our brokerage's catalogues in the twice-weekly auctions.

One memorable feature of my time there were our long trips, in pairs, up to the Darjeeling and Assam tea gardens, particularly the former, almost 7,000 feet up in the Himalayan foothills, facing Mount Everest. We were the appointed brokers for numerous tea garden proprietors there, living their lives in a place of extraordinary beauty.

The brokerage also had an office in Cochin, right in the south-western tip of India, and the assistants took turns to go down there to assist the local director. I stayed there for six months. In Cochin we performed the same work as in Calcutta, but a touch more of it, and the best part was travelling up into the Nilgiri Hills to visit the tea gardens. I went on these trips on my own, just with the office driver, who leant perpetually on his horn as we threaded through the hill villages in our Jeep. Often we drew to the side of the road and stopped for working elephants to pass us by. While the elephants plodded placidly along, seemingly and perhaps actually deep in thought, heavy timbers balanced securely and effortlessly in their curled trunks, their mahouts would sit up on their necks, talking to them, scratching behind the elephants' ears with their sticks.

But one morning we arrived at a village to find that an appalling tragedy had occurred. A mahout – a trainer, a keeper – starts as a boy in the family profession, and is assigned to an elephant early in that elephant's life. The boy and that elephant are subsequently never then parted from each other, and deep, lifelong bonds are formed. On this particular morning, shortly before we had arrived in the village, a young elephant and its young mahout had been playing around together as they did each breakfast time, spraying water at each other, all their usual games. One of these games, played over many months, had been for the elephant to pick up the mahout in its trunk, wave him around a bit and then put him gently back to the ground. But this time, thinking to make it even more fun, the elephant lightly tapped the mahout on the trunk of a tree. Not lightly enough, unfortunately. The boy's neck was broken, and he was dead.

When my three-year contract was almost at an end, I found myself back in Calcutta. While there, I met Josh, my father's cousin, whose son had spent time in England in order to qualify as a civil engineer, and whom my parents – horrifyingly, shamefully – had refused to have to stay with them, despite his loneliness, in case anyone thought he was my father's son. Josh had three of his other children with him, and I asked after their mother. He showed me a snapshot of the two of them together, he and his Indian lover, plump and lovely in her sari, their arms around each other's waists, she with her head resting on his shoulder, both of them smiling and content and safe. It was a beautiful picture, and, of its time, iconic, for she was of simple, peasant stock. I have never forgotten it. Josh and his lady were never parted and spent decades together of mutual fidelity and love. They died, I believe, within a week or so of each other.

In my time in Calcutta I also had the opportunity to make acquaintance with the nuns at Mother Teresa's Order of the Missionaries of Charity, who were dedicated to helping the poor, and it was from them that we were able in later years to adopt, as a three-month-old baby, my daughter Maya into our family. I also came across a retired English regimental sergeant major,

Jim, who spent every night of the week, every week of the year, in his van on the streets of the Calcutta slums, handing out free bowls of soup and rice. This was paid for by him, from his army pension, and also by a small team of donors, most of them from his old British regiment, in which he had served his entire army life. He lived alone, in a single room, and Mother Teresa made it her task to ensure that there was a clean glass and an ice-cold bottle of beer there waiting for him each and every morning, when he returned from the streets.

Meanwhile, with consummate idiocy, I had failed to take one of my scheduled top-up vaccines against typhoid. This resulted in me promptly contracting it several weeks later. I have no idea how severe my experience of typhoid was on the scale of things, but anyone getting it worse than I did has my most profound sympathy. Perhaps today it is easier to treat, because I don't think the specific antibiotics that are now used against it were then available. All I can say is the abdominal pain, the headache and the sky-high fever made me perfectly happy to die, if that was to be the result of it all.

I don't remember anything of being carried off to hospital, but I do remember the point when I gradually started to recover there, a week or so later. The fever was easing, the body rash fading, my bowels gradually regaining control, and a sense of life and health was slowly reassuming a place in my mind.

One morning I felt well enough to at least open my eyes, and there on the other side of the room I saw that there were three burly men in tropical suits, sitting around the bed of what I could see was another man, eyes closed, lying still, breathing erratically. One of them saw that I was awake, and he raised his hand in greeting. I managed to raise mine in return, then promptly went back to sleep.

But later, on reawakening, and beginning to feel stronger, I said something or other to one of these men, trying to find out who they were. In hesitant, heavily accented English he explained that the ill man was a sailor from a Russian cargo boat, that he had been put through surgery on arrival at the hospital, while I had been too ill to know what was happening, and that he and his two colleagues were from the Soviet Union consulate, and were there to make sure he was safe. Then one of the others swung around to face me and said, 'What he means is to make sure he doesn't run away.' He grinned broadly and the three of them laughed, while the ill man himself appeared to smile, perhaps a little nervously.

Since all this was happening at a time when the Cold War was at its coldest – indeed, only a couple of years after Kennedy and Khrushchev had squared up to each other over the Cuban Missile Crisis, with all the consequent global fear that had brought about – I felt a touch of the invalid's nervousness myself. But over the next week or so, as I slowly recovered, the bodyguards and I became positively friendly, the sick man now comatose after having had a second operation. There was not much therefore for the three of them to do, so they said they wanted to practise their English with me. I thought the easiest thing to do was to teach them a poem to recite and the second poem from A. E. Housman's *A Shropshire Lad* seemed appropriate as it was Eastertime:

Loveliest of trees, the cherry now
Is hung with bloom along the bough,

And stands about the woodland ride
Wearing white for Eastertide

At least two of the three men learnt the three little verses of the poem diligently, and were so pleased with themselves for having done so that they kept on repeating them. They seemed to like best:

About the woodlands I will go
To see the cherry hung with snow.

Maybe the image reminded them of home. At any rate, Housman had struck a chord, and I was glad of that. So I tried another short Housman poem with them, 'Here Dead We Lie', and they learnt that too:

Here dead we lie
Because we did not choose
To live and shame the land
From which we sprung.

Life, to be sure,
Is nothing much to lose.
But young men think it is,
And we were young.

I think they realised I was offering that poem to them as a statement of admiration for their country's heroism in the Second World War not twenty years past, and as an acknowledgement of my country's debt to them. I nearly said as much, then didn't, hoping they would merely catch the hint.

By the time I was free and away from the hospital, and had shaken hands and hugged and slapped backs and expressed enduring and life-lasting friendship with the Russians, I had lost a simply prodigious amount of weight. The brokerage contract was almost over, so I was due to return to England in any case, but I was too weak to make the trip. I remember trying to get my legs back to strength by walking up the first hole of the Tollygunge golf course and back to the clubhouse. This was a distance of about four hundred yards or so each way. I proved unable to do so without someone running out from the clubhouse and putting a supportive arm about my waist before the distance was up.

Every day I tried to walk a little more, and about five weeks or so after leaving the hospital I was able to catch a Swissair flight back to London. I remember it was Swissair because I ate a little Swiss butter during the flight, and, being Swiss, the butter was so rich that my post-typhoid stomach rebelled against it.

Back in England I slowly mended, and regained some weight. After a month or so it was time for me to gather myself and set about finding a career. I knew that the India honeymoon period, such fun as it had been, was over. I was just about to turn twenty-five, and I must move my life on.

CHAPTER 17

I married during my time in Calcutta. We were extremely young: I was only twenty-three and Tricia had just turned twenty. She had come out from England to join me, and we had three perfect children together, all in quite rapid succession. Tricia was delightful, but in just a few years we broke up, and it is best for all of us if I keep the statement as plain and unvarnished as that.

Four years after we broke up I married again. Claire was twenty-five, and she too was delightful. Again, we had three perfect children. Again, in time we broke up. And, again, it is best for all of us if I keep the statement as plain and unvarnished as that.

Unconnected with all this – or was it? – a year or so into the period between the two marriages I'd had the biggest depressive breakdown of all time, or so it seemed to me. It happened quite suddenly, and I have no recollection as to what the trigger of it was, or if there was indeed a precise and identifiable trigger to it at all.

Perhaps all breakdowns seem like that. I am sure they do, and that mine was conventional and commonplace, but it felt at the time as if it was the end of me. I was rescued, somewhat bizarrely, by my dentist, who was actually a doctor with an interest in issues around mental health, to which, in later years, I believe he devoted his professional career.

At this time, I was attempting to lift myself out of a dark, dark melancholy that had served to wholly flatten me. I got to the point where I was almost incapable of speaking, or indeed even of physically moving. Quite literally that. Physically speaking. Physically moving. You have to have experienced that condition to know the lack of exaggeration in that statement of mine. But I was fortunate. Most generously, I was quietly released for a period from my desk at Allied Breweries to allow me time to get help and to recover (more of Allied in a moment, but I should say at this point that such swift and sympathetic action on the grounds of mental health was, I can assure you, rare, perhaps even unthinkable, in the corporate world of those benightedly ignorant and prejudiced days...).

Trying to rebuild a discipline, a structure to my life as a route through, I thus honoured a simple check-up appointment with the dentist that had been scheduled many weeks before. I knew him quite well, and liked him, and made an attempt to smile as he showed me through to his surgery. I was ushered to sit, but as he talked to me he began to look puzzled, and then gazed at me thoughtfully, his hand on my shoulder. Then he went to his house phone, and called another doctor who had a practice within the same Harley Street building. He came up and joined us a few minutes later. He talked to me as well, although I cannot recall whether I was in a condition to make anything beyond a cursory response to his questions. What I do remember, though, was that there was then a further phone call or two made by the pair of them. They then came back to me and said that they were of the opinion that I needed an immediate professional assessment. A car was arranged to take me straight to a hospital and they said I would be seen on arrival.

An hour or so later, there I was, at the Maudsley, in south London. I was assessed and they arranged a bed for me in a general ward. I do not remember much else of what turned out to be, I think, the next five days, or perhaps at most six or seven. The majority of that time I must have slept under some form of sedation. I remember some things, however. I remember a particularly kind West Indian nurse. I remember another kind and extremely young houseman. I remember a consultant, and his quiet, persuasive voice, and the clarity of his assessment and his advice. I remember sitting in a day room, and the squalid, rank odour of spent cigarettes and full ashtrays and furniture polish. I remember wanting to go home. I remember asking to see the consultant once more, and saying that I felt much stronger and that I wanted to go. I remember that he tried to dissuade me, almost to the point of insistence – legally enforceable insistence, he stressed, but then gave way. He asked if there was someone to look after me at home, and I lied about that. He arranged a taxi for me. He gave me some drugs to bide me over for a day or two, and a prescription. He told me that it was too soon, much too soon, and that I would be back. Indeed, he said he was certain that I would be back. But he wished me very well. And he repeated that. Then, 'Hold on,' he said. 'Hold on.'

He was a most likeable man. In a couple of weeks I threw the prescription drugs away. And as it turned out he was wrong. I was never back at the Maudsley, nor anywhere near being back at the Maudsley. Never again in my life did I experience that step over the line into the black pit of a breakdown of mental facility. There were times ahead of melancholy – of course there were – but they were of an entirely different order. Gloom, sometimes, greyness, sadness – that happens to us all. But even at a particular moment, decades later, when the heaviest of personal blows struck me, and unexpectedly so, I never experienced that collapse again. Nor did I come anywhere near to doing so. I was very fortunate to come out of that period as decisively and as quickly as I did. But I remember still what it felt like and I know how lucky I have been in my escape from a recurrence.

Now that part of my story has been told, as it needs to be, and we won't return to it. So let's go back.

*

It was 1964, I was about to turn twenty-five, and my life must move on. And move it on I did through the next fifteen or so years. Initially, though, it was a messy process. The dream was there – to bring my Heffers epiphany, Waterstone's, into life. But that was going to be years away. I knew perfectly well that to get there I needed over time to make huge and steady strides in my confidence, my knowledge and my maturity so that when the moment arrived I could credibly take my chance and go for it. And I knew exactly what *it* was. The image of Waterstone's was always there at the back of my mind.

My initial thought was to start that process by going into book publishing, which seemed a logical step. As it turned out I was put off that particular step by an amateurish and dispiriting interview I went to with a small to middle-size, low to middle-quality literary house (which lapsed, some years ago, into extinction). In fairness, I knew I didn't want to join them the very moment I walked into their chaotic office, and I no doubt showed it, perhaps offensively so, as they never wrote to me after our conversation that afternoon. At that age I didn't possess the grace or the tact or the sheer common-or-garden communication skills to deal with that sort of encounter. For, as the conversation between me and the publisher ground on, I realised for certain that I didn't want to be an editor, that I didn't want to be a salesman, and that I didn't want to employed in their publicity department – and these were the only three roles that my conversation with him that afternoon suggested were the paths into publishing. Apart from that, I had no desire to work for him, for he struck me as second-rate and culturally void. If he was typical of publishers, I concluded, then that world was not for me.

Of course, it was a most juvenile piece of analysis that I made and I am embarrassed to write of it now, as you can imagine, but it does serve to illustrate how much growing up I had to do before I could convert my Waterstone's dream into reality. For all my crassness, I did know that my mind was at least already set on my ultimate goal, and that I was fortunate to actually have a goal when so many did not, and that I must calmly plot my way through to it. I knew that I had to get myself to the point where I truly knew enough about, well, so many things: money, building a brand, leadership, financial engineering, and all the other requisite skills. I had to educate myself and I knew I had a long, long way to go in that.

So, if not publishing, which industry would teach me the lessons I had to learn, and get myself to where I wanted it to be?

Perhaps a big brand advertising agency or a big brand marketing company? Either of them seemed to me to be possible and potentially useful routes. However, I couldn't persuade myself that the schmoozing and the constant purposeful socialising required of an account man at an advertising agency would work for me – and how right I was in that. While starting out in life on an alternative route in advertising, as a creative man, or perhaps a copywriter, which I knew I would enjoy, was not going to lead me anywhere near to my final goal. Perhaps a career in marketing would be a better bet.

So, late in the autumn of 1964, I drove up to Cambridge to discuss matters with the man who ran the Careers Advice department, who I had previously got on with as an undergraduate. I didn't mention to him my Waterstone's dream, sensing that he might think my aspiration laughably absurd. But I did hint around it in general terms so that he came to understand where I was at, and followed my own line of thought in suggesting that I went for the route of a marketing role in one of the major brand consumer companies. Proctor & Gamble, perhaps, or Dunlop or Unilever or best, of all maybe, Allied Breweries? The latter was a relatively recent and huge new corporate entity that had been created by the merger of five or six very large, mostly family owned, breweries together with their related subsidiary companies. On its public listing it was pretty much immediately placed amongst the largest one hundred companies on the stock market. He said he'd had dealings with the group and admired them, mostly because of what he considered an unusual and enlightened approach to graduate recruitment, and – particularly – to graduate training. That all sounded fine to me. He said he would call the relevant people there and tell them to expect a letter of application from me. He told me to write it immediately, so that they would recognise my name from his introduction. I did so, that evening. Three days or so later they called me in for interview. Two weeks after that I was called in to meet one of their executive directors. Then two weeks after that I started work in their Clerkenwell headquarters, and was immediately placed on their six-month graduate training course.

That course gave me an immediate insight into how a corporation that emphasised leadership (in deliberate contrast to management) can work for the good of itself. The focus was on decent, courteous, civilised and open interaction with the workforce, including absolute clarity as to corporate objectives and strategy, and respect for manual operatives and their unions. All this was totally out of step with the corporate manners of the age, and it was exhilarating stuff.

What's more, the course threw us straight in at the deep end. For a couple of weeks, we worked all the long day standing on bottling lines. We were sent to climb down into the depths of the mash tuns to shovel and clean and clear, and sent back down again if the foreman considered our work to be sloppy and casual, which in my case he once did. Before dawn, we went out on the lorries that delivered the barrels of beer to the pubs, which was unbelievably heavy work that lasted all day. The first stop at five a.m. each day was at a greasy-spoon cafe for a gargantuan full English breakfast at its very, very fullest, eaten side by side and in cheerful companionship with the lorry driver. We worked in a customs bonded warehouse amongst the towering fine wine stacks, which had a strict seven a.m. clock-in time, and if our card showed us as being even a few minutes late then there'd be a dressing-down from the foreman. We packed and lifted cases, hundreds of them a day, and carted them around; drove pick-up trucks, and made tea for all the warehousemen, washing up the dozens of stained mugs afterwards. Meanwhile, we turned a tact-fully blind eye to the way the traditional Customs' 'allowance' of 'breakages' was applied. This allowance, in the Thameside bond where I worked, was dealt with by the warehousemen, who were predominantly West Indian, and uniformly good company. Having calculated from the day's work schedule what that day's breakage allowance would comprise, they would then calmly knock the necks off whatever number of bottles of wine that represented, thereby providing for themselves that day's refreshment. And all of this was openly done under the perfectly contented and compliant eyes of the supervising Customs office. The warehousemen seldom bothered to do this with anything other than that King and Queen of Sauternes, Château d'Yquem, and who can carp at their taste in that...

As my training programme came to an end, I was offered a brand manager role within the wines and spirits section of the group, which was a major player. That sounded interesting, but, just before I started, the marketing manager, a man in his mid-forties, dropped dead at his desk one morning with a heart attack (absurdly, this was the second time this had occurred in my life – the first being my opportunity to go to teach at Gresham's). I thus found myself promoted all the way through to the marketing manager role instead, with immediate effect, overseeing the health and development of our complete range of brands. I was just twenty-six, and way too young for the role really, and certainly too inexperienced, horribly so, but I learnt as I went, or, looking back, I certainly hope others thought that I did.

My immediate superior was Derrick Holden-Brown, then in his early forties, who was certainly the most brilliant man I worked for. This was the 1960s, and labour relations in British industry, wherever you met them, were beset by class separation, prejudice, antagonism and discourtesy. Not in Allied Breweries, though, and certainly not with Derrick HB around. I was sometimes at his side when he was touring our plants, breweries and warehouses, and to be there beside him was a master class in good manners and friendliness and, best of all, true, impeccable leadership. He had in his history an extremely good war in the Royal Navy, and I imagine he had learnt a lot of that there. Always a word for everyone; a smile here, a compliment there; never a rebuke, always praise; all names, first names, these totally and magically and instantaneously at his fingertips. And one other thing, too. We had been together in some plant or other all morning, and I witnessed, as I had before, one of his attributes I had come to admire most. It was this: if one of the workers wanted to come over and talk to him, to ask him questions, to challenge something the company was doing, to offer suggestions around the solving of problem X or Y, he always, *always* had time for them. Then and there. He would have the conversation and answer the questions and listen to the advice.

For me, in only my mid-twenties, it was a lesson and a model that I have never forgotten. All the more so due to the fact that it was done, as I have said, in total contrast to the miserably class-ridden, separatist, amateur, confrontational style that was the accepted norm by most management figures across British industry at that time, let alone those in positions as senior as that which Derrick held. The historian Correlli Barnett is damning in his assessment of the British industrial directorate of the forties, fifties and sixties:

> At the summit of the industrial system stood an elite pre-dominantly blessed with the accent of the officers' mess: men bowler-hatted or homburged, wearing suits of military cut either bespoke or at least bought from such approved out-fitters as Aquascutum or Simpson's of Piccadilly; gentlemen indeed, confident of manner, instantly recognisable by stance and gesture.

While British middle management:

> ... were all denizens of that unchartable sea that lay between the two well-defined shores of the upper class and the work-ing class. All spoke in regional or plebeian accents, with the original roughness sandpapered down to a greater or lesser degree; they ate dinner at midday (though this was chan-ging); bought their ready-made suits from Meakers, Dunn's or Horne Brothers; (and) wore at the weekends blazers adorned with the crests of such un-crack regiments as the Royal Army Service Corps.

My poor father...

For those of us who experienced industrial leadership in those times, this description of John Hanbury-Williams, chairman of Courtaulds, and a social grandee, by the historian David Coleman, would fit a thousand faces:

> Hanbury-Williams knew little or nothing about production technology, despised technical men, remained ignorant of science, and wholly indifferent to industrial relations... He was contemptuous or patronising to those he could refer to as 'technical persons'... His tactical ability to rule in a small and fairly homogenous group, and to give suitably beneficent and urbane nods to the doings of the executive directors, allowed dignity to masquerade as leadership... (but) there is no evidence that Hanbury-Williams had had any innovative ideas whatsoever.

And it was in this way, in his contrast to the lamentable norm in industry overall, though not at the admirable Allied Breweries, that the classless, technically brilliant Derrick Holden-Brown was such an unorthodox and exhilarating leader. Although he was a chartered accountant, he was by nature something of an adventurer, a risk-taker, a man not for the pettifogging detail, but for the big, bold and colourful picture. He had, for example, a habit of setting our annual corporate budget by simply telling us what profit he required us to make in each of our divisions, so we had to work backwards from that and figure out for ourselves how we were going to achieve it. And we had better achieve it. Then, by hook or by crook, we did of course reach that profit, so he had pushed us to exactly the sweet spot, and all was well. But it was unorthodox, and there was a danger to that approach. It has to be said that maybe it was that sort of style that in the end proved destructive to his career; one final bold risk was perhaps instrumental in, at last, twenty-five years or so later, bringing him down. But the cavalier aspect to him was great fun to be around, and actually, in its way, inspirational in its boldness. He was, as I have said, a brilliant man.

Of the important fifteen years developing my knowledge and my skills before I could take the great step into the Waterstone's launch, around ten of them were there at Allied Breweries, and not a single year was wasted. I learnt a very great deal about brands, and how to identify and exploit the essence of their individuality, their Unique Selling Proposition, as it used to be called in business schools. And then how to market them, how best to position and price them, and how and why to commission and then apply market research. I was operating large budgets and there were some very strong people around me and ahead of me. It was a most professional and competitive environment to be. Standards were very high, and learning to apply those standards was an education in itself.

The Allied years concluded with an interesting experience on my very last day, in Leeds, where I spoke at a conference to an audience of our salesmen. There, sitting in the front row and looking up at me, was Norman Yardley. He had last been in my life some twenty years before, an impossibly glamorous and athletic young Cambridge graduate from Yorkshire, striding out on to the pitch at Lord's as captain of the England cricket team in their test match against South Africa. That was on the wonderful occasion I mentioned earlier, a highlight of my childhood, when my godfather had spirited me away from Warden House to watch a day's play. But the Norman Yardley I saw in the audience that day, two decades on, had grown to be a flushed, overweight man in a crumpled suit. It seemed to be an upsetting decline in the curve of a life, a sportsman's life – a dose of reality as to how all too easily our lives can pan out, really. It has always stuck in my mind.

That day was my last at Allied Breweries because an opportunity to move across into WH Smith had arisen, and I had decided to take it. For some time I had been wondering once again about publishing: books were so clearly the dominant interest of my private, cultural life that it seemed perverse for me not to be professionally involved with them. Particularly, of course, with the Waterstone's dream so locked into my being, and I hoped very much locked into my future too. That moment would come, and I would know it when it did. I'd started to wish that I had carried myself more thoughtfully all those years before when I had been interviewed by that one publishing house, and had not enjoyed the interview, and, looking back, I rather suspected I had not necessarily behaved all that well during the course of it. There were plenty of other publishers I could seek to join now – and much, much more interesting and competent firms I was sure than the first one.

But here in front of me was an offer and the terms were good. I decided to take it, though it was not in publishing, and then learn by it. It might prove to be extremely useful, as the role offered to me was to establish a new book distribution and marketing unit, outside the Smith retail operation itself, there to act as an agent in that respect for a number of publishers, including the Paul Hamlyn lists. This seemed to me to be one final piece of experience that would serve me very well indeed when the time for Waterstone's came along, for it would also give me an inside look at the Smith book retail operation, which was going to be interesting.

My heart sank not a little, though, when I actually took up the place in Smith's head office adjacent to Lincoln's Inn Fields. I had not before, as a complete outsider, appreciated the style and character of the Smith corporate being, which was highly nepotistic amongst the original controlling families from the long years of the company's private status before their public market listing, and excruciatingly feudal in general style, caricatured by an embarrassingly deferential interface from the staff towards their implied social superiors. All this nonsense was absolutely painful to me. And I found that amongst the ranks lurked others who were similarly discomfited, all of them marked as troublemakers on their staff files I am sure, and all of them 'mildly subversive', in my ex-housemaster's phrase, and no doubt deeply distrusted. It was not my sort of place at all, but that was a matter really of personal taste and style, and I knew if I was going to work there I would have to put up with it. Allied Breweries had certainly been my sort of place, but it was a player in an industry that I had no personal affinity for or much cultural interest in. I also felt that Allied and its brands had taught me as much as I was going to learn from there. So, here I now was at WH Smith, which was foreign territory for me, but at the same time I was listening, and I was learning, and I knew I need not necessarily stay there for long.

There was the added bonus that the more I saw of the traditional WH Smith retail book operation from the inside, or somewhere near to the inside, the more likely my Waterstone's plan was to succeed. My difficulty – my agony, really – was how I was to finance that plan. I had mapped out a detailed model, and endlessly fiddled with it, endlessly adjusted it, but it was so unorthodox (and I will explain more around that a little later in the book) that I increasingly realised how complicated it was going to be to pull it all off. But then, suddenly, my circumstances changed, and abruptly so. This was how it happened.

I looked at him, the chairman of WH Smith, Simon Hornby, and he looked at me. It was April 1981, and we were in the Smith's New York offices. He had flown over from London for one of his holidays. He had got this holiday of his under way, straight from the airport, by firing me.

It was he who had asked me to go out from London, two years earlier, to work through a business plan his people had prepared for an experimental foray of WH Smith into the US market, not as retailers, but with a trial operation, a marketing and distribution unit, on the lines of the one I had established for them in London, for a wide range of British-published books that for one reason or another had failed to find a home with an American publisher. The moment I had first seen this plan I thought it was an absolute hospital pass, with the prospect of an extremely limited upside set against an unpleasantly deep downside. It was a suicide note. If Smith wanted to go to the US why couldn't it have been as retailers, which was of course their main play? So, of course, I should have rejected this offer. And, of course, I didn't. I took up the invitation and went.

Hornby looked as if he was feeling cheap and embarrassed, and no doubt he was. He coloured, muttered something about transition arrangements, and set off hastily for the door. He opened it, and then turned back. 'We don't really mind what you do now,' he said, suddenly sounding rather braver with the door handle in his grasp. 'Though we wouldn't want you to go straight out and open a load of bookshops in competition with us. That we would stop. We'd stop that.'

He closed the door behind him, and I knew immediately what he was referring to. One day, not long before, I'd had a conversation with him about Bowes & Bowes, the literary Cambridge booksellers, and actually the oldest in the land, having sold books from that 1 Trinity Street building of theirs since 1581, no less. WH Smith had bought Bowes & Bowes in the early 1950s, but had really done nothing with it, and he had asked me to lunch with him to pick my brains as to what I felt they should be doing to make it a decently high-profile commercial and cultural success. We had a long chat. He must have been surprised at my quite instant and extremely detailed opinion on the subject, all of which of course came from my private workings on the prospective Waterstone's business plan. So that, I am certain, was why he made that parting remark to me.

It was years before I saw him again. I gazed at the closed door, thought things through, and knew then the moment had finally come. I knew exactly what I was going to do. I went off and did it. I was angry, but at the same time I was exhilarated. Wildly exhilarated. Heaven knows where the money was going to come from, but come it would, and the future was going to be magic.

And that was how Waterstone's, finally, was born. And it was magic.

CHAPTER 18

I n *Through the Looking Glass*, the Red Queen says she lives in a world where it takes all the running you can do to keep in the same place. If you want to get somewhere else, you must run at least twice as fast as that. How often have I thought of that, as my life absolutely exploded into action in the years that came next.

It was no longer a question of how long I should stay at WH Smith. That decision had been made for me. Now was the time. I was free. I had acquired the experience that I knew I had needed, and now I would create my own company. I had identified a niche, a slot, a tantalising gap in the market, a place for magic to be made. I had seen that opportunity, and brooded over it, and had gone through dozens and dozens of drafts of the business plan. I had learnt many of the lessons I had needed at Allied Breweries, and that had been time well used. At WH Smith I had at least had an inside view of how the then 35 per cent market leader in book retailing worked, and I knew the flaws and the gaps in what they were doing. I had also seen their decision to pull back on their bookselling activity to make increased room for other, unrelated products – videos, music, and yet more toys, for heaven's sake. All of this made me even more certain that Waterstone's would succeed. And now I was free, and I would do it. I would bring Waterstone's to life.

I was absolutely plumb certain that I was right, and that it would work. I had pretty well no money, but I had no intention of wasting the sheer weight of that opportunity on a small, hesitant, reduced scale. I was going to do it on a national scale – and quickly. And the beauty of it, the perfection of it, was that from now on I was to be in a company that was to be mine, within a market that felt like mine too: books. The passion of my life, from my earliest days of Miss Santoro, and The Book Club in Crowborough, and sitting in that wonderful village shop of hers and reading, reading, reading. Then Richard Bradley at Tonbridge, and the school literary prize he pushed my way when I was barely fourteen, and the heroically fecund assistant chaplain's wife, and through her my sudden understanding as to what literature is actually about. D. H. Lawrence and Robert Browning. And so it went on. My first class at Gresham's, teaching English to thirteen- and fourteen-year-olds, and the senior school drama society there, and the white wine and the Rattigan. And Cambridge, and being taught Virginia Woolf, erratically, eccentrically, by my postgraduate friend Francis Warner. And the twenty years of my life that followed Cambridge, reading, reading, reading. And that last, wholly unexpected encounter with the Richard Bradley lookalike from Gresham's, so greatly aged of course, at a Cambridge college dinner party. To me, it was all of a piece.

But what I was about to do was no longer just the fanciful dream of an undergraduate having a moment of epiphany standing in Heffers, gazing around, bewitched. It was real. It was business. It was dangerous. It was going to be the make-or-break of me.

*

As Alexander Dumas, fils put it:

> Business? It's quite simple.
> It is other people's money.

Yes – and that's true, it is, but it's exhausting work to secure it. Now I had to put the money together – 'Other People's Money', as Dumas suggests – to launch Waterstone's.

I bought a dormant company off the shelf, renamed it Waterstone's, and put into it every single penny I had, following my exit from WH Smith. This was £6,000 (equivalent to, say, £18,000 today) and I then borrowed £15,000 from my father-in-law to add to the pot. In the interim, trying desperately to keep this £21,000 intact and untouched, I went to sign on the dole. I stood in line at my local unemployment office, but, just as my turn came up, I turned away and went back to my borrowed car. I was bigger than this. I was not going to stand in line for the dole. I had six children who looked up to me. Waterstone's was on its way. Waterstone's was going to win.

And if Waterstone's was going to win, now was the time to seek a significant financial partner. I realised it would probably prove extremely difficult to find one for an untried, low-technology start-up, particularly one in a consumer market showing sluggish compounded annual growth, but I was determined to do so. I knew how far and fast I wanted to drive the business, and I reckoned the earlier I had an institution on board for the ride the better.

After some early turn-downs I came quickly to the conclusion that the only realistic player for me was ICFC (or 3i, as they subsequently transmogrified into), whose business model was in those days almost wholly focused on the financing of start-up and early-stage companies. Eventually, after one meeting and a constant battery of telephone calls from me – on the hour every hour – they agreed to subscribe the sum of £10,000 into our 10p ordinary shares, to sit beside the £21,000 investment in those shares that I had made concurrently with them. I believe this was the smallest initial equity subscription that ICFC ever made in their long history. They did this simply to get me off the telephone, I was told later.

Now I had £31,000 in equity funds, but I needed at least £100,000 more in funds to get the first store open. I asked ICFC to help me raise that amount in debt, explaining to them that I had tried raising money for the company on my Putney house, but was unsuccessful due to the fact it had developed severe subsidence problems as a consequence of the 1976 London drought, and needed to be underpinned. They told me that my only hope therefore was what was called in those days a small business loan guarantee scheme facility, in which banks, taking their fall-back security from the Department of Trade, would lend to small early-stage companies up to a limit of a £100,000.

I asked them where to pitch for a loan of that description, and they suggested that I called a young Barclay's manager at Cranleigh in Surrey, who they had heard was really on the ball.

So I did. He told me that I could come down to Cranleigh to talk to him. I made the most colourfully impassioned presentation of my plan, explaining that within ten years Waterstone's would be the biggest bookselling chain in the world outside the US (which, as it turned out, proved to be exactly the case). All I needed to achieve that was a little temporary help from him.

How very interesting, he said, and did I have another fifteen copies of the plan. I told him I hadn't, but rushed off down Cranleigh high street, found a photocopy shop, and made fifteen extra copies. I ran back to the bank and gave them to the manager. He flipped through them, and said he would be in touch. He never was. I found out a little later what he had done with my lovely business plan: he had used it that very afternoon at a regional Barclay's seminar as an example of the sort of company you should not lend money to under any circumstances whatsoever...

Anyway, we still lacked our small business guarantee loan, and we couldn't get under way without it. So I called ICFC again, at least every hour, as before. This time they suggested I went to a certain NatWest manager in Covent Garden. Once again I made an impassioned presentation, and when I had finished there was dead silence. He stared at me, and I stared at him. Then he told me that I was either a madman or a genius, he couldn't make out which, but he didn't mind much either way as he was retiring on Tuesday, and I could have the money...

Other People's Money, indeed. We were on our way and had concluded our first round of funding. I then found the site in South Kensington that I thought ideal for the very first branch. We were off. And, as I mentioned in the Prologue, I immediately had a stunning and totally unexpected success, for from my initial recruitment advertisement in London's *Evening Standard*, four of the six booksellers I needed for the branch came to me from Hatchards, in Piccadilly.

These recruits really were a gift to me. They were led by Julian Toland, who was both well known and well respected amongst publishers' sales people, and his presence in our ranks gave out to the book world some invaluable initial reassurance. But it wasn't just Julian. All four of them were so knowledgeable and so experienced, and so wise in the dark arts of charming books into customers' hands, and thereby gently extracting money from their wallets. Thirty-five years later, they are still, in my heart, my friends. They taught me how to make it work.

With our first tranche of money in place and our initial staff recruited, we were ready to go. There was, however, an immediate problem, as a number of major publishers initially refused to supply us at all, in the fear that, because of me, and only because of me, they would suffer reprisals from WH Smith. Brave souls. I feel resentment at the memory of that still, and I remember the consequent stress as to how we were ever going to get this first shop open. But help was at hand, for Penguin and Oxford University Press, both key publishers for Waterstone's, given the quality and style of their lists, now led the way in getting strongly and immediately behind us, and emphatically and publicly so.

Those initial dealings with Penguin were pivotal, actually. Peter Mayer, their iconic CEO, asked me to visit his Chelsea office and go through our business plan with him in detail. He had been encouraged to do so, I know, by Paul Hamlyn, the brilliantly successful popular illustrated books publisher, who was my friend, and who knew the ambition of what we intended to do. Mayer wanted to understand the arithmetic as to how our working capital was going to be funded as we opened branches moving forward, for the plan, as it had been described to him by Hamlyn, assumed very heavy stock levels, indeed stock levels that would be totally unprecedented in UK bookselling.

I argued out the model with him. Bit by bit he came to see that we needed both purchase discounts and credit days well beyond the then norm in order to succeed. And that was what we were asking from him. I was with him for a couple of hours. Suddenly he made a decision. OK. We could have those discount percentages and the credit days. He called in one of his fellow directors, Peter Carson, to explain what he was doing.

'He's the only one who is going to try to open the bookshops Penguin needs to see across the high streets of Britain,' Mayer said. 'The terms he is asking from us are ridiculous. But I'm going to give them to him. And if he ever, ever lets us down...'

He spoke then, I believe, to OUP, who immediately followed suit. No doubt he spoke to others. In any case, one by one the other publishers (but not for a time all), seeing their example, crept in too, and, at last, we had our stock.

So – the dawning of our very first day – the very first day of our very first branch. The seven of us – me plus the four Hatchards stars and two other enthusiastic young graduate booksellers we had poached from elsewhere – flung open the doors of Waterstone's Old Brompton Road at nine o'clock in the morning. The telephone rang, and, as earlier described, Dane Howell picked up the receiver and purred into it, 'Waterstone's?' A man bustled in, walked straight over to the reference section, pulled out a copy of the Koran, and took it up to the till. A surprising start to our life.

The day passed. We closed the shop at ten p.m., all the staff staying, unasked, well beyond their contracted hours. I let them out, then emptied our solitary till, extracted its tray, and carried it upstairs to the safe. The safe wouldn't open. I tried the password numerals again, and it still wouldn't open. Once again, and it still wouldn't. It was too late to call the people who had installed it the previous day, so I stuffed all the money into a Waterstone's bag and took it with me to the underground station. I fell asleep on the train, woke up a few minutes later at St James's Park, and jumped out.

I jumped out rather too hastily, as it happened. Our ICFC man rang me in the morning to ask how the first day had gone.

'Good news and bad news,' I said.

'What's the good news?'

'We took over a thousand pounds,' I said.

'That's wonderful – wonderful! Well done!! So what's the bad news, then?'

'I left it on the train...'

*

Then – on we go – back to Other People's Money once more, so that we could find and open a second store. We had been trading at Old Brompton Road for no more than three or four weeks, when one late evening I saw a headscarfed Ava Gardner browsing the fiction tables. But much more interesting than that was the woman I noticed alongside her: Christina Foyle, owner, of course, of the famous Foyle's bookshop, which for all its much parodied imperfections was at that time still a most powerful force.

I was behind the till, and she came over to me, introduced herself, made some pleasing compliments and invited me to come for a drink at her flat in Charing Cross Road the following evening. I went. With astonishing generosity she offered me the building beside Foyle's on an extended lease at a peppercorn rent, simply because she liked what she had seen, had understood that we had virtually no money, and wanted us to have a chance to succeed. Between me and the surprised ICFC, who were delighted with this gift, we each managed to find a little further cash down the metaphorical back of the sofa (mine from finally maxing out each one of my, I think, five credit cards). Then one or two friends came in and invested a little each, and I opened up there beside Foyle's in Charing Cross Road on 30 December, only four months after Old Brompton Road, and just in time for the New Year weekend. The staff had been recruited for an 8 January opening date, and were due to join us on 5 January, but as it happened I had got pretty much all the stock into place by myself, and so I went for it, and opened up with me as the one and only bookseller in a store of almost 8,000 square feet and several floors. There were open boxes everywhere, and no doubt casual thefts, but the store was packed with our target market of literary book browsers, and in those five days or so I took through the one till almost twenty thousand pounds all on my own, which seemed like a miracle given our threadbare financial resource, particularly as I had no staff costs for those working days.

Three or four months later the first really substantial opportunity came our way, when a large, 11,000 square foot premises on

High Street Kensington came on to the market. I asked ICFC if they would support me in taking the lease, and they did so, re-investing in us once more, and quite substantially, which enabled me to get a slightly more generous credit line from our bank. Even so, it looked like a desperately close financial call, though it was eased a little by a raft of very welcome small private investors (including, incidentally, Laurence Olivier), which was clearly driven by a most generous and unexpected piece on us by Max Hastings in the *Evening Standard*.

I myself had no more money to give, all the cash that I had or could borrow, every penny of it, already having been put into the company. But by coming clean on this with the other investors I managed to negotiate with them that my stake, irrespective of whatever sums of future equity the board decided to enlist and employ, would, protected by legal contract, be frozen and pre-served at a permanent level of twenty-five per cent ownership of the company (this was done by means of arranging for me to have special convertible shares). As things turned out, my deter-mination to negotiate this fixed twenty-five per cent ownership, and the generosity and indeed the good sense of the others in quite readily agreeing to contract it, made a very great difference to my life.

We did succeed at that point in acquiring a lease on the High Street Kensington site, and the company still trades from there now. After a succession of quite superb branch managers over almost four decades, it is perhaps one of the best known individ-ual bookshops in the south of England. In securing the lease, the freeholder demanded that I personally guaranteed the company's ongoing rental liability. So this I did, accepting of course that as all my money had already been invested in the company, if we were to fail, my guarantee would at best threaten my house, and at worst clean me out completely, and I would be bankrupt. Over the next few years the same demand for my personal guarantee was made by landlords all over the country. I simply went on giving my guarantee, for otherwise we would not have been able to open the rapidly increasing number of stores that we did. Our investors knew of course that I was giving these guarantees, and the exposure I was accepting.

The Waterstone's model was simply this: the highest class of heavily stocked literary bookselling run on a national scale by an unusually enthusiastic and highly knowledgeable young staff. There was an intense desire by all of us in the company that our model, our very own model, would succeed. For it was now the staffs' model as much as it was mine, and I really liked it that way.

New York had great, great bookshops open at every hour, and Paris too. Rome and Amsterdam also. San Francisco had what seemed like dozens of them. So why not London? I wanted the Waterstone's stores to be the most civilised and welcoming places in the world – better even than those in the rest of the world. I wanted them open day and night and for seven days a week. And I wanted in time tens and tens of dozens of them across the British Isles. And so did the staff – they were exhilarated by what we were doing, and they wanted that too.

This was in a climate where most people in the book trade thought that we would fail, and on the retail side many seemed strongly to wish that we would do so, perhaps unsurprisingly. The knowledge of that served to drive us all on yet more determinedly, of course. The Chartered Booksellers Association refused us membership, and did so by means of an insulting letter. And some of their delegates, quite unforgivably, got up and booed one of our young branch managers when, giving his name and Waterstone's as his company, he tried to ask a question at one of their conferences (he was just twenty-three years old).

Thankfully, our Hatchards recruits in particular understood the vision I was trying to describe to them. And they understood it because it is difficult to overstate how lamentable the book-selling scene of the time was. The previous decade, the 1970s, had proved particularly grim. You could say that the three or four prominent university bookshops – Dillons in London, Blackwell's in Oxford, Heffers in Cambridge, and perhaps James Thin in Edinburgh – were doing their job, and generally well. In London there were bookshop boutiques that had a strong follow-ing – Heywood Hill (a sort of cultural annexe of White's Club in St James's, whose membership was wholly aristocratic) was well known if quirky, and you could say the same for the excellent John Sandoe, the vast Foyle's and the specialist Compendium. But having said that, together we all found it inexplicable that a city as great and as culturally diverse as London had within it, apart from the few names above, no stockholding literary bookshops at all, and certainly not one single one – Foyle's, Hatchards, Dillons, not one of them – that was open at the weekend past lunchtime on Saturdays, let alone on weekday evenings. Hilariously, the High Hill bookshop in Hampstead, with the advantage of perhaps the most bookish public around them of anywhere in the British Isles, and quite possibly in the world, only turned on its lights if someone stepped into the shop. They then turned them off again immediately when the departing customer was still stepping out through the door...

Actually, telling that anecdote reminds me of something else. Before High Hill opened in Hampstead there was no bookshop at all in that famously literary part of London. How incredible that is. Every third person in Hampstead is a published novelist, as the joke runs. There had been no bookshop for them. What an indication that is as to how appallingly empty and bereft Britain's bookselling scene was during the post-war decades. Come 1982, and the vacuum was still there. That is what we spotted (if you can spot a vacuum), and that was our opportunity.

In 1985, Paul Baggaley joined us, and is these days a most influential and respected literary publisher. I think his reflections tell us a lot about the flavour of Waterstone's in those early, driving years:

... Working at Waterstone's (inverted comma crucial) was the go-to job when I tried to leave academic life for the first time. It initially gave me a gap year between Oxford and starting a PhD, and then I stayed for another ten years.

After a brief interview, and the offer of a £5,200-a-year salary, I was assigned to 183 High Street Kensington, one of the five London branches. It was – though I'm sure we all thought that about our own branches – the best one. The area was classy and wealthy, but also fashionable, with Hyper Hyper down the road, and a bit grungy, with Kensington Market if you turned left out of the tube station. Most importantly the area was full of potential readers who could easily be tempted by a convincing pitch and it had not one but two incomparable managers – Dane Howell (failed child actor, happily married father of four, with a very interesting past – and, it turned out, future) and Julian Toland (still a bit of a counter-culture hippy, with a wife in the rag trade, chain-smoker and a bundle of nervous energy). Both of course ex-Hatchards, from the original magnificent bunch.

This was my finishing school. Dane taught me about the coolest writers you never studied for an English degree: Patrick Hamilton, Colin MacInnes, Derek Raymond and Ronald Firbank, and for Julian I refilled the Picador spinner with the books he loved – hardboiled American noir and contemporary druggy classics. At least this is how I remember it. This was an education it would have taken years to find elsewhere. It was always frantic, manic, exciting and very sociable – which it had to be as the shop was open every day late into the evening; it was your social life as well as your job.

New Waterstone's branches were opening in market towns and cities and my colleagues all took up management jobs in places such as Bath, Guildford and Cheltenham. But I stayed on in London, studying during the week, bookselling at weekends and in the holidays – whether I was needed or not. Soon I moved up to help open the Hampstead branch where the complacent and complaining existing bookshop lasted only a few months before it threw in the towel.

And that was because the Waterstone's shops were extraordinary: art sections full of new books, but also a remarkable range of out-of-print books sourced by the maverick Andrew Stilwell; fiction sections featuring books from the most obscure small publishers, and others ordered lovingly from America – something only Compendium in

Camden seemed to have done before; and you could browse bays and bays of poetry books – run of course in each branch by poets, so you could find not just the Neruda that featured in films, but dual-language editions and exquisite collectors editions. In the shops I worked in artists ran the art sections; screenwriters and film-makers ran the film section; and of course everyone who worked in the fiction section was a novelist waiting for their moment. And for so many of these that moment came – and we would be soon selling their first novels.

When I became a manager in the Mecca of bookselling, the Charing Cross Road, we cajoled, bribed and begged publishers for our favourite writers to read in the shops: we had Mailer and Vidal, Amis and Barnes, Said and Chomsky, the first Rushdie reading after the Fatwa, the first Donna Tartt reading from *The Secret History*.

So long as sales kept growing, you could do pretty much whatever you wanted. It always surprises me for how short a time Waterstone's remained independent, that the sale to WH Smith was only eleven years after the first store. Those eleven years seemed mercifully free from competition: the Net Book Agreement was in place; Amazon was still in the future; digital books hadn't arrived; and the supermarkets didn't bother with products they couldn't undercut everyone else on.

So we just had to be the best; in the best locations; offering the best books; served by the best booksellers; and bringing to our public the best authors. And most of the time Waterstone's branches were the best; not perhaps the most efficient in stock turn; not the most tidy (everyone over-ordered because no one ever wanted to be out of stock of an important book); and certainly not always with the most socially adept booksellers (loving reading doesn't necessarily give you US-style customer service skills).

What also happened was that Tim Waterstone gave young graduates in particular an extraordinary level of respons-ibility – for running often £5m businesses; for hiring, training (and occasionally firing) staff; for managing costs and stock levels; for choosing (and occasionally returning) all the books in the store; for deciding which to display and promote; and for inviting every author in to read and talk.

We all learnt about the sharp end of business by trial and often error. But, above all, it was the most fun place I ever worked. I made friends for life – who found their ways into writing, publishing and literary journalism. Waterstone's was a stepping stone for the ambitious, but also a haven for the sensitive and a meeting place for the like-minded...

Paul Baggaley soon introduced his Oxford friend John Mitchinson to us, and how fortunate we were that he did, for only three or four years later I promoted him up to our board, as marketing director, realising by then that I had recruited an absolute jewel. John Mitchinson recalls:

My college friend Paul Baggaley had suggested it to me: he worked at the branch in High Street Kensington. I had never heard of Waterstone's and assumed they were some vener-able carriage-trade bookseller that had survived from the nineteenth century – the name seemed to suggest as much. In many ways, they were that, but also much, much more. It took me a while to realise that I had stumbled into the middle of a revolution, perhaps the most civilised and humane revolution of recent times: the reinvention of the high street bookshop.

I was 'interviewed' by Julian Toland, a tall, intense, awkward man, who I later discovered was a human version of Books in Print, a bookselling legend. He asked me what I'd been reading (Boswell's *Life of Samuel Johnson*). That was it. I was in. I asked him the same question and discovered he had the entire last decade of new book releases in his head (and had read most of them).

It was people like Julian, and the irrepressible Dane Howell, who ran the Kensington branch like some west London version of Warhol's Factory (*jeunesse dorée* behind the tills; a constant string of celebrities queuing to buy their books), who helped make early Waterstone's so beguiling. They were experienced booksellers – people who knew the trade – people Tim Waterstone had plucked from Hatchards – now given carte blanche by him to run big, bold emporia.

And so we thrust onwards, opening initially two shops or so a year. At this point I must say that Waterstone's has often been accused, or more accurately *I* have been accused, of having had too little regard for the health and safety of the many independent booksellers around the nation who, in the days before Waterstone's existed, could be said to have been labouring mightily and nobly in the task of providing for the nation decent quality literary bookselling. All that in contrast to WH Smith, who had interest only in bookselling in the mass-market, non-literary, non-specialist area. But I think that misses the point. Look back at our birth in 1982, and then indeed follow our history through the years that followed – we were an independent bookseller ourselves, and at first a very, very small independent bookseller indeed. To stay with the example that Paul Baggaley quotes, when the people who ran the High Hill bookshop heard we were to open a branch in competition with them in Hampstead, they poured public scorn on us through the pages of the local Hampstead press, labelling us a bumped-up, financially precarious newcomer.

However, it was not us who were precarious, it was them. There was no reason whatsoever why they should not have tied down the Hampstead literary market for themselves, and secured it for ever, and irrevocably so. After all, they had been trading there for almost thirty years before we arrived on their patch. But they hadn't secured that market. They hadn't tied it down. We arrived, and we were simply better than they were. Much better. We were far more heavily and widely stocked than them, and far better staffed, and far better sited, and we were open for incomparably longer hours. So, we opened, and after all their insults, in very short order they closed down. They gave up. High Hill fled. We had won.

And what enabled us to do that, to defeat them like that, to drive them away? It's simple. Above all else, of course, there was the marked superiority of our offer. But that aside, we did it by me, yet again, personally guaranteeing the rent to the landlord, and by me tramping around the City, day in and day out, trying to source access to more debt and more equity in order to get our new branch open, and riding the blows, and taking the turn-downs, and then, in the end, succeeding in getting our money and getting another branch on its way.

So why didn't the High Hill people do that? Do what we did? Finance the vast literary stock? Recruit the superb, mostly young graduate staff whose drive and enthusiasm and literary expertise Paul Baggaley so vividly describes? Take a big store on a prime site with a rent passing so substantial that it had to be personally guaranteed by the owner? Why didn't they do that? Why didn't their owner do that?

Knowing Hampstead's potential, we put in an absolutely crack team to take on High Hill. David McRedmond, who in later years has had a brilliantly successful career in Ireland as a Telecom's executive, as a broadcast owner and as a CEO, was part of that team:

In those early days Waterstone's expanded so rapidly, and so quickly that anyone with ambition would become a manager. I was appointed by Tim Waterstone to be assistant manager for the to-be-opened Hampstead shop, working with the colourful and talented Dane Howell as manager. We opened just before Christmas in 1988 in the wonderful London village, one of the great literary oases: Jewish, bookish (a favourite word of TW's) and exceptional. Dane and I matched the brilliant customers with the best booksellers from across London. Dane and I knew exactly what we were going to do. The store would not distinguish between hardbacks and paperbacks; it would have no crass window displays; the till would be in the centre of the shop, and the ground floor would only have Fiction, History, Biography and Art. This was Waterstone's.

So – we drove on and on and on. By the end of 1985 we had ten wonderful big and profitable bookshops. By the end of 1989 we had forty-eight of them. On to the next one, on to the next one, on to the next one. Five in London, then, for example, Cheltenham, Bath, Newcastle, Edinburgh, Aberdeen, Belfast, Cardiff, Norwich, Canterbury, Birmingham, Manchester, Guildford, Liverpool, Exeter, Perth, Bristol and Leeds, where again, as so often happened, there was a very well-known literary bookseller in place, and they had been there for decades. But they weren't good enough – in an excellent local literary market, Julian Toland and I thought that they carried weak, thin and unbalanced stock, with indifferent staff, and laughably reduced opening hours. They hadn't properly secured and taken possession of their local literary market, and we sensed that.

All over again, as in every one of the towns listed above, my personal guarantee was made on the rent of a large and prominent property, and again there followed my endless tramping around the City to raise the requisite money, taking the blows, and waiting for the win, knowing that in time it would come. So why didn't they do that? Why didn't their owner do that? Then, with my personal guarantee put in place, and the money safely in our bank, we opened a couple of hundred yards away from them, in a handsome and striking building right in Leeds city centre. There again we immediately outclassed them in our drive and our site and our stock and our opening hours and our staff. And, after all those years they'd had in proud possession of the city, instead of raising their game to combat us, in very little time they gave up and they packed their tents and they had gone, they too complaining away at us in the local press.

The story was repeated all the way around the country, and at increasingly rapid speed – in England, Scotland, Wales, Northern Ireland and, initially to loud, shrill abuse and astonished, deeply unpleasant outrage, in the Republic of Ireland itself, as we opened first of all on Dawson Street in Dublin, and then in Cork. The story in fact was repeated wherever we saw weakness and comparative neglect, however long the incumbent had traded. Where there was a really effective literary bookseller in existence, we kept well away. Good for them – they had secured the market and thus deserved it. We did not attempt Oxford for a very long time, for instance, such was Blackwell's quality. Likewise Cambridge, with Heffers almost as strong on their home patch as the admirable Blackwell's was on theirs. Similarly, on a different level, Chelsea, where the tiny, quirky and magnificent John Sandoe in Blacklands Terrace had the local literary market absolutely and totally sewn up, and admirably so. But not in the end in Edinburgh, where we decided after a time to have a go at Thins, who we thought were showing an offer not quite good enough for that extensive university and general literary market. So into Edinburgh we went.

David McRedmond again:

As Waterstone's grew from one to three to five to ten to twenty and to thirty and forty shops, TW faced the challenge of ensuring the standards for his remarkable chain were the highest possible. It was before the technological revolution of the 1990s. Outside the head office there were no computers, no email between shops, almost no central management apart from TW himself (other than the wonderfully diffident and talented Julian Toland).

It was at this point that he developed his mantra, communicated to us all more with determination than heart – *Perfect Stock, Perfect Staff, Perfect Control.* As a statement of intent for the business it encapsulated exactly what mattered: a reliable and brilliant range of books (he would spend literally hours checking up on the range of books in each store), bookish staff (but definitely not 'bookworms') and then Control, and this remained the burden of TW's. We were all massive enthusiasts, purchasing every book published (I remember especially buying the whole print-run of Oscar Hijuelos's *The Mambo Kings Play Songs of Love* because I had read a proof on my honeymoon). He loved that sort of thing, absolutely loved it, but I had always detected in TW something that maybe some of my colleagues missed: he was also, or perhaps firstly, a businessman. It was clear that the bookshops would drive the top line by being brilliant. But he would somehow manage the P&L and the balance sheet, and manage them he did. This way there would be no compromise. His simple formulae: driving sales per square foot; managing debtor days; relentlessly improving gross margins; ruthless management of overheads; all underpinned a generous literary vision and a simply and perfectly expressed brand.

The journey was so marvellously enjoyable, it really was. Forget the stress, it was worth every second of that. Looking back, I am spoiled for choice as to selecting my favourites amongst all those dozens of branches we opened, and there are some wonderful memories for me around pretty well all of them. Yes – all of them. But Cheltenham, for example, where we opened one of our earlier branches outside London, would be a star memory. Cheltenham was a wealthy town with a population of well over a hundred thousand people, and a number of well-known and high-profile schools. It was and is a town of long and distinguished literary profile, as typified by its annual Cheltenham Literature Festival, founded in 1949, which is the longest running festival of its kind in the world, and amongst the most distinguished.

Julian Toland and I spent a day exploring the town, and together we took the view that given the quality and size of the present and prospective literary market it was surprising that there was no one truly dominant bookseller there. It seemed to us that all the town's bookshops were way too small, too indifferently sited, and too thinly stocked, with more of an eye to tourist trade than to the literary reading public of the town itself.

I got the money together (with absolutely all the usual ghastly, nailbiting dramas), and our funding was sufficient for a large branch in a pleasant building in the city centre, overlooking Montpellier Gardens. We placed there a very strong pair of booksellers, now promoted up to managers, to run it. One of them, Will Atkinson, now a very senior London publisher, claims to remember that I waved him off from Paddington Station as his train drew out for the west in a manner suggesting I was seeing him off for a lifetime of service in the colonies, we two never to meet again...

The pair of them put together an exemplary, erudite, marginally eccentric stock (with, I discovered, the eleven-volume Byron letters kept hidden under a table in case anyone wanted it!), and they recruited a strong support team. The store was kept open for long, long weekly shopping hours, and within a month or two it became an absolutely classic literary bookseller. It was a jewel, really, and of a standard as high as the similar-sized London branch in Hampstead, which is saying something. Thirty-five years later, the Cheltenham store is still there, dominating the local market, unchallenged in its home marketplace.

A little later we opened a rather similar store in Canterbury. It was spectacularly pretty, and right up near the cathedral, and in time it was fully Cheltenham's equal in every way. There we were fortunate enough to be able to place a newish member of our staff as manager – Martin Latham, who had joined us just after taking his doctorate at King's College London. He proved to be one of the best, and the most long serving of any manager Waterstone's were lucky enough to have. Here he recalls those earlyish days:

> After some initial months at a couple of Waterstone's branches, High Street Kensington and Cheltenham, I went to open as manager a new Waterstone's in Canterbury. At the interview Tim asked why on earth I should get this sought-after branch, perhaps one of the most beautiful we ever had. My answer – this was the dreamy eighties – was 'because I will set the town on fire'. He laughed, and gave it to me.
>
> Shortly after this, I sat at my kitchen table and ordered, by marking publishers' catalogues, over £100,000 of stock for the shop. After we opened, locals complained about the Sunday opening, about the casually dressed staff and about the books

on paganism (Tim always encouraged in all branches a big and catholic selection on Mind, Body and Spirit). By contrast, when the shop recently closed down on the termination of the lease (for us to relocate only a few hundred metres away), several customers wept and even offered to chain themselves to the doors in protest.

My Canterbury St Margaret's Street Waterstone's was a rebel ship in the Waterstone's fleet. Tim rather liked and respected rebellion: one of his favourite anecdotes was the tale of Robert Topping, the Manchester manager lovingly nicknamed 'The Major' by Alan Bennett, who Tim finally, finally sacked one day for pushing even the Waterstone's envelope too far, but then he turned up for work the next day as usual. Tim pretended not to notice and Topping simply carried on as before... Robert was always a great favourite of Tim's, and rightly so. There was a day when Tim called in on Manchester unexpectedly, to find, to his total delight, Irvine Welsh, at the height of his fame, giving a foul-mouthed talk on one floor, while downstairs a Buddhist monk was simultaneously leading a large meditation event... Tim always represented that incident to be an example of Waterstone's at its extraordinary and eccentric and inimitable best, and so indeed it was.

The independence which Tim granted in those early Waterstone's days was truly absolutely exceptional. I had fifty-two staff running the bookshop and café, and I followed Tim's mantra: 'I love the company so much, why should I work with anyone who doesn't?'

The first fiction buyer we had at Canterbury was a young dreamer who said he was writing a novel: David Mitchell, author of *Cloud Atlas*, and James Henry, who ran our sci-fi section, wrote for the sitcom *Green Wing*. The basement was run by a published poet and anarchist, fluent in Anglo-Saxon and Latin, who spent every lunch hour in the cathedral archives pursuing a lifelong analysis of medieval church court records. Annually, he spent eight consecutive weeks in a Provencal nudist camp. James, the history buyer, visited London once a month in his own time, to go around our London branches to make sure none of their history sections was better than his – they never were. Canterbury St Margaret's Street had the best Waterstone's history section in the country.

And the authors... How wonderful all that was, endlessly working the phones to get star authors to visit us; it was all in our own branch hands, no one at the centre interfered, and how furiously, furiously we branches competed with each other in this. Although Umberto Eco's London publisher told me he would never visit for a talk, after I phoned his Milan publisher he agreed to come. He wanted to work in the bookshop for a day; few customers suspected the identity of the strange bookseller in the black hat! And it was all done on a major scale. I invited, this with no exaggeration, more than a thousand authors over the years to give evening talks. For multiple visitor Antonia Fraser, Canterbury was 'the Versailles of England and Waterstone's its Petit Trianon'. She meant, she explained, not that we dressed in milkmaid costume as Marie Antoinette did at the Trianon, but that we kept a garden of literature alive amid the turmoil of literary faddishness. For David Mitchell, the shop was 'the Piccadilly of my psychogeography'. Peter Cushing called it 'Hatchards Piccadilly in

Kent'. To A. N. Wilson, it was simply 'the nicest bookshop in England'. The Dean compared it to the cathedral, a place of solace for all-comers. Tony Benn described it as 'the real University of Kent', because we hosted such diverse voices. Political speakers included Roy Jenkins and Alan Clark, John Major and Edward Heath. Feminists like Naomi Wolf and Susie Orbach gave talks early in their careers. Before apartheid fell, I invited the ANC military commander Ronnie Kasrils to talk about his memoirs. I received hate mail for this, and the Home Office initially said they would ban his visit, but he came, and moderated a stormy debate.

Yes – there really was such superb energy in the branches, such ambition, such pride, such knowledge. My responsibility was to support all these people by getting the finance and then driving us straight on. And as fast as possible. Then do it again.

John Mitchinson writes:

In many ways, for me retelling the story of Waterstone's is to unravel the mystery of my own twenties. It feels very personal and to this day I still can't go into a Waterstone's and not feel proprietorial about it.

Despite the reassuring burgundy and gold livery, early Waterstone's were nothing like other shops. It felt like a business that had been kidnapped by students. Everyone was young; most were, like me, arts graduates. On my first day I was given responsibility for the Science Fiction and Photography sections. I remember being shown the ropes by Richard Hayes, another experienced bookselling legend and son of Tubby, the famous English jazz saxophonist.

We learnt on the job and we learnt fast. There was no manager's office, no stock cards, no bureaucracy. Tim Waterstone encouraged us to read and take books home, to pore over the review pages of newspapers, to explore and experiment with stock. I knew little or nothing about SF or fantasy but after a couple of months, by watching what sold and listening to customers and to the publisher's reps, you soon began to see patterns. I still remember being given my first proof by Martin, the kindly, scholarly Gollancz rep. It was *Mort* by Terry Pratchett. I still have it somewhere.

Everything important happened on the shop floor. Well, almost everything. Waterstone's was radically decentralised – there was no central buying department – and almost everyone who worked on the shop floor was a graduate. In fact, as the company grew, it became almost a rite of passage for arts graduates with 2:1 degrees to do a stint in a Waterstone's to give them time to figure out what to do with their lives.

Some of us ended up staying. And part of that appeal was the Waterstone's staffroom. They were not tidy or clean places, but the conversation was fabulous. I remember working my way through the novels of William Faulkner not long after I arrived and finding myself embroiled in long and stimulating discussions about modern fiction – much better than anything I'd experienced at Oxford. I began to read contemporary fiction – and what a golden age the mid-eighties was for British fiction! Martin Amis, Julian Barnes, Ian McEwan, Angela Carter, Bruce Chatwin, Salman Rushdie, Graham

Swift – most of them coming to prominence in that first and astonishing Granta Best of Young British Novelists promotion in 1983.

I've often thought that the emergence of that generation, the adoption of the B-format paperback as the perfect form for the literary backlist and the arrival of Waterstone's all at roughly the same time were what transformed bookselling from a strange semi-academic profession into something universal and mainstream. And the conversations in Waterstone's staffrooms – knowledgeable, passionate, unashamedly egg-headed – were an essential part of that culture. We stocked writers we loved and wanted to tell others about. I remember the launch of the publishing house Bloomsbury not long after I joined – bold and exciting books with jackets to match – and reading *Dreams of Leaving* by Rupert Thomson. The excitement of finding a new and original voice! I loved that book and have read everything he's written since.

That was how it worked. The Waterstone's staffroom taught me how to read, and how to turn that reading into something valid, something helpful for others. When, years later, Andy Miller (another Waterstone's alumnus) and I started our books podcast Backlisted, the reference point for the tone and quality of the discussion was a Waterstone's staffroom of the early nineties.

David McRedmond says:

The effort to open a bookstore was immense. And the relief of customers flooding in, seeing books sell that you were worried you had overbought, and young, new booksellers coping with the myriad questions was the reward. It was unbelievable fun. We all became the best of friends and we were on a mission. The stores were highly competitive with each other. Who would have the best events, the most perfect stock, the coolest staff?

So much energy, so much drive. It was not that we had insufficient regard for other independents. I repeat that – 'other independents', for, as I have said, we were one of their number – we were an independent too. We did have regard, especially for those who had the guts and drive and skill to nurture their marketplace. We left those fellow independent booksellers well alone, and were very wise to do so. However, we had rather less regard for those who were not serving their local literary markets to an acceptable standard, and had not taken the proactive, challenging and – yes – frightening route of boosting their energy, girding their loins and funding themselves up to do so. We had. We took that route. And we then had a go at those vulnerable and attractive local literary markets ourselves.

Robert McCrum wrote in the *Guardian* in March 2014:

In retrospect, the turning-point in British writers' fortunes came in 1980. The Booker Prize was televised for the first time, and the subsequent year *Midnight's Children* won. After that, literary life began booming – a mirror to the irrational exuberance of the economy. Tim Waterstone's bookselling revolution was transforming the trade. New writers were making headlines. In the feeding frenzy that followed, publishers' advances entered a never-never land in which commercial prudence was thrown to the winds.

That 'bookselling revolution' of ours, as McCrum generously calls it, was led by the branches themselves, rather than by 'head office' – that ghastly and deadening term, which is satirised in the deathless old joke: *I'm from head office and I'm here to help you.* It was in the branches where the energy, the quality, the ambition was to be focused, with the hope that it would be passed on from me. Our central office would be tiny, in essence just me, my assistant (a close friend and a previous colleague), a finance director and an accounts department. Apart from the indispensable guiding hands of Julian Toland, that was the sum total of it.

Our branch managers themselves would be responsible for the quality of what they/we offered to the public. Though that of course was on the premise that the branch managers had first accepted and bought into our concept of very heavy investment into £ stock per square foot across an extremely wide selection of titles, with a corporate voice that was emphatically literary rather than mass market. Actually, they could hardly do anything other than buy into that concept. That was all we did. We embraced the concept of heavy £ stock per square foot because we knew that it would lead to heavy £ sales per square foot, and, given our high gross margins and deliberately low overheads, the result would yield high profit.

Perhaps I should linger on these concepts for a moment to illustrate their significance.

First, the £ sales per square foot. The fixed £ costs of a bookshop lie in such things as the rent and the rates, the lighting and heating of the place. There is nothing the branch manager can do about these. In a conventional bookshop chain there would be nothing much she or he could do about sales either, as all the stock in the shop would have been selected for him or her by head office, the manager allowed no input into that.

In Waterstone's, however, the branch manager and the section staff could make a huge difference to the profits of their branch. They couldn't lower the cost of the books they bought in for their store, as buying term contracts between the publishers and bookseller chains have to be negotiated in the centre, and once contracted, remain in place indefinitely. Nor, in the days of the Net Book Agreement, which had been established in law in 1900 and only came to its end in the mid-1990s, could they alter the price the books were sold for, as these were set and printed on the books by the publisher, and had to be adhered to. But what managers could do – and here lay the very essence of their skill – was to select stock for their branches, section by section, title by title. A medium-size store, of say 10,000 square feet, would carry roughly 50,000 titles in stock. A really skilled manager would get annual sales of, say, £500 per square foot off those constantly replenishing 50,000 titles, and do that by running a superbly skilful selection and balancing of the stock. A less skilled manager would get, perhaps, £400 per square foot from those 50,000 titles, because the stock balance and selection would be that much less skilfully bought in. A huge difference – in that example the highly skilled manager would have sales that year of £5m, whereas the less skilled manager would have sales of £4m – a difference of £1m, or perhaps £500k in gross margin. That sort of differential, over an estate of a hundred branches or so, makes a colossal impact on the company's affairs. And that was the very reason why we never so much as gave one moment's thought as to whether we should go the orthodox route and buy centrally...

As to the £ stock per square foot, we arrived by experimentation over our first ten or so branches at what seemed to us as bold and generous an allocation as was physically sensible (and a vital note – for control reasons none of the branches were allowed stock rooms or outside warehousing – all stock bought had to be physically out there on the shop floor, so we all could see it). Relating that to the example above, a 10,000 square foot store had just about enough room to carry the 50,000 titles. Multiply therefore 50,000 individual copies by the average cost of our buying them in from the publishers and you have your £ stock per square foot.

It is interesting perhaps that unlike our competitors, we had no particular interest in £ stock turn as a concept. (i.e. the number of times a single copy of a title sells in a year). Indeed, we thought it basically flawed, and potentially harmful. By carrying such a heavy stock, tens of thousands of titles in each store, we were maximising, optimising that store's £ sales – the £ sales per square foot. If we had carried a lighter stock, our £ sales would have been less. But the cost of running that store – rent and rates, light and heat, staff salaries, etc., – would be the same in each case. So the greater the sales the better (and remember that gross margins were essentially fixed, as under the Net Book Agreement there was no discounting). And so we placed great emphasis on £ sales per square foot in our assessment of our managers' performance.

Their skill in perfecting the balance and shape of what those 50,000 titles should comprise – rising to well over 280,000 titles in our largest store, the Piccadilly Waterstone's in London – was and is an exquisite art. In a single branch you might be lucky to sell twelve copies a year of, let us say, Frederick Manning's 1930 novel *Her Privates We*, but it had to be there in place on the shelves, such an iconic work as it was, for that was a statement of our worth as an interesting, literary, highest grade bookseller. Conversely, in that branch you would sell at least a hundred copies a year of, say, the new William Boyd novel, probably more, so the stock turn on the latter might well be a dozen times 'better' than on the former. But that is irrelevant. Each title needed the other. People came to browse and buy at Waterstone's because of the quality, the range, the diversity, the magic of its stock. So that's where they came for their William Boyd, which actually they could have found in any half-decent bookshop in the land. They came to us, though, because with us they could buy the Boyd, and then spend time in a wonderful browse to see what else they might find. Twelve times in the year it might be that copy of *Her Privates We*...

And, thus, by all of that...

Wonderful Waterstone's on Manchester's not so wonderful Deansgate is a gem, and a large one at that. I could quite easily spend half a day looking through the biggest bookshop in the north of England... highly recommended, says a local Manchester guidebook.

The extraordinary energy that had built amongst the managers was then applied to authors' events in their stores – readings, signing sessions, lectures – all to be organised by the managers themselves, liaising with the publishers' marketing people.

David McRedmond recalls:

One event at Hampstead highlighted an essential facet of Waterstone's. The company would always be something bigger than a retailer, with a purpose beyond bookselling. Every new store opening was heralded as the revival of a particular town. (I remember especially Waterstone's opening in my native Dublin at a time when nothing ever opened in Dublin.)

One quiet morning in November 1990, TW phoned me (I had recently become the manager) to say that I was about to receive an important call from the Special Branch of the Met. Five minutes later the call came through: I was asked if I would agree to Salman Rushdie, who had been in hiding for eighteen months or longer, holding a special pretend book-signing for *Haroun and the Sea of Stories*. There was a security lockdown as staff were informed two minutes before the event to clear the store and close it. Salman arrived and we set up a book-signing with staff acting as customers.

The next day the picture of Salman with me beside him and the staff posed as customers went around the world on the front page of every major newspaper. Not one member of staff was concerned about the serious security threat (although I was instructed to be anonymous) but revelled in the publicity for the shop. This was us; this was Waterstone's.

These days, literary festivals are ten a penny, and are admirable, but in my view nothing in them quite matches the sheer energy and informal bustle and intimacy and fun of what the

Waterstone's branches ran throughout the land in those heady days. No one else was doing them. Martin Latham is right in what he says – intense rivalry sprang up between the branches as to which could book the best authors, and for me that was the fun of it. I could sit back and watch. Hardly an evening passed without me being there at one or another of these branch events. They were always, always good, and sometimes they were quite superb. To take one example, amongst a plethora of the richest of memories, I recall Ted Hughes one evening in the basement of our Camden High Street branch in north London, with hundreds and hundreds of local people crammed in to the store, sitting packed together on the floor, standing on the staircase, there to hear him read his poems, to ask questions of him, to listen to his memories, to touch the hem of his garment. Faber had arranged for him to stay one hour with us. He was there for three. It was totally magical.

John Mitchinson remembers some of those occasions:

The first secret events for Salman Rushdie at Hampstead. A reading in Charing Cross Road for an ailing Raymond Carver, with Richard Ford and Tobias Woolf. John Irving reading from *A Prayer for Owen Meany* in the same shop. The first Waterstone's Debate at Stationers' Hall on fiction vs. biography (A. S. Byatt and Anthony Burgess vs. Michael Holroyd and Philip Ziegler – declared a draw).

David McRedmond writes too of the sheer living joy at being at the cutting edge of the company's literary obsession, and, vitally, his own too:

Throughout it all, all our work is peppered with great books. The connection with authors was effortless: they wanted to be part of our tribe! I recall arranging a tour of nascent Irish writers in Waterstone's stores across London in 1990: Colm Toibín, Dermot Bolger, Anne Enright... now all literary stars. And nights with Tom Wolfe, John le Carré (a good Hampstead friend), Julian Barnes, Oscar Hijuelos and many more.

And all our branches' energy in working side by side with literary authors in this way not only led to superb support of their new titles but also helped to sell their backlist. Indeed, the result of it all was in sales that were heavily weighted – at least 80 per cent weighted – towards backlist rather than current bestsellers (and thus the absolute direct opposite to WH Smith, and very deliberately so). This was to my pride, and relief, as it exactly proved the point I was making in all the drafts I made of my business plan. We found that our average sales per square foot was around four hundred plus pounds per annum (about a thousand plus pounds today), which was rather more than twice what was then the norm across the industry – an extraordinary win, and a win that progressively made fundraising for rapid expansion so much easier, as we were able to show to prospective backers the documented evidence of our model's success.

Our range would be an expert selection in the literary sense, made by the branches themselves, of individual titles for their individual markets, with a guide, no more than that, of a basic core title list chosen and drafted by the staff. To do this we would invite one of our people with a reputation amongst us for exceptional knowledge and interest in a particular genre to be that genre's champion for the whole company. Thus Nick in Waterstone's Manchester, an acknowledged expert in crime fiction, would compile for his colleagues throughout the Waterstone's estate his view of an 'ideal' crime fiction range. Gill in Waterstone's High Street Kensington, whose main interest and expertise was in travel narrative, would do the same for that. Alice in Waterstone's Bristol, fresh from Cambridge with a first-class degree, admired by the staff throughout the company, and most of all by me, for her expertise and knowledge in presenting an ideal literary fiction range, would list that range, author by author, title by title, for all the other branches to consider.

And so it went on. One particular trick, or rather one particular characteristic that we wanted all our branches to have, was to ensure that where we were supporting an author we would have on the shelves not just that author's major selling titles, but also all the minor ones too. Take Thomas Hardy, for example; we would stock his short story collections, such as *Life's Little Ironies*, alongside *Jude the Obscure* and the like. This in the full knowledge and acceptance that for every one copy of that collection we would sell in a year, we would sell thirty of *Jude* or *The Mayor of Casterbridge* or *Far from the Madding Crowd*. That wasn't the point. The point was to show to the public that we knew what we were doing, and if they came to muse around our shelves and tables they could be certain of a huge range of interesting stock. They knew and loved Hardy's great novels, and of course his poetry, but were perhaps barely aware of his short stories. Here they were. Just on impulse, they would pick up *Life's Little Ironies*, leaf it through, and take it up to the till.

For the impulse buy is, of course, at the very heart of good bookselling. I remember a research project, commissioned at a time when we had perhaps thirty or forty branches, showed that over 70 per cent of books bought from us arose from a sudden impulse decision when the person was there in the store, which was extraordinary. People would come through our doors with perhaps a single title in mind, find that title, and then spend another twenty minutes browsing. Such was the richness of our stock that eventually they would find themselves taking a further four or five books up to the till, none of which they had planned to buy before entering the shop. The same piece of research concluded that the majority of our sales came from the very heaviest of book buyers, the category set at the level of people who bought more than fifty books a year.

'What are you going to do about the browser problem?' asked one banker of me on one of my perpetual journeys into the City to raise funds, so that we could open further branches. I must have been in the City for these meetings well over a hundred times over the first seven or eight years of Waterstone's life, as we forced the company on, financing each branch individually as it came our way. Often it proved to be only to meet these sorts of dumb questions, but on I had to go. I'm not sure this particular young banking ace had quite caught the point of what I had been saying and trying to illustrate...

All the branches operated very long opening hours, including Sundays, though in those days opening on Sunday was illegal, but we thought the law an ass, and we did it. We ran a public campaign on this issue, protesting that bookshops offered urban communities an unmatched cultural and leisure amenity on dreary Sunday afternoons. As a result of this we were almost entirely left alone by all the various borough councils wherever we opened.

Our central control of the branches was limited, in essence, to just two factors. First, a monitoring of their £ stock level values, to ensure that the individual branch managers were running their branches at not less than the stock value levels required (which were hugely above industry norms) and, at the other end of the scale, not significantly higher than those levels. And second, that their individual branch staff costs were running in line with what we had budgeted for them, thus giving the individual managers the task of deciding how to balance full-time staff against booksellers working part-time. This is simply impossible to do accurately at 'head office'. Easy to do, though, by the branch manager himself or herself – mostly herself, I should add, as women predominated by about sixty/forty, and deservedly so. What was so stunning too, as Paul Baggaley was quoted earlier, was that many of them were in their early twenties, just a few years out of university, and they were running at least twenty or thirty staff, as well as their branch's entire stock range, the cleaners, the branch's cash, the constant calls from publishers, and the constant calls from me, and doing it all with the greatest of verve, confidence and enthusiasm. I have never seen, before or since, young people so competent and engaged.

Added to all this was the promise to our staff that all promotion would be from within the company itself. No one would be brought in from outside to take a branch manager job, each of these posts being reserved for our own booksellers. Because of this policy our staff turnover was much lower than we had forecast. Our policy as regards to recruitment was, as I have said, only to bring in to the branches young people with not only a demonstrable and profound knowledge of literature, but also clear enthusiasm. I tried to get to know everyone who came to work with us, and I mean really get to know. To make real contact with them and get to know their lives. I made sure that I interviewed everyone coming into the company, or at worst had a chat with them as soon after they had arrived as possible.

David McRedmond writes:

TW, in the early years at least, interviewed for every role. My interview was unremarkable except that he didn't ask me about books. His interest was life, the person, my studies (an average history degree). Instantly he changed my perception of the job from being a shop assistant to something much more important: a 'Bookseller in Waterstone's'. He understood the value of ennobling work, creating a new profession called 'Bookseller in Waterstone's' and translating this into a vibrant enterprise.

Within weeks everything he promised came through. I would be a buyer as well as a seller of books. I would work with a collegiate group of like-minded people. It would be fun and it would be important as the company would grow.

The first book I acquired for sale was six copies of *The Athenian Trireme*, a Cambridge University Press history of the reconstruction of an ancient vessel. I persuaded the nearby Greek Tourist Office to put the book in its window with a 'for purchase in Waterstone's' sign. The six copies were sold in a week. It was the start of the most fun career.

*

I always made a point of stressing that I didn't want them to necessarily think of Waterstone's as a long-term career (though for some it has proved to be exactly that, and how very good that is). What I wanted from them was not only great knowledge, and a desire to use that, but also a bubbling, joyful enthusiasm. And one more thing I asked of them, and it was highly unorthodox – I asked them to promise me that the moment they became bored with life with us they would come to me to say goodbye. That was why I told them that I didn't want them to think of Waterstone's as a long-term career. The moment they were bored with life with us was the time when they should move on and away. After our reputation had started to spread we had literally dozens and dozens of arts graduate applicants for every single bookseller vacancy we had. I could probably add a further 'and dozens' or two to that. That's another reason why I asked people to leave us the moment they lost their enthusiasm and spark: so that we could bring in replacements from the vast cadre of other young people who wanted to join us.

And I have to be proud of them, of the Waterstone's diaspora out there now in the world, such clever and talented people who started their working careers with us. Some of the most distinguished and senior names in the nation's arts and literary world spent two or three years of their then young lives with us in one or other of our branches – novelists, biographers, publishers, scriptwriters, playwrights, reviewers, journalists, agents, broadcasters, film-makers, actors, teachers, independent booksellers.

There are some quite astonishing people on the list. I can identify names, several names actually, for every single one of the categories listed above. I am very proud of them. And I am very proud of Waterstone's, for attracting those wonderful people into our midst.

*

In 1986, we had an idea that would provide another way to build our brand and extend our reach, our DNA, which was to publish what we quickly decided to call *Waterstone's Guide to Books*. It was exactly that – a selected overview of books in print in our part of the literary market. We had a first shot at this, in a rather modest form, a practice swing if you like, and learnt the lessons we needed to, and decided to put out a second edition in 1988, which would be more comprehensive and ambitious. Rosie Alison was appointed from our staff as the general editor of this new edition, and she asked if she could work on it with John Mitchinson, a close friend of hers from their Oxford days. We had only just pulled John from his poetry section at the-about-to-be-opened Hampstead for a six-week secondment to compile our Waterstone's literary diary for the following year, 1989, on which he worked every day in the old Reading Room of the British Museum sorting out dates and anecdotes and selecting passages to do with books and reading for the diary. I am sure he was longing to get up to Hampstead and organise his poetry section, but he immediately agreed to join the *Waterstone's Guide to Books* team, and Rosie and he and the five other selected members of the staff set to it.

'The next three months were some the most intense of my life,' John recalls:

I edited the Essays & Collected Prose section, educating myself across 2,000 years of philosophy, art and literature, and contributed many essays to the fiction section. The dead-line was impossible and the small team of seven of us worked for months with no days off. I remember the exhaustion still, coming home late to make an omelette and forming the recipe into blurb-speak in my head: 'A combination of fresh eggs and butter, the omelette is a staple snack that originated in France...'

Somehow we made it. The final book was a beast, the best part of 1,700 pages long, featuring over 60,000 titles, with lists of favourite books from David Attenborough, P. D. James, Saul Bellow (!) and many others. Written and edited on very early Mac Plus computers, in Microsoft Word files and boxes of floppy disks, it was the largest paperback the printers Clays of Bungay have ever produced. Rosie Alison's team of seven had drawn too on the knowledge of a vast team of a hundred and fifty of our booksellers, and the *Guide* still stands as one of the most remarkable achievements of that early Waterstone's period.

It was a commercial failure (we overprinted and the book was too fat to go through the standard letter box). But in its ambition and chutzpah it seems to me to sum up so much of what made the company so different and appealing. Personally, it taught me how to write copy and how to edit: in the most gruelling and intense way. And at the end of it, Rosie asked me to take on the editorship of the third edition, so I can reasonably say it changed the course of my life.

The third edition was a solid bit of work which stemmed the financial losses but lacked the wayward spirit of the second. Perhaps the most significant thing was that we had digitised it. It's important to remember that at this point there was no internet and barely anyone had email. Amazon was six years away (I remember years later pointing out that the *Guide* was essentially a paper Amazon but by then it was too late...).

By the time the third edition emerged, I'd been put in charge of the publications department: which produced the literary diary, the *Guide to Books* and two seasonal catalogues. These were the brainchild of Roger Bratchell, who became a close friend and mentor. As well as lists of upcoming books by subject, he thought we ought to do interviews with authors and asked me to help.

In the Autumn 1988 edition I managed seven interviews in a fortnight, including Julian Barnes (*A History of the World in 10 ½ Chapters*), Redmond O'Hanlon (*In Trouble Again*) and Salman Rushdie for *The Satanic Verses*. This was the first interview with Salman about the book and he seemed impressed that I'd not only read it but also his three previous novels. The interview contains the prophetic line 'I suspect there may be problems'...

The catalogues were popular with customers, but they also began to change our relationship with publishers. The publications department became the marketing department, responsible for coordinating shop openings and making sure the store merchandise was up to snuff. Our combination of enthusiasm, knowledge and fearlessness was new in the book trade – Waterstone's opened fourteen shops in 1988 alone: the revolution was under way.

CHAPTER 19

Yes – the revolution was indeed under way. My dream, the picture in my head, my bottom-of-the-barrel £6,000, my cry for literature, my personal statement, my name (I still recall the rush of intense pleasure as I saw that name go up over the door of that very first store), the public encapsulation of my own personality. My bookshops. Waterstone's would be better than any bookshops anywhere. We would open them all across the land, and trade from them as many hours as we could.

We told our staff to regard their bookshops not so much as stores within a national chain, but as independent bookshops which just happened to carry the Waterstone's name. Independent bookshops of the very highest quality. And we told them to accept personal responsibility for the achievement of that, and to relish doing so.

And in doing that, as Andrew Stilwell, one of Waterstone's earliest staff members, reminisced a few years ago in the *Guardian*, they accepted that:

> ... we Waterstone's managers, as part of our autonomy, were also encouraged to become good business people, rigorously mindful of profit and loss, balance sheets, business plans,

budgets and forecasts – with the result that some of the most successful independent bookshops are now being run by former friends and colleagues from Waterstone's... We strove to achieve the key skill of a good bookseller and the source of his/her pride in the job; not just intelligently stocking what people will expect to find in a bookshop, but second-guessing what customers will be surprised and excited by.

In giving our branch managers this power, we hoped that a by-product would be that they would like to invest themselves in Waterstone's, however modestly, thus encouraging their sense of ownership yet further. And some did.

'He encouraged everyone to take out shares,' says Ray Monk in an interview in the *Independent* at the time of the launch of his deservedly acclaimed biography of Wittgenstein. Ray was an early staff member at the Charing Cross Road branch, and the proofs of *Wittgenstein* were corrected as he sat at the Charing Cross Road front till. I know. I once caught him at it...

So that was Waterstone's and the vision. Hardly rocket science, and the better for that. Passionate book people running individual, passionately committed bookshops, and, free of centralism, taking personal responsibility for the quality of their bookshops and their financial results. Perfect Stock, Perfect Staff, Perfect Control.

As Paul Baggaley said earlier, we rolled out the stores across the country pretty well straight away, immediately after our success in High Street Kensington. And we did that – rather than concentrating on the London area, as we had originally planned to do – because we became convinced that, outside a few specific travel books, literary reading tastes are universal rather than local. Our managers barely changed our style of offer at all, region by region. We believed it would succeed anywhere. And we backed our hunch, a few years down the line, opening for example a large branch in Gateshead in the north-east of England, an industrial town with raging unemployment and very low further- and higher-education demographics – probably amongst the least promising social demographics you could find for literary bookselling anywhere in the country. Our star manager there, just two years out of university, confident from having worked for a few months in a couple of our best northern branches, gave Gateshead our standard high literary offer, exactly as we would in Cambridge or Oxford or Edinburgh or Dublin or Bristol. We saw what she wanted, and we hesitated for a moment, but we didn't interfere. And it worked just fine, to our great pleasure. In fact, because of the low Gateshead rents, it was very profitable. Give people access to books, possibly for effectively the first time in their lives, and many of them will find within themselves an interest and a cultural capacity they perhaps never thought they had. This we believed, and passionately so.

Bit by bit new investors came on board to help us finance new branches. Notably, three or four years in, three quite excellent professional private equity investors – the DC Thomson family, Apax Partners and Quester Capital Management – offered to invest in us, alongside ICFC. There was also a steady gathering of private individuals, and always – this is very important – each time equity rounds would be set at an increased entry price, thus driving the company ever upwards in terms of demonstrable market value (and that was beginning to represent some millions of pounds). This highly unusual and unorthodox funding strategy carried within it a very positive feature, and it was actually that feature that ended up being taught by means of a case study on Waterstone's written at INSEAD, one of the world's leading business schools, based just outside Paris at Fontainebleau. The INSEAD thesis was that start-up and early-stage companies should always have only just enough cash for each incremental development step. Too much, and it is wasted on infrastructure and administration and an excess of options. Just right, and each incremental step is made in tight, hard focus. That leads to a great positive – step-by-step higher new investment values. And this was the Waterstone's funding model that I had been drafting and redrafting all that time before. We would always work on just enough cash and no more for each new branch. And thus the endless rounds of financing we undertook. And thus the ever rising investment values in the Waterstone's shares on each and every funding round. And thus the company's step-by-step acceleration in its demonstrable market worth.

I have said earlier that we undertook no market research. Actually, that is not entirely true. There was some, but it was free, and was of incomparable quality. It related to site selection, rather than anything to do with our offer as such. Site selection was largely a process of following in footsteps. Specifically, in Marks & Spencer's footsteps. If their property specialists and their highly developed demographic models were good enough for them, then they were certainly good enough for us. So, on the streets where they opened, we looked to open. But we did so with one crucial difference. We could not take on prime rents, so what we did was to open near to Marks & Spencer, but around the corner; off-prime sites, and preferably – and this was quite crucial – in buildings of architectural interest. We really liked that. There were many of this description, but perhaps the two best examples would be our stores on Grey Street, Newcastle, and Milsom Street, Bath, both sited in notably beautiful buildings – Grey Street of the 1830s and Milsom Street of the 1760s. We trusted in our belief that if our stores were good enough – more than merely good enough, wonderful enough – then within a period of just a few weeks the word would get out, and people would set out to find us. People love good bookshops. And when they had found us, we would get our £ sales per square foot that we aimed for, but at much more moderate ongoing rental cost (not just in the short term, but with increasing benefit throughout the whole tenure of the long leases we sought).

We opened near WH Smith too, but that was for a very different reason.

We liked to join combat with WH Smith by opening our stores as close to them as possible, and taking them competitively straight on. Right beside them if we could, and another one right across the street. If our appetite in those days for so aggressively, angrily, overtly competing with WH Smith surprises, all I can say is there is nothing like enmity, edging into personal vindictiveness, to get the entrepreneurial juices flowing. It is all part of the mindset, and it works. 'We're good haters,' Charles Dunstone of Carphone Warehouse is quoted as saying, in the early years of that company. Think Branson and his bitter battles with British Airways; James Dyson and his furious wars with Hoover; Bill Gates in the early days and an ultimately cowed IBM. I objected to being the fall guy for WH Smith's distribution experiments in the US, but I was additionally irritated, actually contemptuous, to learn that their directors were – publicly, and no doubt in their eyes amusingly – at that time engaged in running a book, all welcome to join, wagering on exactly which month Waterstone's would go belly up.

I was alerted to that at an early stage from inside their camp, by my good friend Michael Pountney, who in the 1980s, around the time I was setting up Waterstone's, was the chief book buyer for the Smith retail operation. Another 'mildly subversive' type, was Michael. It was he, reacting to the Smith board of directors forbidding him to stock a particular and prominent literary novel of the gay world, who pointed out to them that according to the Kinsey Report 10 per cent of the UK population was homosexual. As there were ten directors on the Smith board (all male, of course... heaven forbid...), would the one director who was therefore a homosexual give his personal view on that decision? This was not, perhaps, a wise career move by Michael, but actually it proved in its way to be exactly that, as he settled very shortly thereafter into a deservedly long and happy senior editor position at a well-established London literary publishing house...

The legendary Sam Walton of the mighty Walmart once again:

If you love your work, you will be out there every day trying to do it the best you possibly can, and pretty soon everybody around you will catch the passion from you – like a fever.

I did love Waterstone's/Waterstones, apostrophe, no apostrophe, it is all the same in my eyes, and of course I absolutely still do. Waterstone's defined my life. I believed I had a winner – both culturally and financially – and committing myself passionately and unswervingly to that win was as necessary to me, and as instinctive, as breathing itself. I am proud of all that happened in those early years. Like Sam Walton, I was out there every day trying to do the best I possibly could. And others around me did see that passion and ran with it.

There is a cussed independence of spirit in a true entrepreneur. And how lucky I was to find that I had beside me in the early Waterstone's a group of brilliant young people so cussedly independent of spirit themselves. They saw what I was trying to do and liked it, and they cussed away beside me at our establishment enemies, and they drove us through to the winning line.

Let's look again at that seven-point checklist that I mentioned in the Prologue – a list that is, or should be, in the pocket of every person setting out on an entrepreneurial journey. We can relate that to the early years of Waterstone's life.

1. *How can I inspire?*
To me, the most vital part of the equation was to bring into the company people, and almost entirely young people, who had a real knowledge of literature, and a demonstrable enthusiasm for showing that to the public. That was why I talked with everyone personally as they came into the company, not only for me to gauge them, but, most importantly, for them to gauge me, and for me to show them that I, too, possessed that knowledge and enthusiasm.

So it wasn't just us trying to find a way to inspire our new recruits. In a way they all brought their own inspiration with them, and that's exactly what I wanted to happen. Our job was to ensure that their working lives with us enabled them to show their inspiration and knowledge in every way: in the way they talked to the public; in the way they bought their books for their sections first, and then, later, for their stores; in their enthusiasm in the sale of those books, and, above all, in their taking of personal and clear responsibility for all their actions.

Kate Gunning, an excellent bookseller who in due course moved from us to a long publishing career at Random House, wrote:

I feel so fortunate that I worked for Waterstone's during that earlyish period. The company was small, dynamic and entrepreneurial and, if one was keen and able and flexible, it was possible to move through the ranks fairly quickly – there was a strong policy of promoting from within. But it was more than that. We were trusted to run our own businesses, and that freedom was enthralling. The grounding gained by Waterstone's managers meant that many of them went on to run their own superb independent bookshops and to further enrich this country's bookselling ecosystem...

2. *How can I ensure that my dream can best be driven on its way?*

In essence, it was my job to keep the company moving forward. But how? By keeping it constantly financed to enable a regular and speedy flow of new branches, thereby opening up opportunities for staff to take on responsibility and move their careers along. By weeding out from the ranks those whose hearts were not sufficiently into the task. By making the staff feel that our profile was ever growing – more, that we were part of a cultural revolution – and encouraging them to be proud of that, and to be inspired by that... To make them feel they were doing something both immensely worthwhile and thoroughly enjoyable. And by endlessly working to improve and develop, all of us together as a team, the quality of our offer, which meant superb bookshops, with superb, highly knowledgeable staff selling a superbly selected stock.

3. *How can I lead more and manage less?*
By getting the right people into the right jobs – back to that interview process again – so that we could fully delegate responsibility to them. And by ensuring that they had a constant flow of management information to enable them to work to perfect their skills and their performance.

4. *How can I inspire creativity and imagination amongst the whole team?*
By high levels of delegation, encouragement, and by a leadership style that is quick to praise and slow to blame.

5. *How can I know who our market is, and deliver to them what I know they want?*
Waterstone's initial range selection was effectively modelled on me and my personal tastes – a stock range that I felt would provide a perfect bookshop to spend lots of my time and lots of

my money in. I just hoped a couple of million or more people out there felt exactly like me. We tried it. We were right. That's the basic reason why Waterstone's worked so well. And I felt a vital key to our model was to deliver to the public a staff in the branches who were intensely knowledgeable and intensely motivated. I was right in that, too.

6. *How can I let our people show what they can do?*
Peter French, one of our earliest recruits and later a superb branch manager, before in time leaving us for the teaching profession, wrote:

It was just that we liked books, and we liked people who liked books, and we knew what we were doing. We could find things in the shop for customers, and we could identify and acquire books for them that we didn't have in stock. And we could have an enjoyable, intelligent conversation at the same time. It was in many ways a very simple job, but with endless variety, because we were dealing with the public, and our product was the entire sum of human knowledge...

We let our people operate within a company model of total delegation, and by a leadership style that congratulated success, and made a point of not dwelling too long on a mistake or two, provided a lesson had been learnt.

Again, Peter French:

He entrusted me with managing one of the first branches outside London. There was no formal process involved. This meant that I felt simultaneously deeply trusted (which I was) and hopelessly out of my depth (which I also was). Some managers crashed and burned given this responsibility, but most didn't. For most of us it gave us the opportunity to develop as people (we were mostly young), and to learn what our own style was, of being a person as much as of managing. He enabled and facilitated us by (mostly) staying out of our way and leaving us to get on with it, having first made it clear what the key priorities were. He was visionary and inspirational, but left the details to us. He was a great believer in the power of leadership, and both embodied it himself and inspired it in others.

7. *How can I let them believe that they are capable of anything, that they can reach out, and that they can grow?*

By all of the above. By delegating total responsibility to young, enthusiastic people, thus giving them a chance to show their quality and their drive and their competence unusually early in their careers.

All of which leads us back again to Sam Walton:

Communicate everything you possibly can to your colleagues. The more they know, the more they will understand. The more they understand, the more they will care. Once they care, there is no stopping them. If you do not trust your associates to know what is going on, they will know that you do not really consider them partners. Information is power, and the gain that you get from empowering your associates more than offsets the risk of informing your competitors.

And that is exactly what we did. We told our staff everything. In time we got to the point where the branch managers received summaries of our branch-by-branch management accounts, in exactly the same form as our shareholders did (and a few of them were of course shareholders anyway). They could see where we were winning and where we were losing. They saw their £ sales per square foot in comparison with the other branches' sales per square foot, and their stock per square foot against the other branches' stock per square foot, and they could draw their own highly competitive conclusions from those things. And because they had decentralised power of action, they could do something about it. Branch staff costs were shared too. We were wholly indifferent as to whether this level of financial detail leaked into the hands of our competitors. What we did know was that our highly intelligent staff were supercharged by means of this empowering access to sophisticated management information, and ran their branches better on the back of it. They were there to embrace and enhance the Waterstone's culture, but they were also there to be custodians of our money as we all drove the company forward together. And we were very, very seldom let down by any of them.

Bestselling business visionary Tom Peters has said that it is wonderful people that make wonderful companies, and that is all there is to it, and Waterstone's certainly had wonderful people. But my view is that those wonderful people are most truly empowered not by 'freedom' in itself, but by freedom within the parameters of a company with a strategic vision so clear and articulated that all can understand the joy of working within it. I hope that we had exactly that, and that the staff had a total grasp of it. Once again – Perfect Stock, Perfect Staff, Perfect Control.

One thing you can be sure of. As an entrepreneur, you carry within you a wonderful mindset asset, common to all true entrepreneurs: you have the instinct to make all business life as unfussy as possible. You concentrate each year on just a very few, absolutely clear management initiatives, the context and importance of which all the staff can understand and support, for with an excess of management initiatives everything becomes a muddle. You go for decisive action. You keep decision-making crisp. You keep the centre just as small as is sensible, knowing that too many people will lead to too many competing initiatives and insufficient clarity. You look to build productivity in each and every member of the staff, concentrating particularly at the lower management levels, the newer recruits where, if you really look for it, you may well find jewels (and we certainly did that...). You avoid like a plague the dreary, fearful, bureaucratic torpor that big corporate life can become. You strain to reserve for all time the fun, bustle and drive – and the humanity – of entrepreneurial companies on their way to the winning line.

*

After three to four years of constant, seamless success, suddenly all was not plain sailing. Our most recent store, in Glasgow – which was huge and very expensive to stock and staff – was performing in its first few weeks a country mile under our expectation. The economy had suddenly gone absolutely dead, sales everywhere on the high street were slack, and our bank was growing very uneasy. For the first time, we found ourselves momentarily above and beyond our negotiated overdraft limit.

I was increasingly concerned that the bank would bounce the monthly payroll, which they were threatening to do. One of our main shareholders warned me, along with the other three institutional investors, that it would be organisationally impossible for them to support at such short notice an emergency call on shareholders to plug the short-term cash gap, so I must not depend on them for that. Meanwhile, I had developed an abscess so agonising that the only way to cope with it, and work, was to rinse my mouth out every few minutes with tepid water – nothing else would reach it.

I was also trying to open that major new store of ours on Dawson Street in Dublin, which David McRedmond mentioned earlier. The Irish unions were encouraging the builders fitting out the store to demand daily cash sweeteners in brown envelopes from us, or walk. Or worse. And 'worse', in Ireland at that time, might well mean getting a fire device dropped through your skylight, which is what eventually happened to us on the eve of our opening day. Fortunately the device flared momentarily, and then fizzled out.

On top of that, our brand-new mail order division was clearly failing in data capture, as we were losing track of who had ordered what, and, disastrously, whether they had paid us for it. A famous politician's mistress was threatening to sue us for some vast sum because one of our biggest branches had failed to remove from their shelves a book on the politician which defamed her.

While all this was going on I read a piece in the *Harvard Business Review* by Tom Peters – the all action!, all drive!, all revolution! management guru *sans pareil* – summarising his thesis in his then current bestseller, *Thriving On Chaos*. It is always better to try a swan dive and deliver a colossal belly flop than to step timidly off the board holding your nose – that sort of thing. People thrive on chaos. Great companies thrive on chaos. Chaos is meat and drink to entrepreneurs. Tom Peters – I thought – you wish *more* chaos on me? I would *thrive* on that?

Whenever I speak in business schools, my personal advice is always a lot less furiously aggressive and apocalyptic. Rather, I take this sort of line: be subservient to no one and to no received wisdom. Trust your intuition. Keep absolutely on top of cash flow projections, and never, never stop drafting them out (and don't leave them to the accountants to do for you – calculate them yourself...). Think for yourself. Give a clear-cut sense of direction. Be brave. Lead through example. Inspire. Above all, create a business which by virtue of its spirit and originality and sheer quality will survive. Keep in play. Get to the winning post of a secure future. Finally, work together to make it.

The last point is a great feature of life within small, ambitious start-up and early-stage businesses. You are a team and you learn from each other, free from big corporation career jealousies. There really is no time for career jealousies. Survival is the name of the game, and when life is dangerous people stick together. They use their individual strengths and learn from the strengths of other members of the team.

In this scenario forgiveness is very important. Inevitably, and with the best will in the world, people make mistakes. There is no time for checking and counter-checking, and people do not want that. Everyone has to learn, everyone has to forgive, and everyone has to resolve privately not to make that same mistake again. This works so well in the young, entrepreneurial company, and so badly in almost all big corporations. In their case they all too often use their appraisal systems and confidential files to record errors and misjudgements, rather than to identify areas of achievement and success. Chastise people for failure and in the future they will make it a point not to expose themselves, or risk wandering one inch off the beaten path.

That's not how vigorous new businesses can be made to work. Furthermore, I believe that the mindset that allows you to spend your working life thanking and congratulating people rather than criticising and being unpleasant to them is a mainstay of good leadership. If your leadership style is to treat good performance and good conduct as the subject of sincere, open approval and congratulation, and reduce criticism of underperformance to the minimum, it is a very pleasant way indeed of conducting one's affairs.

Criticism can be done subtly, sometimes by not what is actually said, and it's way more effective because of that. It doesn't have to be head-on. David McRedmond tells this anecdote:

Several months after opening the Hampstead shop, which had quickly achieved an almost celebrity status as London's best bookstore, Dane and I received a call from TW's assistant to ask us to see him in Hay's Mews. This was unusual. We knew that some customer complaints had built up; the pressure of the most erudite clientele had started to tell on staff: we took longer breaks, boozy lunches; our standards had slipped.

Coyly we went to Hay's Mews and into his office. Five minutes of small talk about recent books were followed by him declaring, 'You are two of my absolute favourite people and I just wanted to tell you how much I admire what you are achieving in Hampstead and how proud I am of your staff and the extraordinary range of books. You really are everything I want Waterstone's to be about. So thank you very, very much, and thank you for coming to Hay's Mews.'

I was stunned. As we were leaving Dane turned around to him and said, 'OK, you're right, it's true, we've slipped, we'll pull our socks up!'

But there is a twist, an interesting conundrum that underlies all this. It is my suspicion that a great majority of entrepreneurs are driven in part by an inability to forgive or forget. There will be some aspect of their past that haunts them and drives them to expunge the memory of it by the overt public demonstration that they are brave, risk-taking people. As I said at the very beginning of the book, I have no doubt at all that was exactly the case with me, and I recognise it. Possibly the main driver of my life had been the beyond painful failure of my relationship with my father. It served to generate an energy in the birth of Waterstone's that was just a little insane. And an insane, disruptive, bottle-hurling foe is tough for the corporate opponent to measure up to.

WH Smith, for example, just weren't up to countering us. We were the aggressive, red-hot, determined, confident challenger. And, as I have earlier described, in quite a short time we had been enthusiastically financed – and this became absolutely crucial – by a broad shareholder list of real diversity and considerable financial strength. In a sense we actually had more money available to us in the task than Smith had. But the Smith predicament was not unusual, for most established corporations – in the US, UK, or wherever – always have trouble in either countering or embracing what the business consultant Professor Clayton Christensen famously called the 'disruptive' innovations that are on their radar screens.

The problem for the big corporates seems to be that they develop mindsets and processes that revolve around one thing: what they already know. Once that pattern has become embedded their managers find it difficult, even career threatening, to justify to others or even to themselves the need to turn their processes upside down to respond to the disruptive newcomers. Make too much fuss and you appear, in corporate speak, to be 'excitable' and 'unsound', and your career card is marked accordingly. The big corporations relish and support a managerial mindset that revolves around what the corporation already does. They want, at all costs, to keep life stable. And above all predictable.

But leave it too late, as WH Smith did with us, and the entre-preneurial newcomer has made the play, got the position and seized a lead. And by securing the lead, the upstart has secured the prospect of a valuable exit by trade sale to the market leader should that be the desired route. Conventional exit valuations based on purely financial performance measures – cash gener-ation multiples or balance sheet net worth – are immaterial if he/she plays the hand right. What absolutely matters is a fast-growing market share combined with a fast-growing public profile, which was exactly what WH Smith faced in us. Almost any price can then be extracted from the corporate, in order that their embarrassment can be buried and the upstart be removed and taken off their computer screens.

In essence, the big corporates can fight away on price, and better operational effectiveness, for that is playing to their strengths. They can bully suppliers, and they have the leverage of a big infrastructure. But these are no more than short-term ploys. Eventually you have to stand apart. You have to be unique – and identifying uniqueness, differential, is what entrepreneurs are good at. This is an intuitive and personal art. Corporates buy up entrepreneurial innovations, then coarsen and ruin them. They so seldom seem to understand the brands they have bought, and the promise they deliver. You have to stand apart. You have to be unique.

Martin Lee, co-owner of Acacia Avenue, an independent marketing consultancy, wrote in 2010:

> I am most interested in looking at the Waterstone's story from the perspective of how markets work. In most consumer markets, it's common to have a big mid-market player with the largest share. They tend to be efficient, appeal to broad taste, and are respected more than loved. WH Smith has held this position in books, Boots in cosmetics and toiletries, Tesco in groceries. It's also typical for markets to have upscale brands with small shares that appeal to the exploratory, passionate consumers in that category – think of Waitrose.
>
> Of course, that's exactly where Waterstone's sat when it first came on to the scene. It was a discovery brand for people who cared deeply about books, and for whom browsing was an end in itself. Now brands that have this characteristic – be they Waterstone's, Waitrose or Oddbins as it was – work by having a shared intimacy or affinity with customers. In

essence, the idea is that the brand connects with its customers around a shared set of values surrounding the product. Although it's a business, the brand succeeds in conveying the idea that profit is a consequence, rather than the objective, of that business. And in fact that's often authentically the case with such brands. It certainly was with Waterstone's, which was ridiculously profitable in the 1990s despite not always making the most obviously commercial decisions.

I have had a good deal of experience of both venture capital and private equity practitioners over the years, and it has been extremely mixed, ranging from the superb to the deplorable. My view after all this is as follows: when these people stick rigidly to their lasts (and, in my view, these are financial engineering, bank negotiations, accounting scrutiny and the exploration of exit routes), they make extraordinarily effective shareholder partners in entrepreneurial companies. The best of them know that, and do so. In Waterstone's that's what I had – the very best of them. They stick absolutely to their area of technical competence and allow the managers, the experts and the motivators in the business itself to get on with it, albeit under as tight a financial framework as is sensible.

The worst of them, however, do not. The worst of them meddle and muddle with the business's operations, and disaffect the very management on whose expertise they depend to make them the money they aspire to. This sort pretends to have market expertise where they have none (see the blindingly disastrous 'commercialisation' of Waterstone's by HMV and their private equity backers later in the book), insists on giving operational instructions, insists on hiring the wrong people into the company, talks of nothing but money, and is impatient of talk around the cultural aspiration of the company they have invested in – the hinterland of those companies, if you like, their soul, the identity upon which their long-term survival and prosperity will depend, long after the financiers have slipped their cash into their back pockets and departed the scene.

I will give you a grotesque example. I think with a sympathetic shudder about a partnership a few years ago of an impresario of global standing and a London private equity house. I talked at a party one evening to one of the partners of the latter. Neither side, it would seem from what he told me, ever had the first idea as to what the other was on about. The private equity people talked about 'product'; the impresario talked about 'artistes'. In this case the private equity investors wanted to turn a number of the impresario's theatres into – wait for it – casinos, for they calculated there was theatre 'oversupply' in private equity speak. The impresario only wanted to mount more productions, and their potential financing support was the reason he had brought them in in the first place. The whole marriage sounded a total nightmare. My sympathy lay with the impresario. Totally.

What I like in life is comradeship, team loyalty, courage and a sense of common purpose towards the achievement of a worthwhile and honourable goal. And a sense of being true to oneself, by means of a compulsion to work one's socks off in a cause or a venture in which one wholly believes. A commitment to life, really. That brings happiness in its wake. And that's what it did for me.

CHAPTER 20

The WH Smith boardroom joke as to betting which month we would go belly up must have palled for them a little when a few years later, in the summer of 1990, they asked us if they could invest in our business, initially with a minority stake, but with the right to buy us out completely after a further three years. The minority stake was partly taken up by cash, and partly by passing over to us forty or so of their Sherratt & Hughes stores, specialist bookstores that they had launched earlier to go into direct competition with us – unsuccessfully, as they just couldn't compete. We would then rebrand them all in the Waterstone's colours.

We negotiated an entry and exit deal from Smith that represented at the end of the day a multiple of almost fifty-three times what our founders and early-stage investors had paid when coming in. WH Smith contracted to pay us on our exit a minimum of 480p a share against the 10p paid by early investors, but because of our escalating profits over the three-year period the final price they were obliged to pay was actually as much as 527p a 10p share. This valued the company's exit enterprise value at about forty-seven million pounds (or about a hundred and two million in today's money).

The joke around the table at the final completion meeting was that the exit price had been boosted at the last moment by one million pounds due to the fact that they had fired me in 1981. All this, I suppose, was intended to be good-natured and generous in spirit. As for me, I could only brood around the old saying, surely inaccurately attributed to Mahatma Gandhi, though it does indeed have a ring of him somehow: 'First they ignore you, then they laugh at you, then they fight you, then you win...'

So, why did we agree to WH Smith acquiring us?

Their offer had come out of the blue, and it was set, cleverly so, at a price which represented such a high reward for the shareholders, particularly of course for the earlier shareholders, that it put us in a difficult situation. A difficult situation for me most of all, perhaps, for though privileged by my hold on a permanent 25 per cent equity ownership, I had actually not been able to personally subscribe further funds into the company for some time. Every penny that I either possessed or could borrow had already been there in the Waterstone's bank account. Others had invested, though, continually, round after round after round, all the way from one branch to fifty or so, with ICFC joined as institutional backers by, as I have said, the DC Thomson family, Apax and Quester. All four of these players had behaved impeccably to me personally, and they had also behaved impeccably to the company itself, believing in it, boasting of it, even, in their various reports to the media. The private shareholders too had been superb, all of them, and by this time there were several dozen; they also followed each round of financing that we undertook in order to grow so fast that no one could catch us.

There were personal friends amongst those private investors too, which, given the size of the eventual reward for us all, pleased me particularly. One, an old friend, Bob S, was a sixth-form college teacher at the very point of retirement. He loved what we were doing and wanted to invest in us but had not a penny of available money to do so. Then, one morning, there was a letter on his doormat from American Express, offering him a Gold Card and on that card a new credit line of ten thousand pounds. He took the Gold Card, grabbed the ten thousand pounds, and invested the whole lot in our shares. Four or five years later, he and his wife were able to sell, at the point of the WH Smith entry, at a multiple on their purchase stake of delicious value, and it couldn't have happened to a more delightful couple. The second example was shortly before WH Smith came in, when my brother-in-law's wife was given a little money by her father, a well-known merchant banker, and she was unsure where to invest it. She asked him about Waterstone's, and he said that given that the amount he had given her was so modest they may as well put it into the biggest risk they could find, and he thought that Waterstone's was certainly that... Well, the six thousand pounds they invested in us was rapidly turned into sixty thousand, she reminded me recently (about a hundred and fifteen thousand pounds in today's money), and she said she had been able to educate her young children on that money, and keep the change. I like that a lot...

And all these people, corporate and private, had invested in us not as a charity, nor just as a statement of support for literature (though this was undoubtedly a major element of it in many or even probably most cases amongst the private investors), but as a business. And one should say that there was also the general sense of a wind of change ahead. The company was now of a size where to preserve its highly unorthodox if highly successful funding style, and indeed operational style, was going to be rather more difficult. A valuation of the company at this level was not going to come again soon. The offer was on the table, and it was very high. The four institutional shareholders told me quietly, gently, that they would like to accept it. I didn't want to. They suggested then that I required from WH Smith a formal letter of intent as to their proposals for Waterstone's in the event of their gaining control. And that I should consider what they said in that before making my mind up – Smith's statements, for example, around the future management structure, their year-by-year capital investment commitments rolling forward, and their understanding of the Waterstone's business model, with its essential emphasis on superb and heavy stockholding and superb branch staffing. So I did so.

Smith's letter of intent duly arrived on my desk, and it was of a sort that was very difficult for me to fault. They knew what I was requiring of them, and they fed all that back to me. I showed it to the main shareholders, but they returned it to me, saying that the decision was mine. I thought about it for a day or two, reading and rereading the letter, but I knew it was the right thing to do. Smith had convinced me that they understood what they were buying in Waterstone's, and that they respected it, and would preserve it, and would invest heavy and immediate sums into building Waterstone's up further. My main shareholders were not out of order in wanting to take their reward. So I agreed. We shook hands with them. We took the deal. And I had the pleasant knowledge that I had a further three years to build the business before Smith were to take over control.

One of the main attractions in my eyes were the forty or so branches of their Sherratt & Hughes chain, which we would now convert into Waterstone's as fast as we could. There was a surprisingly good geographical fit, and we put an absolutely crack Waterstone's team of three on to the task, rebadging, refitting, restaffing, changing management, remodelling and greatly increasing the stock, throwing out stock cards, throwing out bureaucracy, throwing out 'the old ways', lengthening the trading hours – in essence imposing the Waterstone's culture on to those branches just as quickly and decisively as we could. So, before the next twelve months were up, we had eighty-six branches around the British Isles under the Waterstone's flag, and you wouldn't have known which of those had always been ours and which had previously been Sherratt & Hughes.

John Mitchinson remembers:

It was an amazing thing to be part of, that process. I remember going to store reopenings in towns like Middlesbrough and seeing local customers in tears at the thought of having a 'real' bookshop in their town at long last.

In those three years we continued to open branches, bringing our estate up to just over a hundred. It was becoming a chain of such size that some tiny steps towards increased central presence had become obligatory, and it was through John Mitchinson, head of marketing, that this process was concentrated. He writes:

The combative, invigorating culture of Waterstone's taught me a great deal. I remember sitting down with Tim before the very first conference we ever held, this at the point of us completing the successful rebranding and absorption of Sherratt & Hughes. We called the conference primarily to pin down once and for all the essence of our brand, and Tim and I were trying to find the best way of articulating it.

His original idea had been a hybrid – the intimate, knowledgeable boutique style of a John Sandoe crossed with the pile-'em-high swagger of Barnes & Noble, then beginning to expand exponentially in the US – and to this he'd added some simple organisational principles like flat management structure, tiny head office and graduate-only hiring policy. The simple formula of pre-internet, pre-Amazon bookselling was just that: increased stock per square foot = increased sales per square foot. So bigger, better stocked stores + knowledgeable staff = profits. It worked. It most certainly worked. And that is what the conference message was all about.

We told everyone that to traction our increased power we were going to introduce some central promotional initiatives for all the branches to join. As to this, Mitchinson writes:

Mistakes were made. Implementing promotions in a decentralised chain was challenging: branch visits were more like hustings than anything else. You had to win the arguments with a group of highly intelligent people who were used to doing things their own way. It was exhausting but it earned me respect.

The Waterstone's Book of the Month, which arrived in 1990, started as a shared enthusiasm Tim and I had for the remarkable novel by Nicholas Mosley, *Hopeful Monsters*. Surely, we thought, this was exactly the kind of easy-to-miss masterpiece Waterstone's should clean up with. The idea was simple: a big in-store board advertising the book, a large pile at the front of the store, extra discount from the publisher.

The practicalities – never my forte – were troublesome, the store grumbling was loud ('this won't sell in Southend!') but we persisted, using a voting system to help bed down the idea of a group promotion. Some managers got it and knocked it out of the park: in Hampstead David McRedmond bought 300 copies of Oscar Hijuelos's *The Mambo Kings Play Songs of Love* (another early choice) and sold every copy. The most brilliant and wayward manager of them all, Robert Topping, who ran the Manchester Deansgate store, simply adapted the format to his own ends and ran a parallel Manchester Book of the Month, which he delighted in pointing out always did better than the central selected title.

'Waterstone's Recommends' – which gave booksellers the chance to choose and promote their own favourites – followed, and then a massive British Crime Now promotion, the first of the thematic promotions that culminated in Waterstone's Books of the Century in 1997, the most successful and high-profile book promotion of the 1990s.

Practically speaking, our decision to invest all our marketing in helping to support and promote events programmes in the Waterstone's bookshops changed the way publishers' publicity departments operated. Suddenly, bookshops were no longer just venues for celebrity signing sessions, they were genuine arts venues with programmers and publicity budgets, able to attract significant audiences. Some of that legacy remains: most Waterstone's still use author events programmes as a way of differentiating themselves from the online brands.

Thanks mainly to David McRedmond and John Mitchinson all was working out excellently, it really was, and increasingly profitably (and thus that 47p improvement in our final take-out price, from the contractually guaranteed 480p a share to 527p). So I turned my mind then to the US, intending, as my final personal statement in the Waterstone's adventure, to get us up and running there. Boston was my starting point; it was a marvellously cultured three-university town that was most surprisingly lacking in high-class literary bookselling. I couldn't get out there fast enough, particularly as I had found a superb building for us in Boston's Victorian Back Bay neighbourhood. I asked David McRedmond to go out there to run it. He recalls:

TW had often said that it was the great American independents such as Brentano's on Fifth Avenue or the tony Upper East Side bookstores which were the original model for Waterstone's.

I could see that having conquered Britain and Ireland he wanted now to have a crack at the United States. He asked me to lead the charge and in typical fashion wanted me to be in the States in a matter of weeks. So – what a chance for me that was. I had emigrated to London in 1986 and having failed to find any job finally was employed as an impoverished bookseller by TW. Four years later I was on the front page of the *Boston Globe* as I led the charge to bring Waterstone's to the United States. This was no ordinary company.

His American plans coincided, of course, with the timing of the sale of Waterstone's to WH Smith, so in going out to the US I would be employed by WH Smith's US operation based in Atlanta, Georgia. I realised immediately I got there that nothing could be further apart from TW's vision for a great, sweeping literary adventure than WH Smith's calculatedly diminutive potential plan for an add-on brand to its travel retail franchise, but I was of course firmly on TW's side, and within a very few months we were poised to open what was then the very first book superstore in the States, ahead of both Barnes & Noble and Borders.

The audacious plan was best measured by that front-page headline in the *Boston Globe* recalling the battle-cry of Paul Revere, 'The British are Coming!' The 30,000 square foot store would be exactly as a Waterstone's in the UK, predominantly literary, staffed by informative and enthusiastic booksellers and a business built on the top-line.

Finding the staff was our biggest concern. But they proved to be remarkably similar to the UK. That rich vein that TW had recognised and tapped in Britain also existed in America: enthusiastic liberal arts students who wanted to make a difference and have some fun.

Recreating the tribe was effortless (today the ex-booksellers still remain in touch from their positions as national magazine editors, writers, publishers, lawyers, etc.).

Recruiting a manager for the first store was more difficult. I went to New York to interview candidates with TW.
He was staying in the Plaza Athénée (I recall his embarrassment as the porter delivered him his freshly laundered
underpants... he had clearly made it!) and we met a string
of unsuitable managers, either too driven in the American
way or hopelessly pious booklovers. We settled on a candidate neither of us were in truth enthusiastic about (within a
month of Waterstone's Boston opening we swapped him out
for an ex-Waterstone's manager living in New York, Colette
Carty, who understood both the culture of Waterstone's and
the United States).

Boston was an instant and brilliant success. TW was not
uncritical. Just as in Hampstead or anywhere else whenever
he was in town he slipped quietly into the store and spent
hours checking over the detail of the stock. He was horrified,
I remember, that we had every Hemingway in every version except for *A Farewell to Arms*. He didn't like the slightly
crass price promotion (not possible in the UK due to price
maintenance). His natural bashfulness couldn't quite deal
with the success in front of him: a decade after leaving the
United States with nothing he had come back and turned
the book world upside down. He had proven the power of the
Waterstone's brand, its portability and the uniqueness of its
formula, its DNA: an unparalleled range of books, highly
informed booksellers and a great environment. Perfect stock,
perfect staff, perfect control, in TW's old mantra.

Those who had been the more cautious WH Smith exec-
utives were paradoxically now bursting with pride at seeing

themselves (in truth wholly accidentally) having exported to the US a major UK retail brand so successfully. Sir Simon Hornby, the chairman, stopped by on his way to Elizabeth Taylor's (his wife's friend) wedding, and declared it a triumph. The store was not just an immediate literary success but it was also immediately profitable and had established the clear blueprint of a supply chain and an operational model.

Although WH Smith did not take Waterstone's very much further in the US, with problems beginning to rapidly and extremely seriously beset them in their own business back at home, it is to the huge credit of many people that the marvellous, beautiful Boston Waterstone's store remained a cultural and financial triumph in that great city for almost a decade, before tragically being totally destroyed by fire one ghastly night in the late 1990s.

That Boston store was a lovely symbol, a statement for me to end on, for 1993 was now upon us all, and WH Smith paid out to us our 527p a share and I was gone, eleven years after that unforgettable morning when we first opened our doors in Old Brompton Road. I was sad, of course I was sad, but I had been on a quite wonderful journey. There would be adventures ahead. Life hadn't come to a stop. And, anyway, the adventure I had already experienced over those superb eleven years would always be with me, I knew that. Waterstone's had made a difference. Waterstone's had disrupted a market that needed disrupting, because that market was badly served and culturally vital. Culture is vital. Books are vital. We had changed things and we had saved things. And I knew that what we had done was so very, very much for the better.

John Mitchinson, after eventually leaving Waterstone's, becoming first a brilliant publisher, then a founder of *QI*, then, additionally, a founder of Unbound, therefore so very much himself a serial cultural entrepreneur, wrote this in 2017:

I'm often asked how I think Waterstone's changed things. The obvious answer is by putting range in front of people who hadn't had access to it before. Now, Amazon has put an even wider range in front of people at a lower price. Which is why I think my answer has changed from a distance of thirty years.

I am now convinced that the success was as much to do with culture as with convenience or range. Waterstone's created a series of community hubs, staffed by people who loved what they were selling. Who believed that books were the most important vector for spreading ideas and stories and the barometer of a nation's civilisation.

Opening up our discussions directly with the commissioning editors (as opposed to the sales departments) in publishing, encouraging them to come in and talk (with their best authors) to groups of booksellers made them feel they weren't alone and made the booksellers feel they were part of something important. And our customers, despite clear and spirited competition from Dillons, Books Etc, Borders and Ottakar's, consistently responded to the Waterstone's brand in terms of love and commitment that made nonsense of the tired old canard that we were 'elitist'.

It's not elitist to be on the side of intelligence, or experimentation, of individual brilliance. That was what Waterstone's, at its best, was trying to do. It commanded (and still commands) affection that will never be accorded to Amazon. We were the best and best-loved bookshop in whichever town we opened.

Actually, there is a coda to this, and it was all a touch vindictive of me, but elephant-like memories of rejection and the personal vindictiveness that follows from that are not, shall we say, exactly uncommon amongst entrepreneurs. There was for our side of the deal a very pleasant press coverage indeed around the fact that WH Smith had paid so much to acquire us, the media story being centred on the fact that they had fired me, and it was because of this that Waterstone's had been born, and now they found themselves in a position where they had to buy us out. One weekend I put together a file of the cuttings and sent them to that Cranleigh Barclay's manager who at the time when we were desperate to put together the initial funding had used our business plan as a cautionary tale for his colleagues. My little and perhaps rather smug accompanying note pointed out that I had achieved exactly what I had promised him in that plan – that within ten years Waterstone's would become the largest bookseller group in the world, outside the US. *Remember me?* I asked. He sent the cuttings straight back. *Win some, lose some*, he replied.

And – well – one last coda. One night, at that same time, when our exit deal with WH Smith was surprisingly still prominent in the news cycle, I was coming home on the tube. The carriage was packed, and all I could do was to clutch on to a handrail, and sway around in the jostle. I was by a door, and looking down I could see what a sitting woman was reading in her *Evening Standard.*

I wiped my glasses clear of rain spots and condensation and bent a little closer so that I too could read the piece. It was written by a prominent female journalist who specialised in personal put-downs and thus I expected the worst. I was right to do so. She first wasted at least a quarter of the space in comment on my physical appearance, which was at a level of insult that was, let us say, unusually frank, and then she turned to my conversational skills. Here, the insult was absolutely magnificent: *Mr Waterstone is by repute about as interesting to talk to as a lock keeper on a disused canal.*

Magnificent stuff. Swift, Dr Johnson, F. E. Smith – any of the masters of insult would have been proud of it. And as to her comments on my physical appearance, all I can say is that I had met the journalist, and knew her very slightly, and can report this: the lady was no oil painting herself...

CHAPTER 21

After I left the company, three, four years went by, but rightly or wrongly I could never let my concern for Waterstone's go.

It wasn't that the WH Smith ownership of Waterstone's began to fail, because I had no complaint at all as to that. Certainly, there were a rocky few months initially, for the new MD, a Smith man through and through, whom they had installed there in Waterstone's on my departure, was not a literary man in the least, nor did he claim to be. But, having said that, determined remedial action was swiftly taken by the Smith CEO, to whom he reported, and David McRedmond was quickly parachuted back in from the US to be Waterstone's operations director, with John Mitchinson there beside him as marketing director. So, in McRedmond and Mitchinson, Smith had positioned two leaders who were absolutely steeped in the Waterstone's culture. Smith had made formal promises to preserve this culture, and they seemed genuinely anxious to do so, fully minded that in Waterstone's DNA had been coded an original formula that would deliver the richest of rewards for them down the line. They were certainly right in that. It did. And they could see now an example of what was possible for them to achieve right there in Boston, for that was one of the most superb and commanding bookstores Waterstone's had ever opened. So Smith's level of investment was made at the levels promised, indeed quite substantially beyond that, and new branches were rapidly opened in the British Isles, bringing the tally well beyond a hundred. With David McRedmond and John Mitchinson in the team all was now going fine again, but Waterstone's was developing to a size where David McRedmond's task in operations was challenging, to say the least. He writes:

My job was a constant battle to protect the independence of store managers to purchase stock and hire staff while integrating and overlaying the controls that a much larger business needed. Electronic point-of-sale facility was installed across the stores, a mighty task for shops which could contain 50,000 individual titles; area management needed to be strengthened, and the supply chain had to be regularised.

It was the latter that was most controversial as WH Smith wanted to benefit from its higher publisher margins through their central supply depot in Swindon. The teething pains were shocking. Some of the older managers found the retailisation too difficult to cope with. But it worked.

Waterstone's between 1993 and 1997 grew to approaching two hundred stores. The great marketing initiative to have events such as readings across all stores and the start of book clubs (yes, we at Waterstone's recognised the phenomenon before anyone) strengthened the brand across broader demographics. And the results: a top-line compounded annual growth rate for established stores of over 10 per cent; the doubling of floor space; the gross margin gain of between 5 and 10 per cent; and well-controlled costs, eventually defeated the competition. Dillons, TW's rival back to the eighties, succumbed and was acquired by Waterstone's under the HMV Media deal of 1998. The final catalyst was the controversial decision to break the Net Book Agreement. The strength of the Waterstone's brand combined with superior margins made it unbeatable.

For WH Smith the success was astounding, delivering even higher returns than most successful private equity investments. Waterstone's, having been acquired five years earlier for £47m was in 1998 sold to HMV Media for £300m. WH Smith had of course invested heavily over those five years, but that investment had paid off. And TW's model, his formula, the Waterstone's DNA, had held through triumphant, and the results in large part were delivered by us, John Mitchinson and me, TW's very own Waterstone's management.

All that was absolutely fine, but what had changed was very significant indeed, and it concerned the stability of WH Smith itself. From having appeared to be at the time of our deal with them a sound and responsible and conservatively financed corporation of some weight and size, suitable parents one might say for Waterstone's as it had by that time grown to be, by the time these three or four years had elapsed they were beginning to look very, very different. So different, indeed, that WH Smith looked anything but a safe place for Waterstone's to be.

Their high street estate, around 400 stores strong, was fast losing direction and focus and beginning to drift even further downmarket than it had been before, and there was a sense of both muddle and panicked inaction around that. Their board was openly split and openly quarrelling, and there were highly public resignations and a lot of anger. It all seemed to happen at once. A profit warning followed and alarming strains began to show in the funding of the company's pension fund, which the City picked up on. The share price started to go into a persistent and steady decline, which accelerated as, catastrophically, more than a century of profitable trading for them ended abruptly in 1996, when a series of provisions and disposals plunged the group to no less than £194m in the red. It was a desperate, desperate situation.

Unsurprisingly, the financial press and the City were publicly losing confidence in the Smith board. This followed the recruitment and the then hasty departure of the first true outsider this overly nepotistic, family-dominated firm had ever recruited to the chief executive role. The City had considered the new man to have bravely tried in his short period there to change the culture for the better. The climate and perception around the company grew worse and worse, and it got to the point where it was surely heading for exactly the same fate as was later to overcome two other bottom-of-the-market non-specialist retailers, Woolworths and British Home Stores.

I sensed that there was both a problem and an opportunity for me, and over the summer of 1997 I decided to see if I could find the backing for a transaction that would put the entire WHS group under my personal management control. My intention was to not only get some even more emphatically added momentum into Waterstone's, but also, and vitally, to rescue and remodel the

Smith stores themselves. Waterstone's had a proven and superb model. WH Smith appeared to have no model at all.

But I was absolutely clear as to what I wanted to do with those stores. I would push them up away from the rock bottom of the market and move them up a notch or four into a middle-market positioning as a high-quality, well-presented, combined book, news and stationery offer. Just those three – the three traditional core markets for Smith, which not so long before had served the public, and the pockets of their shareholders, consistently, reliably and well. Under my remodelling I was sure that we could trade those markets more stylishly, and more knowledgeably, and more profitably than anyone else in that sector of the high street, and by a distance.

Thus, out of the nearest and quickest possible window I would throw their bottom-of-the-market sandwiches, snacks, chocolate bars, fizzy drinks, vending machines, ice cream, cheap plastic toys, and thinly ranged videos and music. And, indeed, everything else that was extraneous to those three traditional core products. This would free up loads of extra space for a really superb range of mid-market books, a huge range of magazines and newspapers, including foreign language, and a vastly improved and stylish stationery range. Heralding this transformation, I would rebrand the stores, calling them WH Smith Metro. And, finally, I would radically decentralise their stock buying, and thus start to get that and perhaps just a little more of the Waterstone's DNA into their veins.

Actually, it was the prospect of resuscitating the Smith book offer that particularly intrigued me. Not so many years before, prior to Waterstone's entering the market, they had held a

35 per cent, no less, share of the book market (and 40 per cent of the stationery market). They had been totally dominant. That had melted away. I knew exactly what I wanted to do, and it seemed to be so sublimely obvious that I couldn't understand why they were not doing it themselves. At least 50 per cent of the space now made available after the extraneous products had been removed would be devoted to books, and we would carry within that space about four times as many books as Smith were by that time offering. The range would be concentrated entirely within the middle market, which was a large market, and one where Waterstone's was not really a player. For example, the Metro stores I was envisaging would carry every single title Catherine Cookson had ever written, along with, for example, every Joanna Trollope, and we would expertly champion and promote a whole range of additional if less distinguished popular fiction authors. There would be a wonderful and extremely wide range of gardening, cooking and popular reference books (The *Guinness Book of Records*, for example) and, best of all, we would stock children's books absolutely en masse. My styling fit of the Metro stores would be a lot softer and more elegant than the hard, garish, abrasive, overlit, coarsened look that Smith had for some extraordinary reason presented to the public in recent times.

Thus, under my plan, within our one single group Waterstone's would continue to dominate the top of the book market, and a revitalised and reconfigured WH Smith would control the really quite separate middle market, and both of them in a most emphatic and stylish manner. I thought that the Smith chain, with that book offer, and with what would be its lovely new stationery range, and its now uniquely wide news and magazine offer, could not only be saved in this way, but would then prosper. WH Smith after a century and more of profitable trading and considerable public respect had grown profitless, directionless, aimless, leaderless and lost. Above all, it was planless, but I had a plan.

So – it was back to the City once more to see if I could find the backing I required. I started with S. G. Warburg, and as it turned out I needed to go no further. They agreed with what I was saying, and felt that an approach to WH Smith under my business plan might well succeed, given the market's disillusionment with the company and its leadership. They agreed to finance my proposals, and so, in late September 1997, we formally submitted them to the Smith chairman. We offered a valuation of £1.17 billion, comprising 200p a share cash, and a proportionate share in the new firm that would be created thereby, adding up to an offer of 385p a share all in.

The chairman's immediate reaction, along with that of his executive directors, was amateurishly abusive, and indeed 'verged on the hysterical', as *The Times* of 17 October described it: 'The public rubbishing, without any warning to Mr Waterstone, made it easy for the bookseller to insist that he had a right to be taken seriously.'

They were attacked all the more by the press when it was discovered, as reported by the *Independent* on 13 October, that despite their assertion that the decision to reject our approach and refuse a meeting with us was unanimously agreed by the board, actually not a single one of their non-executive directors, a quite distinguished group, had attended the board meeting that day.

In any case, we had immediately moved straight into action when this refusal came and had made contact with the dozen or so institutional investors who controlled between them around 50 per cent of the Smith share capital. On a whirlwind tour, I presented my plans to each of them individually. These investors then called Cazenove, WH Smith's adviser, and the company itself. They directly urged that the Smith board should meet with us, and deal with our proposals in a professional manner. They were supported in this now by the team of non-executive directors, who had been left so exposed and embarrassed by the previous disclosure in the press. Those directors knew, as the *Independent* wrote on 9 October, that the board had wildly misjudged the willingness of Smith's owners to turn a blind eye to a truly pathetic share price performance over the preceding months, the shares having fallen by 23 per cent, underperforming the rest of the market in that time by over 40 per cent. 'Blithely to reject proposals in these circumstances suggests wholly unjustified arrogance,' the *Independent* concluded.

They had our proposal in front of them, and it was a rescue plan that had merit. If they didn't like that, what was the board's proposal as to how rescue should be achieved? What plans did the board have? Or did the board have no plans at all? Why did the board say only a month previously that there would be no strategic review? What thinking was there to address the crisis? Any at all? The *Daily Express* summed up what everyone suspected in an article on 16 October:

There is no evidence that the current management of Smith's has the faintest idea of what to do to reverse this calamitous trend, which is why the bid from Tim Waterstone and his backers has not been greeted with the derision that WH Smith's bosses had hoped for. The initial attempt to pooh-pooh Waterstone's approach has been shown up as just another example of poor judgement on their part. Whatever the merits of the initial offer, it was always clear, as this column pointed out at the time, that shareholders would not stand for the simple, immediate rejection rushed out by the WH Smith board. Investor anger with the status quo is understandable given the dismal performance of the group and its apparent disarray as to where to go next.

Investors Chronicle pitched in the next day, 17 October:

Smith's has to come up with more than a 'no', said David Manning, head of institutional investment at Foreign & Colonial, which controls almost three per cent of the shares. 'If it says no, it has to provide an alternative.'

What happened next was a total surprise to everyone, the City in general, and to us too. For suddenly, out of the blue, the company put out the very next day a dramatic plan which was blindingly obvious to every observer – the press and not least their institutional shareholders – had been cobbled together quite literally overnight. WH Smith, the board announced, was to be broken up. Six weeks before, as *The Times* that day pointed out, the chairman had told the press that such a course of action had been ruled out. On 19 October , the *Observer* stated: 'It is disingenuous in the extreme for the company to say that it has been working on a break-up plan since the summer, when in August and September it insisted that the company should remain as it is.'

But there we go. Now, every part of the group was to be sold off, with the exception of their high street stores, their news booths in railway stations and their wholesale news distribution facility (although in short time this would go too). Everything else was to go to the highest bidder. And that's what they set out to do, and the City, as much as it shrugged, added up what the bits and pieces might get at auction, and said fine, good, about time something emerged from your camp, get on with it then. The chairman resigned, and was gone. The company, despite all its previous protestations, showed that it had no other plan, after a hundred years of trading, but to break itself up.

What an irony it all was. Accidentally, and it was accidentally, we on our side had launched a bombshell on them. So we withdrew, except that we didn't fully withdraw, as Waterstone's was now to be sold out of the group, and I knew I had better put my skates on to find a way to ensure that it came in my direction, rather than in anybody else's.

But before I move on to relate what happened in that context, I would like to pause for a moment to say that I still, to this day, believe that my analysis of Smith's inherent fault lines was right, and that my plan for their restoration as front-line retailers was right, and that it would have worked, and in some style. And I believe that all that has happened to them since supports me in this. For many observers may feel that all of Smith's impending disasters, and they were that, were actually such a pity, as their one hundred and fifty or so specialist stores in airports and other travel outlets around the world, which they have developed in more recent years, have been strongly profitable. But the Smith high street stores, four hundred of them, which used to be the proud core of their business, had become a train wreck. They weren't like that in the 1980s, particularly in earlier times, but they had become that.

It is true that their policy of spending year by year just as little as possible on their high street stores – actually the bare minimum, on presentation, on maintenance, on staff, on anything much at all – has resulted in those stores being cash generative, and has enabled them to return thereby quite substantial funds to shareholders by means of dividends and share buybacks. Yes – true – that's one way of going. It has its point, in the short term. Others, at the cheap end of retailing, have done just this too, though of course it ends eventually and inevitably in the graveyard. But for a company with so long a history as WH Smith I still find it shocking, and sadly lacking in corporate self-esteem, that their high street stores ranked as appallingly as ninety-ninth out of a list of one hundred of the UK's retail majors in the latest (2017) *Which* consumer survey of public satisfaction, on a huge poll of ten thousand shoppers. Ninety-ninth out of a hundred high street retailers... Yes – shocking. Humiliating. 'A high street estate that is withering on the vine...' as *The Times* described it in January 2018.

I can't help but mention that Waterstone's, in the above survey, ranked equal second, grouped side by side with John Lewis and Harvey Nichols. WH Smith ninety-ninth; Waterstone's equal second. Quite a difference. And just work out the list of famous high street names ranking behind Waterstone's. What a compliment that is.

The irony of it all is that it was Waterstone's who over the course of the 1980s defeated Smith, once the dominant high street booksellers, so comprehensively that Smith lost their position for ever, permanently, as a domestic national retailer of any rank. The damage was done, it now seems clear, in those early Waterstone's years, when we took them on, branch by branch, town by town, street by street, week by week, month by month, and sowed the seeds of their eventual destruction thereby. In a sense, Smith bought us too late on our journey, the battle with us already lost and gone.

But to return to the extraordinary fall-out of our bid for WH Smith...Waterstone's was suddenly on the market, and I had to move quickly. I immediately went into discussions with EMI, owners of HMV, whom I had advised in their acquisition of the Dillons book business two years earlier, consequent to the collapse of the conglomerate Pentos, Dillons owners. Now EMI and I agreed to make common cause together on a purchase of Waterstone's, and we set up a joint venture with the American private equity group Advent International, into which all three of us invested – me, EMI and Advent. This was done, and we now set up an entirely new company called HMV Media Group, of which I became chairman. We succeeded in buying Waterstone's out from Smith, and the HMV music chain and the Dillons bookshops from EMI. The Dillons stores were then either closed down or rebranded (in every sense) as Waterstone's, therefore creating a very much enlarged and potentially increasingly profitable Waterstone's chain. Straight away we set about opening Waterstone's flagship London store in a prime Piccadilly location, and at 66,000 square feet, and with a stock of 280,000 individual titles, it was the largest bookshop in Europe, and, with a Barnes & Noble New York store, one of the two largest bookshops in the world.

This is what the *Observer* on 11 January 1998 made of it all:

HOW TIM FINISHED UP FIRST AMONG EQUALS

There is something uncannily tidy about the saga of Tim Waterstone and the bookshops that bear his name. In the world of retailing, this is a Jeffrey Archer of a story – improbable, staccato, but neat in the way it tidies up loose ends.

To sum up for those who haven't been concentrating for the past few years, this is the outline of the plot. Chapter one: Tim goes to work for WH Smith. Chapter two: Tim is chucked out for not doing what was wanted when running a Smith's offshoot in the US. Chapter three: Tim starts a bookshop called (imaginatively) Waterstone's. Chapters four to seven: plucky Tim expands Waterstone's and becomes a roaring success. Chapter eight: WH Smith – yes, the same lot who had chucked Tim out those many years before – buys the Waterstone's business and Tim pockets a small fortune. Chapter nine: Tim dabbles in one or two things like writing the odd novel and setting up a children's shop; meanwhile, Smith's starts looking a bit ropy. Chapter ten: Tim tries to launch a takeover for the whole of the Smith's empire – including his old book chain. Chapter eleven: Tim fails in said attempt, but Smith's says it will break itself up. Chapter twelve: Tim, and some pals of his who run a rival book chain, do a deal with WH Smith to buy back Waterstone's. Tim goes away happy – without control of his old employer but with an even bigger bookshop chain than he would have had with a full-blown takeover of Smith's.

It's a rattling good tale, no mistake. And they won't even have to bother changing the names over the doors of the Waterstone's outlets...

In short, the idea of putting Dillons and Waterstone's in a single venture with Tim playing a leading role seems utterly sensible – and good luck to him.

Well, I laughed at reading this again when I found the clipping very recently, but my laugh was more than somewhat targeted at myself, for as it turned out there were anything but happy times over the decade that followed.

But back to where we were. It must be said that it was unfortunate that the HMV Media Group began life just at the time when the internet was taking off and the likes of Amazon were beginning to make headway. While HMV tried to set up its own online operation in response, the board decided that it did not have 'the scale of operations online to compete' and, in 2001, subcontracted the whole thing out to Amazon. HMV still had to face the challenge, though, of competition from online business (which actually affected the music retail business far more than Waterstone's). Waterstone's also faced increasing competition on the high street, as the second-ranking US chain, Borders, bought Britain's third largest independent bookseller, Books Etc, in September 1997, and then began opening its own Borders UK shops. On top of all that, the supermarkets were also moving into the book market, and aggressively so, albeit only at the popular illustrated book and bestseller end of it, where Waterstone's had pretty well no trading interest at all.

Having said all that, the fact remains that with underlying trading profits of £40m Waterstone's was in emphatically good order when we bought it out from WH Smith in 1998, and had been so for way more than a decade. Emphatically profitable, and with a long history of very strong cash generation, and with our DNA, our original cultural and operational model, left intact by Smith. However, with an eye to as fast an exit from their HMV Media investment as possible, there was pressure on Waterstone's from both Advent and EMI, HMV Media's two other investors, to adopt a more so-called 'commercial' attitude to its business. I absolutely hated this sort of talk. I knew exactly what that 'commercial' euphemism meant and where it would lead: to the destruction of the Waterstone's corporate soul. But they thought that this was a good, simple, seductive media story to feed through to the City and the financial press in the run-up to a public listing. And there was a need for speed amongst our EMI shareholders particularly, as what was quickly becoming apparent was an alarming decline in the fortunes of EMI itself.

I fought as hard against this as I could, day by day, meeting by meeting by meeting, but could find no ally amongst the other directors. Indeed, what I did find was raw personal enmity. And so the vulgarisation – the 'commercialisation' – of Waterstone's proceeded, and at a startling pace. Initially there was an immediate switch in emphasis towards frenetic promotional activity and deep discounting (as had long been the style of the HMV music stores), and thus a high, wholly out-of-character focus on shifting popular bestsellers. Gross margins promptly dipped, of course, alarmingly so, and what this brought about was colossal reductions in the number of books stocked in each shop. The *Guardian* of 1 July 2000 reported on the case of my friend Robert Topping, the manager of Waterstone's in Manchester for the past sixteen years, who had been sacked for 'stocking too many good books', while the trade magazine *The Bookseller* was full of complaints from publishers about the level of books Waterstone's were returning to them. It was raw and unpleasant chaos, and the most senior HMV Media executive directors, who knew very much better, should have had the character and the guts to resist it, but hadn't – to, I trust, their everlasting shame.

During this time both Bertelsmann and Borders made offers to rescue the Waterstone's business from HMV; both were rejected, as was one further fully financed offer from myself. Nevertheless, for a few months more I remained as chairman of HMV, but became increasingly distraught at the direction the company was taking.

It was a bitter and most unpleasant period in my life, as I watched Waterstone's quite simply implode under this pro-gramme of destruction. And so I left the company in early 2001, looking to see if I could fight the battle from outside. Waterstone's was being abandoned to the wolves by the HMV board, and dis-gracefully, ignorantly so. The company was stagnating and dying through a total lack of investment. Everywhere there were empty shelves and tables, increasingly shabby interiors, a puzzled and dismayed public, and a staff morale that was utterly destroyed. Between the years 1999 and 2003 HMV not only ripped out the stock, but failed to open a single new Waterstone's outlet.

That whole HMV transaction had been a nightmare for me as it turned out, but much more importantly, a total, total nightmare for Waterstone's itself and its loyal branch staff, after all those years of fight and guts and achievement. And little had changed by 2005 when the private equity firm Permira made two offers (of £672m in February and £842m in March) for the whole HMV Group, these angrily turned down by the HMV board as a major undervaluation.

So – with the two Permira offers for the whole group refused, early in 2006 I made another formal and fully financed offer of £256m to buy back the Waterstone's business from HMV, with my executive teammate in this Anthony Forbes Watson, one of the most impressive of the new generation of literary publishers. There was considerable media interest and the board should most certainly have accepted the offer, and actually were as good as obliged to do so by their investors, for by this time HMV was a public company, and failing fast. But after a few days I had no choice but to withdraw the offer, after it was clear that the HMV board would not negotiate with me with an open hand, setting conditions for sale on the consortium I had put together that were absurdly, amateurishly, vindictively punitive, and impossible for my investment partners to responsibly accept.

The sheer weight of press and City criticism for that action, barring my chance of completing a fully funded and fully priced bid, then led the HMV board to hastily proceed on another route, making a bid for the rival literary book chain Ottakar's. Complaints from publishers and authors ensured that the initial probings around a possible bid had been referred to the Competition Commission earlier, in December 2005, but the Commission ruled in the spring 2006 that the takeover would 'not result in a substantial lessening of competition' and that they would allow a transaction to proceed. So in May 2006 HMV announced that it was proceeding with its purchase of Ottakar's, claiming that the combination of the two chains would 'create an exciting, quality bookseller'. It was also the trigger for another round of redundancies amongst Waterstone's branch staff, and a number of high-profile departures from the Waterstone's head office team.

As of May 2006 there were around 250 Waterstone's outlets (now that all the Dillons stores had been rebranded), and once the rebranding of the former Ottakar's shops was completed this rose to a total of over 330 stores. In my own time we had also acquired Hatchards in London and Hodges Figgis in Dublin, as well as opening specialist English-language bookshops in Amsterdam and Brussels. But with the Ottakar's stores now folded in, the HMV carnage of the whole of the enlarged Waterstone's estate continued just as before, which made the Ottakar's purchase look so odd. They continued the programme of branch closure, and held stock levels right down, hopelessly so. Branch staff left in droves, and matters continued to decline. It was horrific to watch. I have never witnessed such wanton destruction. Morale collapsed. Profits, which before the so-called 'commercialisation' were, of course, at a way more than admirable level, at underlying annual earnings of around forty million pounds, now totally collapsed. Losses set in, so quickly, and at an alarming level, and were ballooning. The miracle was that the inherent heart of the Waterstone's brand, the soul of the brand, survived, evidence of how hard-wired its DNA was locked into its being.

Since 2003 I had spent extensive time in Moscow, as a founder investor and active director of Bookberry, an experimental Waterstone's lookalike chain of Russian-language literary bookshops in and around that city. It was a most interesting experience, and I met there Alexander Mamut, with me a founder shareholder of Bookberry, a lawyer, a banker oligarch of cultural affinity, and an intellectual from a well-known professional family. I liked him, which is not difficult as he is a congenial man, and in the summer of 2009, six years after we first met, I took to him a business plan for Waterstone's that I had adapted and developed from the one I had used in 2006, when I had made (with my £256m offer) my previous attempt to rescue it from the ravages of HMV. I had adapted the plan to take into account Waterstone's horrific decline over the subsequent three years, and the specific remedial measures that I knew would now have to be applied because of that.

As a genuinely literary man himself, and an anglophile who knew Waterstone's culture and history well, I found Mamut to be readily perceptive. He read and studied my business plan with an eagle eye, and over the following eighteen months or so, until the spring of 2011, we had a long series of interrogative conversations. I was delighted to find that his interest gradually quickened at the prospect of acquiring and rescuing Waterstone's from HMV's hands as soon as an opportunity presented itself. This, given the fact that HMV's reputation and market valuation as a public company were sinking by the minute, was clearly not going to be very long in coming. And indeed their final, desperate collapse into administration proved actually to be just around the corner. Astonishing really, as only a few years earlier, as I have chronicled, they had rejected an offer for the group from Permira edging towards a price of one billion pounds.

By that spring of 2011 it became clear to HMV that the end was nearly upon them, and that like it or not they would be obliged to sell Waterstone's in order to generate some quite desperately needed cash. That April, standing alone with me in London's Pall Mall one afternoon, Mamut asked me what I thought he might now be able to secure Waterstone's for, and I suggested to him between £40m and £60m, probably less than half of its true market value were it to be put out to an orthodox and organised sale process. A couple of weeks later he struck, and early in May the deal was made and rapidly closed for £53m. He installed the excellent James Daunt, who had recently joined Mamut and me in our discussions, as Waterstone's managing director.

And although for a couple of years it proved difficult for Waterstone's to pull itself out of the quite ghastly spiral of trading losses into which HMV's 'commercialisation' agenda had deposited it, by 2013 the tide was beginning to turn. Daunt, bit by bit, started to gain traction by applying all those measures we had been discussing with Mamut in the run-up to the purchase. I looked on in delight as the appalling 2010 rebranding exercise was cast away, the discounting radically curtailed, the inventory both refined and increased, the creeping centralism majorly reduced, and the stores cleaned up and refurbished, this at significant cost but absolutely essential if Waterstone's were to regain reputation and status.

Under Daunt's leadership morale radically improved, confidence was regained, and Waterstone's began to sound and feel and look and trade and be like Waterstone's again. (At this point the apostrophe was dropped, and the company was restyled as Waterstones.) A pattern of large and increasingly alarming annual losses was turned around into first modest and then accelerating annual profits, to the point that by the trading year ending April 2017, six years after Mamut's acquisition, the underlying trading profits (earnings before finance costs, tax and depreciation/amortisation) had reached £40m.

This, of course, ironically, was exactly the £40m level of twenty years earlier, April 1998, the point when the horrors of the HMV 'commercialisation' programme was first set on its tragic way. So twenty years had gone by before Waterstones recovered to exactly where it was before – twenty devastating, wasteful, destructive years, for which, as I have said earlier, some people who actually knew very much better should have hung their heads in shame for having allowed it to happen. But happen it did, and all credit to both Mamut and Daunt for bringing Waterstone's back to life, and not simply in terms of profits, but also in terms of style and bookselling competence, flair and presentation.

*

But then, in May 2018, with Waterstones restored both financially and culturally, ownership changed once again, with control passed from Alexander Mamut to Elliott Advisors, the UK arm of the New York activist hedge fund Elliott Management.

It is believed that Elliott's interest in Waterstones bears mostly, perhaps only, in regard to Waterstones regained capacity for cash generation. If this cash generation is preserved it should enable Elliott to enjoy an annual running cash yield of a highly satisfactory 8 to 9 per cent on their net investment. This of course is classic hedge fund good business. But it has nothing at all to do with the culture of bookselling, and in that fact resides all one's nervousness, and no doubt that of the entire publishing industry, let alone the devoted reading public. But, the optimist in me says that this time, in the search by Elliott for cash generation and extraction, events will by no means prove to be another HMV destructive debacle. I hope I am right, I pray I am right, and I think I will be.

The reason I think that is this: although Elliott's emphasis on cash generation would on the one hand surely remove any thought as to a further expansion of the Waterstones' estate, which is certainly a pity, on the other hand it may encourage, I would say *should* encourage, an understanding that to tamper with the heart of the brand again will do no more than to wreck the very fountain from which that strikingly positive cash flow once again wells.

Perhaps there may be yet further savings, sensible savings, available at the centre – if there are, you can be quite sure Elliott will find them, such is their style, and thereby boost their required cash generation. Perhaps additionally there may be further gains, sensible gains, available at the gross margin level – if there are, Elliott will surely find them, such is their style. Perhaps there are some deals to be made, some very harsh and brutal deals, in regard to each of the three hundred or so leases that Waterstone's holds on its retail estate – if there are, there is probably no hedge fund in the world more likely to emerge victorious in these negotiations than Elliott. All those aspects are fine. Waterstones could emerge much the stronger, much the more resilient, much the more cash generative, much the more entrenched under their control. That's possible, and that's admirable. But if there is to be interference again with Waterstones' superb and unique DNA, then that would prove to be the short route through to disaster...

I don't think that will happen. Lessons, surely, have been learnt from the HMV debacle. Elliott are very, very smart people. All may be well – indeed, very well indeed. Ambitious and single-minded in pursuit of cash generation they may be, but they are buying at a time when Waterstones' fortunes and standing in the book market are again so bright. Why risk that?

'The revival of Waterstones has been such a compelling story,' wrote Sathnam Sanghera in *The Times* in 2017:

> ...Its [Waterstones'] survival really matters to Britain. I am not talking here about the whimsical romance of what books mean for writers, but what a bookshop means for any community, economically and culturally. The survival of a really great branch of Waterstones in my home town of Wolverhampton, for instance, even as the city centre suffers from an epidemic of empty shop units, is more than an important cultural symbol, it encourages reading, literacy and intellectual exploration in a way that the web never will be able to.

Which is sort of saying something that I have always believed. It's not just that Waterstones is a cultural symbol. It's more than that. I believe the nation's cultural good health would not have been the same without us. And I am very proud of that. And I am very proud of Waterstone's.

CHAPTER 22

During the final period of my working life, following those wonderful years of Waterstone's birth and then its explosive, glorious growth, a whole series of intriguing and worthwhile opportunities came my way, even while all my various and prolonged battles with WH Smith and HMV et al raged on. I never applied either formally or informally for any of the posts that were offered in such a steady flow, and I was each time surprised and gratified to receive them, and I hope I was then useful. That's for others to judge. What I do know is that the privilege was mine.

Perhaps most memorable of all, was my time at the London Philharmonic Orchestra as both a director and a trustee. This was at a time when the orchestra was at one of its artistic peaks, never more so than under the baton of Klaus Tennstedt, their conductor laureate by then (after ten years or more of working with the LPO as principal guest conductor and similar roles). My time with the LPO dated from 1990, so I caught only the last three or four years of Tennstedt's concerts with them, but that was enough to know how close the orchestra and Tennstedt were to each other.

It was an extraordinary relationship, much described on both sides as a love affair, with Tennstedt describing the LPO as 'a *romantic* orchestra'. In Tennstedt's early days with the orchestra, during the late seventies, morale was low and they were not a happy and consistent band, but there was something in the genius of this dangerously unbalanced man – self-absorbed, petulant, latterly severely ill, occasionally violently ill-tempered – 'that lifted them up to extraordinary heights, and to the extent that neither they nor the public hardly knew how they had got there', as Norman Lebrecht wrote. 'Every concert was an event: audience, musicians and conductor alike would emerge shaken. His Beethoven in the Royal Festival Hall had an impact unequalled since Klemperer's.'

The orchestra idolised him. 'Seeing him walk on stage,' said one orchestra member, 'you were never sure he would not trip over his feet or poke himself in the eye with the baton.' Indeed, much of the mutual love affair between orchestra and conductor was rooted in that sense of transparent honesty and physical and, above all, emotional vulnerability and uncertainty that Tennstedt carried within him.

Lebrecht, reminiscing of Tennstedt's time with the orchestra, wrote:

Tennstedt set about Mahler with a unique and dangerous intensity. Heeding neither caution nor fashion, he embodied the composer's expressed preference for exaggeration. Every rehearsal became a life-and-death struggle; each concert required a health warning, the musicians fearing for his safety and their own. His Mahler recordings, though subdued in comparison to his live performances, contain the most terrifying of Sixths – a symphony in which Tennstedt heard pre-echoes of Nazi horrors – and the most lyrical of Sevenths. His account of the Eighth Symphony is unaffectedly majestic, the first credible record of that gigantic unresolved question.

In my years with the LPO I used to attend some of those 'life-and-death' Mahler rehearsals. I would hide away in the shadows, way out of Tennstedt's eye-line, terrified of so much as moving in case my presence there upset him in some way. Tennstedt upset was a volcanic and terrifying sight, not least because one was fully aware that he was actually terminally ill at the time.

First there were the rehearsals, and then the performance, and the rapture of the audience, and the sweat and the tears pouring down Tennstedt's face, and the smiles of relief and exhaustion and pride and wonder, really, on the faces of the players as they stood facing the audience for their standing ovation. I got to know some of the orchestra members well enough over the years to become friends, genuine friends, and I knew them as down-to-earth people, almost to a fault, not in the least given to arty posturing or pretention. Actually, it was always a mystery to me, an amateur and layman in these things, how they could so easily slip on their raincoats, grab an *Evening Standard* and be on the train home not ten minutes after one of their wonderful concerts at the Royal Festival Hall, apparently quite unmoved by the music they had so superbly made only minutes before. I'm not sure they managed that after a Tennstedt concert, though. I don't believe they could have done. They had given too much, strived too much for that. They were still drained if I saw them the next day. How difficult it must have been for the next conductor to work with them. In every sense, actually, because they could behave extremely disobligingly with conductors they didn't respect, which I began to grasp was an uncomfortably large number.

There were so many other interesting experiences at that time of my life too, if none perhaps of exactly the LPO richness, but all of them still intriguing and important to me, and all of them a privilege. There were the several great libraries I worked with, either as chairman or director or committee member – the British Library at the fraught time when it was decamping from the British Museum and moving to Euston Road; King's College London library at a moment when – at last – we raised the funds for it to properly and comprehensively present the riches of its fine collection; the magnificent University of Cambridge library, as it wrestled with a strategy for its future in the face of the digital world. There was my friend Christopher Hogwood and his Academy of Ancient Music, which I chaired for a period. In contrast, I also chaired Jazz FM for a couple of years. There was a year around Prince Charles's people while I chaired his Youth Business Trust. Then there was more work with Prince Charles and his staff with the Elgar Foundation, which again I chaired, and which he fussed and meddled around with, I have to say not wholly helpfully. And, very satisfyingly, there was Shelter, which I chaired throughout the period around their main twenty-fifth anniversary appeal, and thereby met Cardinal Basil Hume, who was Shelter's patron, and a very engaged one at that.

One evening I received a call from one of Hume's people, inviting me to have a drink and a chat with the cardinal in his house, The Archbishop's House so called, abutting on to Westminster Cathedral. It was a dark, cold, forbidding place. The whole experience of that evening was in ironic contrast to the Anglican accommodation and hospitality of the Bishop of London, Graham Leonard, to whom I had been invited for tea just the previous week. With him it was all comfy chintz, a pot of Earl Grey and a hint of gossip, accompanied by a blazing fire, fawning young chaplains and hot buttered muffins and plum cake. With the cardinal it was a cavernous, under-lit, under-furnished, threadbare drawing room, absolutely freezing, totally miserable, in which the sweet-natured old man sat smiling benignly in an ancient, cracked-leather chair.

He rang the bell, and in came a nun, who asked me what I would like to drink. In truth I wanted nothing whatsoever, but glanced at the drinks tray by which she was standing, which had, I suspected, been assembled there just for me, and spotted a bottle of gin and a large plastic bottle of tonic water, so I asked for that. I don't think she had ever poured a gin and tonic before in her life, for she took a large tumbler and filled it to within an inch of its rim with gin, and then splashed a drop of tonic on it and proudly brought it over to me. The cardinal was then handed something that I suspected was clearly prearranged, brown and then diluted by the nun with a little splash of soda water. I am sure the drink was non-alcoholic, but brown so that I would think it was whisky, and thus be put at my ease. I didn't need to be put at ease by that. I rather wished I could join him. Then the nun departed, and the cardinal and I were alone, and I looked at the drink beside me, and sipped at it, and wondered how on earth I was going to deal with the rest of the glass.

Cardinal Hume came across to me as a shy man, soft-voiced, gentle, but a man whom one immediately wanted to please, to not disappoint, to be a credit to. He asked me about the Samaritans, totally unexpectedly, and I immediately wondered who could have briefed him on the fact that I had for a period done spells of time (evenings sometimes, occasional all nights, Boxing Day, etc.) as one of those anonymous friendly voices that answered their phones and tried to do what one could to calm and reassure people in sometimes near and actual terminal distress. There were normally, in the Putney branch where I went, half a dozen or so of us on the telephones at any one time, so perhaps there were priests there of his among them, all in plain clothes as they would have been obliged to be, and all following the Samaritans' instructions as to an entirely secular, anonymous, non-preachy, worldly character in their presentation. Maybe one of these mentioned it to him. I don't know.

I was taken aback because I was there to talk about Shelter, but also because I had only done these sessions for the Samaritans for a matter of perhaps seven or eight months, unlike the many, many years which many volunteers had put in, and I had withdrawn myself because I didn't feel I was the right person for the task. I was untrained, of course, as almost all of us were, but in my case I felt I was not patient enough in any of these telephone conversations, short of the obviously highly and immediately dangerous ones. I also thought that women's voices, and indeed mature women's perceptive skills in general, were better than men's, give or take, in a crucial and delicate role of this sort.

One call in perhaps fifty was of such prime crisis in that caller's life that it was, to me, a lottery as to which of us volunteers was free at that moment to pick up the telephone, and thereby be responsible for the conduct and successful conclusion of the call. Just one of those crisis calls had come my way, I said to the cardinal, just the one, and I was still shaken at the memory of it. I remember the fear as to whether I had been successful in getting the police and the ambulance there in time, with that distressed woman held by me on the line, her voice beginning to fade away as the drugs she had taken took hold, leaving only the sound of her laboured breathing. There was at least the relief that I had managed – just – only just – to achieve what we had been instructed was the main task in one of these extreme emergency calls, and that was to get from her an address, and to never put the phone down.

He agreed with me about women, made some comments around their role in the Roman Church, and we talked then of Shelter, and of moments of prime, terminal personal crisis. A particular issue at the front of his mind was the fact that there wasn't at that time one single women-only emergency hostel in London, and the behavioural problems that arose from that. I wasn't aware of this situation, and knew nothing about it, and could only listen to what he was describing. And then we parted, and I did not meet him again before he died. As I walked away from his miserably uncomfortable residence into the winter night I realised that I had drunk the entire glass of gin and minimal tonic that his nun had poured for me.

I later discovered that the cardinal had a method and a purpose, and perhaps a little guile. About two weeks after I met him I had a call from Bill K, a friend from my Cambridge days. He was a Roman Catholic, very actively so, and he, along with David A, leader of perhaps London's most prominent advertising agency at that time, had, I learnt, worked on some initiatives with the cardinal in the past. Bill said that he and David had received a message from Hume's office to say that I was wanting to set up a women-only hostel, the only one in London, and would they please help me in that. I didn't realise that I was wanting to do anything of the sort, but help they certainly did. Bill and David raised between them, and in very short time, almost every penny of the money required for us to get the hostel equipped, manned, decorated and open. I see it now, each time I am driving along the Euston Road, and, twenty or so years later, I am told it is both essential and thriving.

There was much other varied experience for me over those latter years. FutureStart, a charitable venture capital fund founded by British Telecom in 1992, with me and three or four others as founding directors, was an interesting initiative. It's aim was to provide funding access to disadvantaged young people trying to start businesses – the textbook example being a young man from a south London Jamaican family, who had spent much of his childhood and early adulthood in trouble with the police, and had thus been in and out of various correction facilities for most of his life. With that background there was not the slightest possibility of him being able to access equity and debt from conventional routes. He had written a compelling business plan, though, and he brought it to us – and had written it himself, I must emphasise, without one jot of professional advice. That business had grown spectacularly when I last heard of it, in 2009, when my seventeen-year tenure with FutureStart ended.

There were some disappointments and let-downs amongst FutureStart investments to be sure, but it was a worthy example of intent by BT, and I believe the fund did a lot of good (it was eventually folded into the Prince's Trust, in my final year).

During that time I also chaired for a year a DTI Working Group, and watched with fascination the subtle political manoeuvrings in those numerous meetings of ours between representatives of that ministry and the Bank of England. I wrote and published a novel or two, and launched the upmarket children's department stores Daisy & Tom, which, in time, we merged with the long established Early Learning Centre chain, and then sold the lot to Mothercare. I lectured a bit in business schools, both in the UK and in Europe, pottered around with the Labour Party, spoke publicly a lot, and in 2007 became chancellor of Edinburgh Napier University, the product of a decade or so of first the merging together of several Edinburgh polytechnics and colleges of further education, and then their academic upgrading under the single entity of the university itself. Over 80 per cent of our students are from families who have had no experience of higher education, and I sensed more and more the effectiveness of our role, and, in terms of upward social engineering, the good the university does, and will increasingly do as it matures and grows in academic confidence and status.

Along with Bookberry in Moscow in conjunction with Alexander Mamut and some other interests, these final working years of mine have threaded their way through, and rewardingly so. And at the end of these years there is the pleasure, which is for me beyond description, of seeing Waterstones doing once more what it so superbly does best.

And in those years there is, above all else, something I leave to mention until the very last, and I am going to express it very simply: my immense good fortune in meeting Rosie Alison, marrying her, and being with her so wonderfully for so many years. That, to put it mildly, above all else.

POSTSCRIPT

There is a dream I've been having, which is persistent and recurrent and it's painful. It seems to be rooted deeply in my subconscious and has been with me for a few months. I know what it means, without going through the process of a therapist telling me. In fact, I don't want a therapist to tell me.

This is the dream: I am in a party of people deep in the English countryside, and we are on a hiking trip over sunlit summer meadows. With me are Rosie and Daisy, my youngest daughter, who is twenty-three. Otherwise all the others with us are strangers, friendly strangers, people kind enough to laughingly check with me before we set off as to whether I have a hat to wear, and decent boots, and a walking stick, as I am by far the oldest in the group.

We set off on our way, and soon the others start to draw away from me, as with my ankle and hip problems from recent falls I am quite soon a little uncomfortable and cannot keep pace, and nor am I trying to do so. I like watching them all stride away down into the meadows ahead: good people, kind people, happy with each other, the sun shining down on them. And I can see over to the right, on the other side of the hill, a couple of hundred yards from me, Rosie and Daisy walking together, side by side, rather isolated from the others, and talking together, and happy together.

Soon the main body is too far ahead of me and out of my sight, but I can still see Rosie and Daisy, otherwise I would have no idea where to head for. In time, even they are out of sight, and I worry, but I can see a little town deep down in the valley ahead, and feel sure that this must be where they are bound. I am unable to raise my pace, but tell myself that all will be well, and that when I reach the town I will find them.

Entering the town I see that there is a railway station, and make for that, thinking that they might be waiting for me there. As I approach the station I see a train waiting at the platform about to depart. I am limping quite heavily by this point, but make my way to it as fast as I can, and I can see Daisy's face pressed against a window, anxiously, desperately mouthing something to me, Rosie sitting in a carriage seat beyond her. Then the train starts, and draws away, and Daisy is looking back at me, still intent, still anxious, still mouthing some words at me, and they've drawn away, and gone, and that is where the dream ends.

So, yes, I do know exactly what that recurrent dream of mine means. And perhaps no more than a dozen or so other people know – I mean fully, really know – as well. They know, but I am not going to expand on it here. It's not so bad. Life has to be lived, and I have lived mine. In the final reckoning, my life, as with all of us, will be defined, good or bad, by the choices I have made.

And despite the train wreckage of some periods and some aspects of my life, on the whole I know I've done what I could.

On the whole, I've done my best. 'I 'ave a go, ladies,' says Archie Rice in John Osborne's *The Entertainer*. 'I do. I 'ave a go.'

Well, that's a good enough claim for me, and for anyone, really. So let me close this account there.

Me too, Archie Rice, I say. *Me too. I've 'ad a go.*

EPILOGUE

There are times when to give the fullest and truest account of some important occurrence, some crucial moment, the only way to do that is to dramatise it, to fictionalise it.

That sounds to be a contradiction, but it isn't. Nothing else will do the job. As William Boyd writes, 'Fiction adds a different dimension that the purely documentary and historical cannot aspire to.' Ernest Hemingway put it this way: 'I make the truth as I invent it truer than it would be.' And perhaps Mark Rothko's dictum is saying much the same thing: 'There is more power in telling little than in telling all.'

So here, to close the book, are two such stories. I needed to write them both.

Miranda Beeching

The room I used as a temporary office whenever I was in that London branch was actually a general storeroom, with cartons of books stacked all around it and my desk crammed up against a broom cupboard. I didn't use it much but I was fond of it, and the more so when we unscrewed and removed the door, which was shabby and cracked, and anyway impossible to shut. The door having been removed encouraged the staff to come in to chat to me whenever they felt like it, which I enjoyed.

That morning Miranda Beeching walked in to see me, hand in hand with a blushing, smiling, awkward, tousle-haired Philip Stempter. His spectacles were askew, as was his hair, his jeans secured by a thick army belt, his plaid shirt hanging loose on his painfully thin body. I thought the pair of them looked delightful together, and I threw my arms open, shrugged, smiling too, and waited for them to speak.

'Surprised, T?' she asked. 'Surprised?'

'Well – no – not really, Miranda,' I said, smiling back at her. 'Every time I've walked through the poetry and drama room recently I've seen you two looking fondly at each other. And with you two... well, it looked to me to be...'

She turned to face Philip, and reached up to throw her free, plump arm around his neck. She kissed him softly on the cheek and looked back at me, radiating both possession and pride. Not for the first time, I thought what a pretty face she had. Thirty, forty pounds overweight her doctor would have told her, her skin imperfect because of that, I suppose, her hair roughly cut and greasy, her clothes careless; it might have been thought that she was an unlikely lover for Philip. He was about four years younger than her, I remembered from their respective staff files, and for all the messy youth of his appearance he was extremely pleasant-looking.

As it happened he came from the same small, unfashionable Cambridge college that I had graduated from myself twenty years or so before him. I rather cherished the college actually, and was protective of it, probably just because it was small and unfashionable, and as a brother in arms I had particularly enjoyed interviewing him eighteen months or so before. He had come to that interview overdressed for the occasion, which was unusual for us, as most of the young people wanting to join us at Waterstone's made a point of expressing their cussed, arty independence by dressing down to an emphatic degree. Philip, though, looked as if he had been dressed for his interview as a single child would be by a widowed mother, in his neat white shirt and our college tie, and his pressed dark suit and polished black shoes. His hair smarmed down, he had looked that day very young, a schoolboy, and it has to be said very handsome indeed.

I had asked him if he was writing, which was one of my standard opening probes in these interviews, and he produced in reply a total ace, though in his modest, unworldly way he seemed unaware of it. He told me that a first novel of his had just been bought on a tiny advance by a major literary publisher for their New Voices list, I think it was called, and tiny advance or not you can't at his age do much better than that. So, he came to us, and I was delighted to have him. He was immediately given entire responsibility for Drama and Poetry in this large branch where I was that day.

Here Philip was now, dressed down, thank heavens, in conventional Waterstone's booksellers' kit, and in love with Miranda Beeching. Clearly in love with Miranda Beeching. Their physical bonding was absolutely transparent. Standing before me they weren't simply holding each other's hands, they were gripping them, kneading them, squeezing them, hers small and plump with bitten nails, his white and thin and skeletal. All I could do was smile at them. I have always been a fool for other people's love. And best of all love between two people not obviously physically matched. These two weren't obviously matched in any way whatsoever.

'And we've been living together for exactly three months come Friday,' Miranda went on, pink, flushed, proud and pretty. 'And this weekend we are going up to Lincolnshire to see my parents, and we are going to tell them that we are going to get married. And we *are*. We are going to get married. Aren't we, Philip? *Aren't* we, Philip?' she repeated, comically pedantic, seizing his arm, laughing, pinching him, pretending to think that he was going to try to get out of it. He said nothing, but stood there, both her hands now in his, eyes fixed not on her but on me, his wide smile that of a young child, as if at the moment of surprised, blissful receipt of the very Christmas present he had secretly wanted above all things in the world, and thought he would never receive.

I had no idea what to say, so all I could do was stand there and try to beam on to them my good will. I had always liked Miranda, though I knew her not particularly well. Before there had always been a shyness in her around me, a reserve, a hesitancy that I had found difficult to navigate. Not that day, though. She was transformed – self-confident, fluent, bubbly – yes, utterly transformed. I had to say something. I heard myself exclaiming, 'Wonderful! Fantastic!' It was inane, but it didn't matter, because they had turned back to gaze at each other, and seemed to have lost interest in my presence. So I told them to take another day off for their trip to Miranda's parents, and jokingly shooed them out of the office and back on to the shop floor to see to their tasks. I saw Philip say something to one of the other staff, and then they both laughed and looked back at me, standing in my office doorway, and I waved at them and went back to my desk.

Later that evening, when I was leaving that store of ours to go and call on another, I saw Miranda talking to a customer, and waited for a moment for when she was free. They broke off, and I went over to her, and laid my hand on her shoulder, and just told her how delighted I was for her, and how I hoped they would be very happy, and have several dozen kids, and live for ever in mutual delight. 'Oh we will that, T,' she said. 'All of it. Particularly the several dozen kids bit, you can count on it. But, well, thanks, T. It's great, isn't it?'

God, I hope so, I thought, as I stood out on the street trying to find a taxi. Dear God, I hope so. This is the first time she has been in love, I guessed, and she is too exposed, too open, and he is too young, too immature, and I suspect too unformed to carry the sheer weight of that.

It was two or three weeks before I saw them next, as we had a new, large store opening in Glasgow, and another smaller one in Perth, and I was up there in Scotland interviewing staff for both. I had thought about the pair of them occasionally, or, more accurately, I had thought about Miranda. What I liked was the simple fact of seeing her in love, for, as I have said, I suspected it had never happened to her before. All that concerned me was that I just didn't want her to get hurt, so vulnerable a soul as she clearly was. Philip looked so young. And I remembered when first interviewing him that though I thought he was extremely bright, and dauntingly well read, and clearly from the New Voices evidence no mean writer, he was emotionally childlike, perhaps sexually too, untried, shielded, untouched as yet by the world. As a matter of fact, I remember thinking that a couple of years with us would probably do him the world of good, thrown into the company of dozens of young people as bright as he was, as well read as he was, but most of them it appeared to me in possession of a far greater degree of worldliness than he had, of experience, of cutting their milk teeth.

Yes, writing this now I am sure it was that which concerned me when I had heard their news. Philip was extremely intelligent, but extremely immature. As engaging and interesting a young man as you could wish to meet, but, still, he was a child. I wondered what his family background was, and then remembered that I knew it, as it had arisen in his interview with me; father something or other in a building firm, who had become a lay preacher for the Methodists quite late in life, in perhaps his fifties, and his mother a primary school teacher. Philip was their only child. Now a Cambridge graduate, no less. They must have been very proud of him.

I came across Miranda again perhaps four weeks later. She was in one of our other London branches one afternoon, borrowing from them for her own branch a few extra copies of a novel by a first-time writer that had just been published and had caught the public imagination to a wholly unexpected degree. She was looking absolutely radiant. I had never seen her so pretty. I suspected she had crossed London to borrow these books from this particular branch because of a girl there who I believe was her best friend – I seem to remember that they had been at university together, the University of East Anglia. They were over by the fiction tables now, laughing and talking with each other, and I guessed that their laughter was all about Philip, and the trip they had made up to Lincolnshire to introduce him to her parents. I went over to join them, and asked how Miranda was and how the visit had gone.

'Oh, T, they loved him,' she said. 'Loved him. Who wouldn't? And we have fixed the day for the wedding – four months' time, first Saturday in November, in my dad's church in Lincolnshire, and Dad is going to marry us himself. *And*, T, you're going to come. Right? And you're going to make a *speech*. Right? And you're going to say that the two best booksellers you've ever met in your life are me and Philip? Right? And you are also going to say how beautiful I look in my mum's wedding dress, which she is going to have altered for me. Beautiful – get it? *Me. Miranda. Beautiful.* OK? *Mum's dress. Beautiful.* OK? OK, T? Got it?'

Both of the girls laughed, and I did too, and I checked the date and place again, and said I would try to make it, and congratulated her once more. Then I got caught up in a pile of matters that were crossing my desk at that point, not least yet another round of financing to enable us to open a large store in Manchester, on prime Dean Street, which in time became the most successful bookshop we ever opened in England. I had remembered, though, to make a note in my diary as to their wedding date, and when I was next in their branch I would make a point of having a chat with Philip, to make sure all was well with him, and to ask if there was anything particular he would like me to say when I spoke – something about his parents perhaps? Something on those lines? But when I was in that branch, maybe two weeks later, I failed to see Philip around the place, so I asked after him. I knew that Miranda would not be there for I had been told that she was helping out in another branch that was short staffed, but I was suddenly anxious about Philip. Unwell, said one of his colleagues. Been off for a few days now. Some gastric problem or other, I think Miranda said it was.

With the benefit of hindsight, I am sure, and perhaps a rewriting of history, I have over the years told myself many times since that I at that moment felt a prickle of not simply anxiety, but a fear, a terror, an instinct of catastrophe ahead. Or let us say at very least an instinct that something was about to go very, very wrong indeed with the idyll that Miranda had embraced into her life, so dangerously, so precipitately, so without caution, so too much full of hope. The handsome, beautiful, skeletal Philip looked to me too frail, too fragile, too exposed, too open to danger. Too frail for safety. Too frail for life.

And in that I was proved to be immediately and hideously exactly right. For Philip never emerged again from the hospital that he had been rushed to. Jenny, Miranda's friend from university, told me later that initially they had misdiagnosed him, and he sank fast, and then they realised what it was, and tried to treat him accordingly, and for a few days he rallied a little, or appeared to, but then he sank again, and then he was lost.

I told her that I had tried to reach Miranda when I first heard that Philip was ill, but there was no sign of her, and I assumed she was at the hospital with him. Perhaps she was. Perhaps she was with him when he died. Perhaps he knew she was there. Perhaps, as he faded away, their hands were as interlocked as they had been that day when they had come into my storeroom office to tell me of their love. I asked Jenny if Miranda had been with him as he died, but she turned away from me, shaking her head, and I could see her mouth puckering, and the tears starting to come, so I said no more, and let her be.

We had Philip's parents' address in his file, so I wrote to them, not at length, but simply trying to impress on them how deeply we all of us in the company mourned Philip, and how impressive a young man he had been, and how golden a future there had no doubt lain before him. I deliberately did not head the letter with a full address, in the hope that they would not feel bound to reply. But they did, and a letter arrived only two or three days later from them, the lay preacher and the primary school teacher, carefully signed by them both individually, and all the more heartbreaking because the language of it was so heavily drafted and formal, and pedantic, and stilted.

Dear Mr Waterstone,

We thank you for your kind letter of yesterday's date, in which you express your sympathy to us on the occasion of our sad bereavement.

It is of course a loss that seems at this moment too desperate for us to bear, a situation to which you so kindly bore reference. But, as they say, everything is for a purpose, and although we cannot know entirely what that purpose was in Philip dying so young, we must respect the callings of a higher body than we can aspire to ourselves, and rest in the comfort of our knowledge of Him, and the love that He bears us, and bore to Philip too.

Yours truly

Edward Stempter

Noreen Stempter

I remember grimacing when I read this, then putting it aside, and burying my head in my hands. Dear God, I thought. Can't they just howl with grief? Can't they just clutch each other, and weep, and break down, then try to pull themselves together, and then break down again, and hold each other, and simply love and mourn the lovely boy they have lost, and will never see again? 'Sad bereavement.' 'Callings of a higher body than we can aspire to'. 'The love He bore to Philip'. God... Dear God...

So, yes, I put aside their letter, and I started in earnest on my search for Miranda, as she had not been back in her branch, and we all were anxious for her safety. I asked Jenny if she knew how I could find her, but she was unable or possibly unwilling to help. But then I remembered I had jotted down in my diary not only the date of what would have been her wedding day, but also the name of the Lincolnshire village where it was to be held. Through the people at Lincoln cathedral we were able to identify her father's church, and I called the rectory there to see if Miranda was with them. She was, it turned out, but didn't come to the telephone. I spoke only to her mother, who said she would call me back in a couple of days or so, to tell me what Miranda wanted to do about returning to work.

She never did call me back, and I felt it best to leave Miranda and her family undisturbed. But a month or so later one day, quite unexpectedly, Miranda came into my office. I jumped to my feet, guided her to a chair, and just gazed at her. I didn't want to say the sort of words that one is driven to resort to on this sort of occasion – so very sorry; deeply sad for you; such an appalling loss for you to bear – though I would have meant every syllable of them if I had. Instead, I simply sat silent, alert, leaning forward, both my hands held out for her to take and hold if she so wished. She stared back at me, then tried to smile, but that was a mistake, as it led immediately to her face grimacing into a flow of tears. So I just pushed my chair forward a little more until we were close enough for me to take her hands myself, and then slowly release them when she had recovered some level of control.

'I can't talk about it, T,' she said. 'Just can't.'

And so I didn't press her to do so. Of course I didn't. I nodded my head, said nothing, kept still, and waited. Then she said, 'I think I had better come back to work. That's what I've come to say. I think I should. Would you mind if I do?'

'Mind if you do? Heavens above, I would love it if you would. But are you sure?'

'No, I'm not sure. I am not sure of anything much at the moment. But I need to try. So, I'm trying. That's why I took the train here this morning. I am going to move in straight away, this evening, with Jenny. Can't stay where I was. I'm fine with Jenny. It's the right place for me. That's where I am going to go.'

We talked on a little more, but I didn't want to attempt too much. She knew what I felt about her without me labouring the point. She knew what I felt about Philip. She knew I was delighted to have her back at work. She knew I cared about her.

There was nothing I could say at that time about Philip or indeed her that would not be better said on a future, perhaps distantly future occasion. So we let it go, and she said she would be in to start work again in the morning, and I saw her to the door, and smiled at her, and wished her well.

I was not in that branch again that week, nor indeed for several after, but I checked that she was there, and she was, and I thought it was better to leave her alone. And then I had an idea. We were opening a new branch in a cathedral town with which I knew she was familiar, and perhaps had friends there, and we were just at the point of advertising to recruit staff for it. Normally I would simply announce the branch management position to our staff at large, and invite prospective applicants to let me know if they would like to talk to me about it, for we never recruited these positions from outside. What if I simply proceeded differently on this occasion, and went straight to Miranda to see if she would like to take it on? She had the experience, and she enjoyed throughout the company excellent respect for her knowledge. With the news of Philip's death I thought that in this one specific instance the staff would understand why we should give Miranda the first shot at taking up the management position if she wished to do so.

And so I called her, and asked her in for a chat. It was the first time I had seen her since the day she had asked if she might get back to work. When she walked into my office this time my immediate reaction was that I had done the wrong thing. She looked a little thinner, and although the shape of her face was now better defined, the bone structure a touch sharper, all of which made her always lovely smile the more pleasing, I knew she wasn't well.

But I had asked her in, and I would put the suggestion to her, if perhaps a touch less directly than I had previously intended. So I told her about the branch we were opening, and I knew she was familiar with the town, and I said I thought it was a branch that might suit her to manage if she would enjoy that. What did she think? It was about the right size for her, I suggested, certainly a very large bookshop for that particular town, but not vast. The market there was likely to be markedly literary, which I thought she would enjoy, and – well – would she be interested in taking it on? Or did she feel she would rather stay in London, now that she had settled down with Jenny?

'Oh, no – that's not the point really, T. I haven't really settled down with Jenny. I'm not sure I can really settle down anywhere at the moment. And actually it might be better if I got away from Jenny really. It might be better. It might be easier to have a new staff around me, all new to us, none of them familiar with, well, you know, Philip and...'

I could see that mentioning his name, saying his actual name to me, had been a challenge for her, and her face began to buckle a fraction, prior to tears, but she shook her head, looked away from me for a moment, and managed to hold it back.

For a minute or so neither of us said anything further. I wanted her to have a moment to think about it in any case. I didn't want a precipitate decision from her. I wanted her to make a decision after she had properly thought this through. But there was one question I had to ask, because if I had the wrong answer the whole proposal might prove to be a mistake, and a bad one, one that would lead to difficulties for both of us.

'Look, Miranda, I have to ask this – forgive me – where are you on medication at this time? Are you under sedation? God knows it would be understandable if you were, totally so, but in your interests and ours we would both have to take that into consideration. You know what I mean – consideration as to whether in those circumstances you would be able to manage the branch properly. The staff. The money. The stock. Authors. Publishers. All of that. So – well – what is the position? I don't want to be impertinent, but, well, can you tell me? Can you be frank with me about that?'

'Oh, nothing very dramatic, T. Valium – I went straight on to that pretty well immediately, I just had to. But just Valium. Nothing else. It helps. It blurs the pain. It doesn't solve anything, but... well, just that really. It blurs the pain.'

I smiled at her, and nodded, and kept silent for a minute or so, to let her think about what she had told me, and whether she wanted to add to it. She was looking down into her lap, her hands locked together, and then she looked up to meet my gaze, and I was struck by the depth of the terrible, terrible sadness in her eyes. But as it happened I had by that time acquired some personal experience of people that I knew well who were dosing on Valium, and I thought the sadness in her eyes was just that, sadness, acute sadness. Not that deadness, that dull empty deadness that you saw there in the eyes of people who were persistently dosing heavily on the drug. I was relieved by that.

'Yes,' she then said, and it was surprisingly, unexpectedly firmly and decisively. 'Yes. OK. Thanks. Forget the Valium. This step will do me good. Give me a challenge. Get me back into life. Don't worry – yes, I can handle it. Honestly – I can handle it. I like that town, and I would like to run a new branch there. It'll be good. Thanks. I'll do it.'

So that was that. Abruptly – too abruptly – that was that. I would have far preferred a longer discussion with her, a debate with her, a little more detail as to her mental health after the appalling trauma she had been through and was of course still going through. But I wasn't going to get it. Perhaps I should have not actually offered her the branch, but brought the possibility of it out in a less defined way. That would have been better, for sure it would have been better, but I hadn't done so. Now we had a fait accompli. We were in for it, and we had better make it work.

For some months I thought we had. In my anxiety I initially spent an inordinate amount of time up there, talking with her, watching her for an hour or so before going off to another branch, but actually all seemed in control and well. She had sat with me while I interviewed the new staff, and I gave her the sole decision as to which of them we should take, and she had strong views on that, and I was reassured that she did. It meant that she was concentrating. And when the branch opened all her qualities as a good manager came to the fore – in particular her stock was excellent, each section most carefully thought through. I liked her kindly, constructive, positive leadership style with her book-sellers, who had clearly taken to her. Yes – everything was fine. Thank God for that. I could stop worrying.

But I was wrong. Some time later, I would guess nine months or so, she rang me in London and asked when I was next coming up to see her. Actually, I had no immediate plans to do so, but the call worried me, so I pretended that I was thinking of dropping in for a few minutes the following day, en route further north, and hoped she would be there at, say, four o'clock? We arranged that, and the next afternoon there I was in her tiny office. The moment I looked at her I knew there was trouble. She was look-ing disordered and unkempt, distressed, her hair straggling over her forehead, her skin greasy and spotted, her fingernails bitten raggedly, cruelly down to the quick. I thought it best just to sit quietly and look at her, calmly, reassuringly, hoping to be able to reach her, to get her confidence, to encourage her to talk to me, to tell me what was happening. She was silent too, though, look-ing back at me.

'Are you cutting it OK, Miranda?' I asked, and smiled. 'All well? Everyone happy?'

She grimaced, and sighed, her plump, childlike hands folded together on her lap.

'I – let me go. Let me go now.' Her voice was so quiet, whis-pered almost, and I struggled to hear her. I leant forward so that I was closer to her, watching her mouth, straining to follow what she was saying without having to ask her to repeat herself, and thus compromise the natural flow of it.

'This nearly worked,' she whispered, trying to smile, and for a moment I wondered what she meant by that – her Valium? Running this new branch of ours? Moving away from London, and her memories of life with Philip there? Perhaps it was all those things. What did it matter? What did matter was to get her back on to her feet, instil confidence in her again, raise her up so that she could once more live her life less precariously.

So, for the next few hours I sat there with her and tried to do that, and in the end I thought that I had succeeded. She seemed to become over the course of our talk so very much stronger than when I had arrived. Frail still, yes, but much, much stronger, reso-lute in a modest way to pull herself around once more, busy herself in her work, build friendships with her staff, meet people in the town, use her position as the prime manager of what was now the town's only really good big literary bookshop, and thus show herself as someone of importance, a person of interest, of prominence, a woman doing an excellent job in an excellent local public role.

We talked of all those things, and I thought by the end that I had her. I thought I had won her. I was certain I had won her. I thought that now she would be all right. I was certain she would be all right. She saw me out into the street, and did something she had never done before; she laid her hand on my forearm, and left it there for a moment.

'God bless, T,' she said.

'You too, Miranda Beeching,' I replied, and smiled, and went off to find my car.

I never saw her again. None of us did. The moment I had gone she climbed the ramp up to the top floor of the nearby multi-storey car park, hoisted herself up on to the barrier, and jumped a hundred feet down to her death.

The Carriage Clock

I never knew Hugh Manning very well, and I don't think I really had a strong view of him one way or another. He seemed a benign sort of fellow, quietly spoken and courteous, pleasant enough in every way. But there was a reticence in him, a disengagement, or so it seemed to me, and I never quite knew where I stood with him.

That may have been true of how most people felt about him. Outsiders at least. But those in his firm seemed on the whole to be fond of him, and loyal to him, perhaps emphatically so. He led well, I was always told. I never quite made out what they meant by that, but I knew he was considered to be decisive, clear of thought, friendly, and very slow to blame and very quick to praise, and maybe the roots of it lay just there.

Hugh had risen steadily through the editorial ranks at his big literary publishing house over a long career there. By the time I met him, at the time when I was just launching Waterstone's, he was in his fifties, and, comparatively advanced in the day as it was, he had finally and abruptly risen to the very top. He was now both chairman and managing director of the firm, the predecessors in both of these roles having been obliged to simultaneously fall on their swords following an embarrassing and perhaps criminal accounting scandal.

The London publishing community overall seemed surprised to suddenly find him there. He was respected well enough I think, in so far as most people had really got to know him at all, but in general the winners in the publishing profession have within that single tight group of theirs a social flamboyance, a desire to party and to be seen to party, and to gossip and to be heard to gossip. And anything more unlike Hugh than that would be hard to imagine. One prominent woman literary agent, to me a most dislikeable figure but to others a legend, was heard to joke that Hugh always looked as if he was about to burst into tears. Also, and this was an insult of which she was very proud, that in a crowd of two, Hugh was the one you didn't notice was there at all. Those two little *traits d'esprit* of hers travelled the party circuit for a while, and for all I know reached Hugh's ears too. The publishing world is a surprisingly small community and it's not a wholly benign one. Actually, not in the least a benign one. I'm not sure if he would have minded or not. I think he probably would. He never struck me as having much of a thick skin.

Actually, I probably knew Hugh's wife rather better than I knew him. She, Carol, was much, much younger – at least twenty-two or -three years or so, I think, probably more – and was very pleasant-looking, very friendly, and generally much more outgoing than Hugh. She was an intelligent, highly regarded editor in the same firm, and she was perhaps Waterstone's main point of contact there, which threw her and me together frequently. I knew Hugh had been married before, but she I think not. Actually, I am sure she hadn't, for she was no more than in her middle twenties when she and Hugh had married, or so someone had told me, with a touch of jealous admiration mixed with gossipy disapproval.

The marriage had lasted, though, and it looked to the world most happily so. Certainly Hugh and Carol were the most agreeable people to talk to on the occasions when I found them together. Hugh was socially transformed with Carol at his side.

She was too in a way, always seemingly anxious to show publicly her affection for him, and her loyalty, as if it all might be doubted. Yes, together they seemed to be delighted with each other, and proud, and most proud of all, I think, that they had three young children, who in time would all go to the same north London day school.

I wish Hugh and Carol had realised how interesting and, well, inspiring others in conventional same-age marriages found them to be. I don't think they ever did. I don't think that they thought in that way. They were each of them both too modest and too private for that. They in no way set out to be role models for anyone. They had simply fallen in love and married each other. And they had conceived and borne their three children just as fast as they could, so happy were they with each other and their marriage, and so oblivious to the unconventional nature of it.

Except, except, except... I have written it all like that, because I would have liked it to have been like that. And it very nearly was, I realised later, but in fact it wasn't. How do I know that? Well, it may be that I would never have known, had I not one day had a long conversation with Hugh's great friend, Rob D. He and Hugh had been loyal and inseparable colleagues ever since their days together first at school and then at university. Rob and I happened to bump into each other one glorious early-summer Saturday afternoon at Richmond Park, both of us simultaneously setting out from one of the car parks for a long walk. It was some years after I had first met Hugh and Carol. Rob and I knew each other quite well, and I certainly liked him, and he seemed happy enough to find me there, so we joined forces and set off together.

It happened like this. I was conscious that I hadn't seen Hugh and Carol together socially for some time – actually, now that I thought about it, I hadn't seen them together for two or three years, maybe more – and as we walked I asked after them. Rob strode on beside me, and was silent for a moment or two. Then he said that Carol had of course left the firm and moved to the BBC. I told him that I knew that, but nonetheless it had surprised me that they didn't seem to be at the parties you would expect them to attend together. And that I rather missed that, as I had always enjoyed talking to them.

Again, there was a long silence from Rob, and I let it continue, for I suspected now there was something he wanted to say, and was wondering how to express it. Then, he said, 'Does one ever know anything about what goes on within other people's marriages? I am not sure one does really, ever. Even if you think you know the two of them really well. Even then... Even then.'

I felt it better to make no reply, but allow him time to say whatever he had decided to say. I was interested, of course. But I didn't want to push him into an account of a private matter that he might later regret. I would stay silent while he thought it through.

'Well – yes,' he said eventually, sitting down on an isolated park bench, and I sat down there beside him. 'Other people's marriages... I tell you something. Carol loved Hugh, you know, she really did, and I think despite it all she still does. I think so. I think she loves him still. Despite the actions she has taken, and the turn her life has taken. I think she does. I hope she does. I really hope she does. I don't want Hugh to lose that. He needs to think that is so, to believe that is so, he needs to feel that Carol still loves him, despite everything, otherwise I am not sure how well he is going to be able to... well, to be able to cope, to put it frankly. In the long term. She had been once very content in the marriage, I'm sure she was, really content, their three children and everything, and her daily life with Hugh as well, and I am sure I am not wrong in that. I'm sure I'm not wrong.'

Oh my God, I thought, she's broken up with him. She's left him. And I found that little as I knew Hugh really, or indeed Carol, I minded. I really did. I minded. Actually, I always do. I hate people breaking up a marriage with each other. I have been through that trauma, and I know what it is like. I was intrigued by that phrase of Rob's about 'the actions she has taken', but I would leave it be. I wasn't all that certain I wanted to hear any more of it anyway. But I didn't see how I could change the subject. Perhaps Rob would stop there, and talk of something else.

But then: 'Yes – it's true – absolutely – Carol loved Hugh, and had been originally perfectly content in her marriage. Very much so. She's quite highly charged, as you know. And often very stressed, highly stressed, and Hugh was a perfect foil for her in that. Like a horse whisperer, if you know what I mean. He gave her calm, patient reassurance. That quality in Hugh was one of the great strengths of their relationship, I'm sure about that.'

A long pause. Then: 'But there was a fault line there, and that was what destroyed them. For although she loved him, she had never been *in* love with him. Not at all. Never. And there is such a difference in that. Hugh, though, was in love with Carol from the very moment when she had appeared in his office to be inter-viewed for a junior editor job. Instantaneously. Hopelessly. He's told me the story so often. God – so often! It was an absolute, dead-on, immediate *coup de foudre*, in his description of it. He fell in love, just like that, just so hopelessly, that he told her of it pretty well immediately. Within days, I think it was. They had lunch together in a tiny and empty Mayfair restaurant, in which apparently neither of them managed to eat one single morsel of the food in front of them. Dover sole. I always remember him telling me that detail. Dover sole. He said that she had sat there silent, gazing at him, as the words poured out of him. He went on and on. I can just imagine it of Hugh, can't you? He told her that he wanted to marry her, and was determined to marry her, and would never give up from his determination to do just that. He told her he was in love with her now, hopelessly, blindly in love with her now, and he would be in love with her not just now, but for ever, for evermore. And he would have children with her, lots of children with her, dozens of children with her, and love all their children, and love her, and be with her day and night and minute by minute and month by month and year by year for ever and ever, in perfect, absolute, unending bliss. On and on and on he went, as he described it to me. And on then again. And he meant it. He clearly meant it. Just after the lunch, immediately after the lunch, he told me what he had done. He never stopped telling me what he had just done and said to her. He never stopped telling me that this was the love of his life, the love of his life, the love of his life. He laughed when I laughed at this, and of course he knew I was not laughing in scorn, but in affection. So Hugh laughed with me, laughed and laughed with me, and in his case it was in bliss.

'And – no – Carol wasn't in love with him,' Rob continued, seemingly determined now to tell the whole story. 'At the time she was barely more than half his age, of course, but she seemed to be a young woman who preferred physical intimacy with older men – father figures, one would say in the caricature. Nothing wrong in that, nothing surprising in that, it was just what Carol was – wouldn't you agree? I mean – it seems likely to be the case, don't you think? And anyway, does one have to search for reasons for it? Why should one? It was certainly not that she was damaged in any way, for I am certain she wasn't, given the wonderful ebullience of her personality. Or at least I think I am. I think I am. Perhaps I'm wrong, of course. Who knows about that either? On a milder level it might have been that she had developed an emotional attachment to someone or other in her childhood, an adult, perhaps protective, perhaps someone in authority, perhaps whom she in a sense fell in love with in a childlike way. But again – who knows?'

Again the long pause, while he stared out across the park. And again I remained silent too. And then: 'And anyway what does it matter? The point is in the negative. The point is that she didn't fall in love with Hugh when Hugh fell in love with her. And she never did thereafter. She just didn't. And that's where the fault line lay. And given her personality, not being in love with Hugh meant that she was going to fall in love with someone else. Some time or other, she was bound to fall in love with someone else. It was always going to happen. But she did love Hugh, in a simple, affectionate way, she did love him, I'm really sure of that. And her love for him did indeed grow in her when his total devotion for her became apparent. And the more so when they started living together. And she accepted him, and she married him. Not without a certain flicker of hesitation about it, and I do know that because she told me that once, in front of Hugh, and they both laughed about it. Because no one would suggest that Hugh was exactly a person of physical beauty. And Carol wanted to have children, and she would have liked them to be good-looking, pretty children, as she herself was, and, well, she looked at Hugh sometimes and wondered if that was what her children would turn out to look like with Hugh as their father. Actually, she needn't have worried, for I know her children, and they look just like her, and they are gorgeous. But I agree with her – it was as well they look like her, and not in the least like him. But she said it in jest, if meaningfully. And that would become a favourite joke between them. But she would love her children anyway, I am sure she told herself that, whoever they had taken after, of course she would love them anyway. And Hugh wanted to have children with her, he never stopped saying that he wanted to have children with her, and she believed him. She knew he did. He really did want to have a real marriage with her, children and all, lots of them. He clearly did.

'So Hugh bought a house for them, and they first lived together for a couple of years, and then they married, and there were those who went to their wedding party who found it to be one of the most moving that they had ever attended. He was and is a good public speaker, is Hugh, and an experienced one, and he struck what was perhaps exactly the right note in his brief little speech, given the fact that their age difference gave such an unconventional colour to their wedding day. So, standing in front of that audience, he simply opened his heart. He simply told the truth. He told it as it was, for him. For him, Hugh Manning. And he did it by quietly, simply, from memory, reciting a Christina Rossetti poem. And all of that poem was resonant with the intense, sharp reality and truth of Hugh's love for Carol.

'You read English at Cambridge too, I know, as Hugh and I did. So – you know the piece of course. Who can forget it?

> My heart is like a singing bird
> Whose nest is in a water'd shoot;
> My heart is like an apple-tree
> Whose boughs are bent with thick-set fruit;
> My heart is like a rainbow shell
> That paddles in a halcyon sea;
> My heart is gladder than all these,
> Because my love is come to me.

> Raise me a daïs of silk and down;
> Hang it with vair and purple dyes;
> Carve it in doves and pomegranates,
> And peacocks with a hundred eyes;
> Work it in gold and silver grapes,
> In leaves and silver fleurs-de-lys;
> Because the birthday of my life
> Is come, my love is come to me.

'I remember all that so well,' Rob continued. 'When Hugh finished speaking, when he finished reciting the Rossetti, he stood for a moment, silent, gazing at the floor. Then he nodded his head, as if in affirmation, and returned to his seat, passing me as he went, but not looking at me, and I could see the effort he was having to make to stop himself from crying. No doubt half the audience felt like crying too, as it happened. Me amongst them.'

Rob turned to me. 'Look – you hardly know these people, this is ridiculous, I'm not boring you or anything, am I?'

I shook my head, and smiled, and gestured to him to continue, and he did.

'And so the years went by, and in short order one by one the children appeared, and they were loved and cherished, and their marriage wended its way on. There were frequent dramas in Carol's professional life, and she was easily hurt by those, and brought them home with her, which Hugh much liked actually, as it enabled him to use his powers of calming and encouragement, which, as I have said, were considerable. You know – the horse whisperer bit. In happier, earlier times, I remember Carol calling it just that, and laughing at it, and hugging Hugh as he laughed too.

'So – yes, the years rolled by. The youngest of the three children was – I don't know – perhaps nine, ten, something like that, and there was a party one evening, a birthday party for Carol. In their home. I was there. It was good fun. I had a chat with Carol about midway through, and it surprised me, as normally in conversation she was marvellously direct, concentrating on you, holding eye contact with you, never doing that awful thing of looking over your shoulder to see if there was someone more interesting she could talk to. Well, this time she was looking over my shoulder. She would say something to me, then not listen to my reply. She was – how do I say it? – she was not with me, let's put it that way. Disengaged. Distraught, actually. I would go as far as that. Distraught.'

He stopped, and fell silent again. This time I did speak.

'So what did you do? What did you say? Did you ask her what was wrong?'

'Yes – yes I did. She told me it was nothing, nothing. It was just that she was waiting to see if someone had arrived. Someone she had invited. And then she tried to pull herself together in so much as she smiled at me, apologised, laid a hand on my chest and moved away. Just that. Only that. But that's when I first realised that something was amiss, though I didn't know what. Or rather I should say I didn't know who. And it wasn't long before I found out. For Hugh told me, not more than three or four days later.'

'Told you what?'

'Told me that Carol had come to him the morning after the party, and sat with him on a sofa, and told him. She told him that she was in love, and told him who she was in love with, and told him that she had been in love with him for at least the past two or three years, and would be for ever. And she needed to make it clear to Hugh that it was the biggest thing that had ever happened to her in her life. The biggest, the most wonderful thing that had ever happened to her. And that the man she was in love with was Marcus B. She told him again, and then again, that this was by far the biggest thing that had ever happened to her in her life. And that she was very sorry to hurt him. And she realised how badly she had hurt him. She was desperately sorry to do so. But she felt she had an obligation to tell him, because she wanted to be honest with him. And now she had. Now she had told him. So – now he knew.'

There was a long pause. I feared for Hugh when Rob told me Marcus B's name. He was of at least Hugh's age, at least that, and a man with a notorious history over the years of many affairs, and many women. But I knew him just a little, and I would never have dismissed him as just a philanderer. That would be too harsh, too uncompromising, too unimaginative a term. He was... well, despite the public appearance of things, Marcus was a tortured soul, a wounded, damaged, unhappy man, I think. But his record would suggest that he was, let us say, romantically irresponsible, and I would certainly pitch his behaviour over the years at that level. Romantically irresponsible. Just that. And it was a pity, perhaps a disreputable pity, yes – a disreputable pity – if he had encouraged or even actively pursued Carol, persuading her to join him in whatever was the course of their relationship together. I don't know if he did. All I knew, of course, was what Rob had just told me. It was a pity because – perhaps only because – I was sad for Hugh. From what Rob had said Hugh was too much in love with Carol, and too loyal to her, for him to be able to handle this. But from Rob's description of events Carol had seemed to have fallen too much in love with Marcus to take into account the damage this would inflict on Hugh. Or indeed to care much either way. Yes – to care much either way about the damage done to Hugh. Which was pretty well exactly what Rob next said to me.

'There was a lack of consideration in the way that Hugh was told of her affair, it seemed to me,' Rob continued. 'I don't mean that pejoratively – I mean it literally. So in love was she that she just couldn't take into consideration what she was doing to Hugh. She said the words of appropriate contrition to him, but they were just formulaic, in Hugh's description of it, nothing more. And I suspect there was an aspect to it that once she had unloaded the truth on to Hugh then it had become his problem rather than hers. Basically, she just couldn't worry about what this would do to Hugh. She couldn't. She was too much in love with Marcus.

'But if Carol was incapable of thinking about the effect of all this on Hugh, then Marcus should have done, in my opinion. He really should have done. And, actually, all these years later, and it's apparent that he never has. Never. For Carol was in his hands, not Hugh's. In Marcus's hands lay Carol's entire emotional life, indeed her whole emotional sanity, and I mean that, sanity. She was his responsibility, his personal responsibility. So he should either have released her, totally and immediately released her, if in real truth he wasn't serious about her, or, if he was truly serious about her, he should have followed this thing through. He should have acted decisively either way. Either drop it or pursue the relationship honourably. If the latter, he should have taken her, gone with her, belonged to her, lived with her, openly so, and she with him. That would have been a commitment, and in its own inverted way an honourable commitment. But an affair... God... whatever Carol and Marcus thought about their relationship, however it felt to them, well, frankly, to me, an outsider of course, all this stuff looks just like a standard, run-of-the-mill, rather depressing affair. But in this case an affair that was spun out endlessly, over a period of years, for God's sake, spun out over years and years of Hugh's treasured marriage, years and years of *Hugh's* life. *Hugh's* life, all of this was *Hugh's* life, think of it that way. Well, it carried no honour with it at all. For me. In my way of looking at it. Dishonour, just that. Well, let's moderate that, I should moderate that, there may have been more honour between Carol and Marcus than I had imagined. Perhaps there was. How could I know? But that didn't stop me from being most deeply concerned for Hugh. And insulted for Hugh. And sad, beyond sad, for Hugh. And as it turned out I was right to be.'

Right to be? I thought. What does that mean? But I said nothing, and meant to sit still and silent and wait for Rob to conclude the tale. But I wanted to hear some reassuring news now, some indication that in the end all of this so familiar, so sad, so clichéd a human story had some sort of happy ending – for Hugh certainly, but for Carol too, and indeed for Marcus, if he was as precarious and vulnerable a human being as I suspected he actually was, despite what the world imagined him to be.

'Carol left Hugh in the end, you see,' Rob said now. 'Hugh told me that he found a letter for him to that effect one morning on their hall table, and that he rushed up to their bedroom to find all her possessions had been stripped out and removed while he was out delivering one of their children to Heathrow. There was a certain justice in it, according to Hugh, for he said that his patience with Carol under the strain of everything had deteriorated badly, more than badly, continually aggravated by the rawest, rawest sexual pain and jealousy, and there had been a number of scenes between them when Hugh had been furiously, unacceptably angry with her. Or perhaps not so much angry with her in person, but with the pain of the position he had for so long been forced to bear. They were bad, bad moments, however you explain them. Moments when Hugh was simply unable to hold himself in check. But for all that they had continued together for some seven or eight further years after Carol's revelation to him on the sofa that morning after the party. And much, perhaps most of that time had apparently passed well. The shadow of Marcus hung over them in everything, but they concentrated on being pleasant to each other, even affectionate – yes – what am I saying? – they were genuinely affectionate to each other, I saw them together and often. They were. I'm sure of that, I'm sure they kept their fluency going, sharing the mutual happiness of bringing up their children together, whom they both idolised. And Hugh told me that he had never stopped being in love with Carol. And that he thought, genuinely thought, that Carol continued to love him, just as she always had, though she was never in love with him.

'So every day, every month, every year of that period Hugh told me that he thought that if he simply held on, waited, kept going, then in time it would all resolve itself, her relationship with Marcus would eventually wither and fade, and Carol would come home to him, as he thought of it. It must burn itself out in time, he constantly told himself, if only he could simply hold on. Wait. Stick it out.

'But it never did. Year by year by year, it never burnt itself out. In his worst moments I think he thought his forbearance, year after year after year, was a mistake. That he was being toyed with. Humiliated, really, and for far too long. He told me that on one occasion he happened to bump into Marcus in a club passageway, and he was within a millisecond of stopping him in his tracks and telling him to leave his wife alone, to get the hell out of both their lives. But in that millisecond he thought something else as well – that if he said that to Marcus then Marcus would probably do exactly as he was being told to do, and let Carol go, and let her go for good. But what would then happen to Carol? And Hugh knew all too well what would then happen to Carol. What would happen would be that she would be utterly, terminally broken. And that she would blame Hugh for it, for having pushed Marcus into that position. And in a way she would have been right to do so. For in essence it would have been Hugh who had broken her heart. And by that the chances of her ever reconciling with him, ever coming home to him, in Hugh's phrase, would be gone for ever.'

'Did he forgive her?' I asked then.

'Well – yes – I asked Hugh that once,' Rob replied. 'He told me he had no concept as to what I was talking about. He told me that he had never blamed her, so there was nothing for him to forgive. She had fallen in love. It happens. After all, he said, he, Hugh, had fallen in love with her. That had happened. There was no difference. There was no question of blame. She'd done nothing wrong. Falling in love just happens.

'A little later I remember asking him if, after all that had happened, he regretted the marriage, and he told me that if he had known in advance every detail of how matters were to evolve in Carol's life he, without the slightest, slightest hesitation, would still have married her, and with joy. And I believe him. He would have done.'

Then Rob muttered something that I failed to catch, and got up, and suggested that we finish our walk. Neither of us spoke for some minutes, and then I asked Rob what their situation was now.

'They live apart,' he replied. 'They sold their family house, and Hugh split all their money with her, and he went off abroad for a period, travelling around, alone of course, but he's quite good at being alone. He always has been. And then he came back to London, and lived in a hotel. For a long time. For too long, really, but he didn't seem to mind. No – it wasn't being alone that was the problem for him. It was simply the devastation of having finally lost Carol, after all those years of trying to hang on, trying to be stoic, trying to see it out. I don't think he was bitter. I don't think bitterness crossed his mind, or enters into this at all. As I say, he didn't think she had done anything wrong, so there was no blame to it.

'No, it was simpler than that. He was just intensely, intensely unhappy, that is what it was. All those years, all of them, he had been so proud of her, so proud to be married to her, so proud that she was his wife. And the unhappiness might well have been weariness as much as anything else, for those last few years, with the dark shadow of Marcus looming always, always over him, had certainly taken their toll. Taken their toll, but the love he bore Carol, and had always borne her, was damaged not in the least. Not one scrap. It still isn't. It never will now. Never.'

'And Carol?'

Rob made no immediate answer, and we walked on together, side by side. We reached the car park, and he stood with me there.

'You asked about Carol,' he said. 'I've seen her once or twice over the last four or five years. She seems well. She seems in good shape. She's as good-looking as ever – actually, now, as she has matured, even more so I think. She is intensely involved in her BBC career, and is known to be a rising star there. She loves her work, she has bought herself a pleasant house, in Maida Vale I think it is, and she loves her children and they love her.

'I have no idea where she is now with Marcus. I have no idea where she is now with Hugh. All I know is where Hugh is with her, and I have just told you of that. He is still in love with her, and always will be, and blames her for nothing. So there we go.'

He raised a hand in farewell, but then turned again.

'One odd little detail,' he said. 'Hugh split his money with her, but wanted none of his possessions. None. They are all there in Carol's new house – everything – every single item – everything he and she had put together in their quarter of a century of marriage – the books, the furniture, the carpets, the pictures, the photographs. Everything. He seems to be content that this new house of hers should be like a museum to the family life that they had once built together. So he has nothing. He took nothing. He left every single thing with her.'

He paused, and shrugged.

'Well – this is it – everything but for one insignificant, plain, valueless little Victorian carriage clock. It predated their marriage. I know he has had it since he was a child. It seems to be important to him. It's the one physical link left in the narrative arc of his whole life from his childhood through to his now final years, alone. I guess that's what it is. I think it's that for him.'